BEST

SHORT STORIES

Middle Level

10 Stories for Young Adults

with Lessons for Teaching the Basic Elements of Literature

Raymond Harris

JAMESTOWN PUBLISHERS

a division of NTC/CONTEMPORARY PUBLISHING GROUP
Lincolnwood, Illinois USA

Cover Design: Steve Straus
Cover Illustration: Lori Lohstoeter
Interior Design: Patricia Volpe
Interior Illustrations: Units 1, 3: Timothy C. Jones; Unit 2: Marcy Ramsey;
Unit 4: Maurice P. Dogué; Units 5, 10: Joel Snyder; Unit 6: Thomas E.
Malloy; Units 7, 8: Heidi Chang; Unit 9: Lois Leonard Stock

ISBN: 0-89061-664-7 (hardbound)
ISBN: 0-89061-662-0 (softbound)

Published by Jamestown Publishers,
a division of NTC/Contemporary Publishing Group, Inc.,
4255 West Touhy Avenue,
Lincolnwood (Chicago), Illinois 60712-1975 U.S.A.
© 1983, 1994 by NTC/Contemporary Publishing Group, Inc.
Manufactured in the United States of America.

9 10 11 12 13 14 15 16 044 / 055 09 08 07

Acknowledgments

Acknowledgment is gratefully made to the following publishers and authors for permission to reprint the stories in this book:

"First Confession" by Frank O'Connor. From *Collected Stories* by Frank O'Connor. ©1951 by Frank O'Connor. Reprinted by permission of Alfred A. Knopf, Inc. and the Joan Daves Agency.

"Raymond's Run" by Toni Cade Bambara. From *Gorilla My Love* by Toni Cade Bambara. ©1971 by Toni Cade Bambara. Reprinted by permission of Random House, Inc.

"Marigolds" by Eugenia Collier. Reprinted by permission of Eugenia Collier.

"The Treasure of Lemon Brown" by Walter Dean Myers. ©1982 by Walter Dean Myers. Reprinted by permission of Walter Dean Myers and *Boys' Life* magazine, published by the Boy Scouts of America.

"The Moustache" by Robert Cormier. From *Eight Plus One* by Robert Cormier. ©1975 by Robert Cormier. Reprinted by permission of Pantheon Books, a division of Random House, Inc.

"Sucker" by Carson McCullers. ©1963 by Carson McCullers. © renewed 1990. From *O'Henry Awards 1965 Prize Stories,* Doubleday & Co. Reprinted by permission of Floria V. Lasky.

"Naftali the Storyteller and His Horse, Sus" from *Naftali the Storyteller and His Horse, Sus and Other Stories* by Isaac Bashevis Singer. ©1973, 1976 by Isaac Bashevis Singer. Reprinted by permission of Farrar, Straus & Giroux, Inc.

"A Sound of Thunder" by Ray Bradbury. Reprinted by permission of Don Congdon Associates, Inc. ©1952, renewed 1980 by Ray Bradbury.

"A Cap for Steve" by Morley Callaghan. Reprinted by permission of Barry Callaghan.

Christine Powers Harris has been a companion author for all four *Best-Selling Chapters* and *Best Short Stories* books. Teachers will once again recognize her critical insight and appreciation for literary technique throughout the lessons in *Best Short Stories,* Middle Level. The author also thanks Louise Loewenstein, Educational Consultant, for her contributions and suggestions in choosing the stories for this second edition.

Contents

To the Teacher

Introduction

The new *Best Short Stories,* Second Edition, has been revised to give your students more writing experience and more practice in critically discussing short stories.

The popular format of *Best Short Stories* has not changed, but you will find new features in this Second Edition—an expanded writing section within each unit and a writing process reference section. Every lesson helps students improve their writing skills by giving them insights into how an author builds plot, develops a character, creates a setting, or uses language. Seeing the short story through the author's eyes gives students a new awareness of just how a writer writes. In other words, students learn to read *and* to write from the writer's point of view.

Most students who use this book will become aware for the first time that stories don't just happen: they are created with great care and diligence by people with a special talent. For this reason you will find that the lessons often refer to the visual and performing arts to show students the various ways in which feelings and ideas are communicated through the things that people create.

Students can often intuitively appreciate the colors in a painting or the majesty of a tall building, though they may not understand what it is about those art forms that evokes a response in them. But these same students may not be able to appreciate a well-drawn character or story setting without some guidance. They must first recognize and understand the basic elements of literature—character, setting, plot, tone, and theme—and how they are used in a particular story, before they can understand and appreciate the ideas and feelings embodied in the story.

To help students understand that the ideas and feelings that exist in literature are *created,* just as the ideas and feelings in other art forms are created, consider beginning your literature course by exposing your students to a wide range of graphic, structural, and musical arts. Your school's woodworking shop, for example, would be a good place to start. Follow this with a visit to the art and music rooms. Explain the planning, feeling, and skill that go into any creation. Point out the ideas and feelings that can be communicated through artistic craftsmanship. A table, for example, may be severely practical or luxuriously ornate; strong and massive, or delicate, with flowing lines. Music may be stirring or soothing, depending on the composer's intent. And don't overlook the world of movies and television. Even the poorest sitcoms hold valuable lessons in elementary plotting, setting, theme, and character development.

Young readers must also have good reading skills in order to readily appreciate literature. It is essential, therefore, that readers continue to practice their reading comprehension skills while they are learning new literary skills. To this end, each unit in the book contains a set of reviewing and interpreting questions. The students' reading comprehension scores can be plotted on the charts at the back of the book, making it easy for you to see improvement or difficulties students may have in the eight comprehension and interpreting areas. As a student's reading comprehension skills improve, you will probably also notice an increasing appreciation for literature.

The stories in this book have been carefully chosen to give students as broad a reading experience as possible. They range from the uncompromising ferocity of Jack London to the powerful feelings expressed in Carson McCullers' writing to the visionary folk style of Isaac Bashevis Singer. All the authors are masters of their craft and have proven themselves favorites with millions of young readers.

The Contents of a Unit

The book has ten units. Each unit contains the following:

1. **The illustration and discussion questions.** Each unit begins with a two-page illustration that depicts the characters in a key scene from the story. This illustration enables visually oriented readers to place themselves easily in the story situation. The page that follows contains questions based on the illustration.

   You will notice that the illustration serves as an introduction to the lesson as well as to the story. The accompanying questions also direct the students' thinking to essential ideas they will encounter in the lesson. In discussing the questions, students will be previewing both the story and the lesson. This activity will heighten students' anticipation of participating in the story (because they will be anxious to know if their interpretations of the illustration are correct) and will sharpen their perception of the literary concept that will be discussed in the lesson.

2. **Introduction to the story.** Each unit contains a brief, four-part introduction. The first part, About the Story, sets the scene and explains a bit about the characters and the story situation. Experiences that are alluded to in the story but may be beyond the knowledge of most young readers are explained. For example, the Catholic confessional and some Irish colloquialisms are explained in the introduction to "First Confession." This part of the introduction also provides information about the author and suggests other books and stories by the author that the students may want to read.

   The second part of the introduction, About the Lesson, simply and concisely defines the literary concept to be studied in the lesson.

   The third part of the introduction consists of four questions intended to call the students' attention to particular passages in the story that are used to illustrate the four major points discussed in the lesson. The students should keep these questions in mind and look for the answers to them as they read the story.

   The fourth part of the introduction offers a variety of writing suggestions directly related to what will be discussed in the lesson. For example, if the lesson discusses character, students are asked to list ideas and suggestions for creating their own characters. Students will use their ideas for writing activities within each of the four lesson sections. Most of the writing exercises will take some time, so you may want to set aside a class period for students to work on a writing project. You may want to discuss with your students the reference section Using the Writing Process at the end of the book. Remind students to refer to that section, beginning on page 445, and to the checklist when they begin a writing assignment.

3. **The short story.** Each of the ten stories in the book is complete and unabridged. These stories were chosen both for their literary excellence and for their proven appeal to young readers. Each story is particularly suited to illustrate the literary concept taught in the accompanying lesson.

4. **The literary lesson.** Each lesson begins with a general explanation of a major literary concept. Then four major elements of the concept are discussed individually, and each is illustrated with an appropriate passage from the story. After the literary element is explained in relation to this passage, the students are presented with a second passage from the story that illustrates the same element. This passage is followed by two questions that allow the students to critically discuss what they have just learned.

Each of the four major elements discussed in the lesson is followed by Writing on Your Own, which helps students analyze a literary technique and apply that technique to their writing. For instance, within the four lesson sections that deal with setting, the students are asked to create a setting of their own. But first they build from basic elements of setting: the first exercise asks them to write about setting and the action; the second, setting and the feelings it creates; the third, putting your reader into the story; and finally, setting and how it reinforces ideas or themes.

Six of the ten lessons deal with elements of literature: plot, character, setting, theme, language, and tone and mood. Three lessons serve as an introduction to genre. The first lesson in the book introduces the short story as a special kind of literature. Later lessons examine two types of stories that are popular with young readers—science fiction and the folk story. The last lesson in the book—Judgments and Conclusions: Discussing Stories—is an easy first venture into criticism and critical thinking.

5. **Reviewing and Interpreting the Story.** Sixteen comprehension and interpretation questions following each lesson provide a quick check of four major reading skills: remembering facts, following the order of events, understanding word choices, understanding important ideas; and four interpreting skills: understanding levels of meaning, understanding character, understanding setting, understanding feelings. Each question is labeled according to the skill it tests. A Comprehension Skills Profile is provided at the back of the book so that you can keep track of the kinds of questions each student misses most often. There is also a Comprehension Scores Graph that can help you keep track of overall progress in reading comprehension.

6. **Discussion Guides.** Through nine discussion questions in each unit, students are asked to consider three aspects of the story: the literary concept emphasized in the lesson, general ideas and implications of the story, and the author's technique or special relationship to the story situation. These questions encourage students to critically think about their reading and give them practice in critically discussing literature.

7. **Writing Exercise.** The writing exercises have always been one of the most popular elements in both *Best-Selling Chapters* and *Best Short Stories*. You will find that the expanded exercises within the

lessons and the final writing exercise in each unit are directly related to what has been presented in the lesson and will encourage students to apply ideas and literary concepts to their own work. This exercise asks students to pull together all the elements they have discussed and written about in Writing on Your Own to create their own stories.

How to Use This Book

Best Short Stories, Second Edition, has four major objectives:

◆ To help readers understand basic structure and the elements of literature

◆ To sharpen reading comprehension skills

◆ To encourage critical reading

◆ To give readers an opportunity to make a conscious effort to introduce elements of literary style into their own writing

Here are suggestions for ways to use the various parts of each unit:

1. **Discuss the illustration.** Ask the students to look carefully at the illustration. On the page following the illustration there are a key question and several supporting questions. Read the key question aloud. You can have the students respond spontaneously or ask them to hold their opinions until they have discussed the supporting questions.

   Have either an open class discussion or small group discussions of the supporting questions. Then return to the key question and ask the students to respond to it in light of the answers they have arrived at in their discussions. Emphasize the importance of supporting or clarifying their opinions and conclusions by pointing out supporting details in the illustration.

   These questions help students focus on both the story they will read and the lesson that follows. Read the story and lesson first yourself so that you can direct the discussion of the illustration to assure that it is a good preview of the story and lesson.

2. **Have students read the introduction to the story.** You may wish to add information to the introduction from your own experience with the story or the author. Point out that the author has

written other works that they may want to read. Some of these works are mentioned in the introduction.

Call attention to the four questions that conclude each introduction. The students should keep those questions in mind as they read the story. Point out how each of the questions is related to the definition of the literary concept given in About the Lesson. Discuss what the students should look for in the reading selection in order to be able to answer the questions. The questions guide the students, as they read, toward an awareness of the literary concept discussed in the lesson.

The introduction is followed by a writing exercise in which students list story ideas related to the literary concept discussed. You may want to provide time for the students to discuss their ideas before they make their lists.

3. **Have students read the story.** Tell the students that you want them to enjoy the story for its own sake, but point out that you also want them to read the story *critically*.

To keep the students' attention focused on the literary concept discussed in the lesson, you may want to have them keep a copy of the questions from the introduction beside them as they read, or write the questions on the chalkboard. Also, remind the students that they will have to answer comprehension questions in Reviewing and Interpreting the Story—another reason for reading critically.

4. **Explain the literary lesson.** Each lesson is divided into five parts. It begins with a general introduction to the literary concept that will be covered. After the students have read the introduction, discuss it with them to make sure they have a general understanding of the concept. Then have the students read and study the other four sections of the lesson, one at a time. Each explains a different element of the major literary concept on which the lesson is focused. The students should also complete the exercise at the end of each section. After they finish each section, pause for a discussion of the lesson so that the students can find out whether their answers or opinions to the questions are right or wrong, and why. Because many of the questions ask the students to draw their own conclusions or give their own opinions, it is important to explain that the Answer Key gives *suggested* answers.

5. **Have students discuss Writing on Your Own.** Each of the four lesson sections is followed by a writing exercise that focuses on the

separate literary element discussed in that section. Provide time for students to discuss their ideas with classmates before they begin Writing on Your Own. These prewriting exercises help students prepare for the final writing exercise in the unit.

6. **Have students answer the questions in Reviewing and Interpreting the Story.** In classes in which reading comprehension is the primary concern, you may want to have the students answer these questions immediately after reading the story. They should answer without looking back at the story. The comprehension and interpreting questions focus on eight important reading skills:

Remembering Facts	Understanding Levels of Meaning
Following the Order of Events	Understanding Character
Understanding Word Choices	Understanding Setting
Understanding Important Ideas	Understanding Feelings

7. **Have students correct their answers.** Students can check their answers to the Reviewing and Interpreting the Story questions by using the Answer Key that starts on page 457. Students should be encouraged to correct wrong answers and to consider why one answer is wrong and another right. Have students count the number of *each kind* of question they get wrong and record these numbers in the spaces provided at the end of the comprehension questions.

8. **Have students record their progress.** Students should plot the number of *correct* answers they got for each story on the Comprehension Scores Graph on page 468. Instructions for how to use the graph are given on the page with the graph. When students plot their scores, a visual record of their progress quickly emerges.

   Students should mark the number of *wrong* answers they got in each comprehension skill area (there are two questions related to each of the eight skills) on the Comprehension Skills Profile on page 469. This shows at a glance which skills a student needs to work on. Students usually enjoy keeping track of their progress, especially when they are allowed to manage this task themselves. Seeing visual proof of improvement in scores invariably provides the incentive to strive for even more improvement. You should also monitor the students' progress so that you can recognize any problems and deal with them early.

9. **Spend time on discussion.** There are three kinds of discussion questions for each story—nine questions in all. The first three

focus on the literary concept studied in the lesson. These questions give students a chance to demonstrate their new skills and allow you to expand upon the lesson if you wish. Questions four through six are more general and allow students to use their imaginations and apply themes in the story to their own experiences. Finally, the last three questions deal with the author's experience and technique, and focus attention on the subjective aspects of literature.

10. **Have students do the Writing Exercise.** The writing exercise at the end of each unit allows students to improve their writing through imitation. Each writing exercise asks students to apply what they have learned about the literary element discussed in the lesson. If the students have not done the four Writing on Your Own exercises within the lesson, you may want them to go back and do them now. To make use of the truism that we learn to write by reading, encourage students to imitate the authors of the stories, if they wish. But an individual, freewheeling style may also be encouraged, especially among the better writers in a class.

11. **Using the Writing Process.** This reference section, beginning on page 445, is an extended lesson on what a writing process is and how to use it. The lesson helps students with the writing assignments they will encounter in the book. It explains the three major parts of the writing process: prewriting, writing, and revising. The reference is followed by a checklist of the major points. Students should refer to this checklist each time they begin a writing exercise.

Before students begin the first writing exercise in the book, you will probably want to review Using the Writing Process with them. Read each section with the students and discuss and illustrate the main points. Make sure they understand that the three steps in the writing process are not strictly sequential. Point out that good writers move back and forth from one to another, focusing more on prewriting at the beginning and revising toward the end of the project. You may want to spend several class periods discussing and experimenting with the various stages.

To the Student

If you follow the adventures of Snoopy, the world's most famous beagle, you know that one of his ambitions is to become an author. He sits on top of his doghouse with a little typewriter and begins:

"It was a dark and stormy night . . ."

And that's where he gets stuck. He just wasn't meant to be a story-teller, it seems.

The same is not true, however, of Snoopy's creator, author/cartoonist Charles Schulz. Schulz is a first-rate storyteller. The "Peanuts" gang, created from the author's imagination, is known all over the world. Through the antics of these characters, Schulz is able to entertain millions of people everywhere. And there is something else he does, as well. Through his stories and his characters, Charles Schulz is able to communicate his own thoughts and feelings to a vast audience. It's as if he had some magical power to charm people into listening to him. In a way, he does.

Storytelling is an ancient art. Stories were told around campfires long before anyone thought they could be written with pictures, symbols, or letters. And people who could tell stories were usually considered very special. Such people must surely have a gift from heaven, it was thought. Today we call this gift *talent.*

You have probably read many stories in your life. You have also had other people read to you. And you have seen many stories on television and in the movies. People still love a good story today, just as they always have. In this book you will find ten stories that we hope you will enjoy. You will have a chance to see *how* the stories were constructed, or created, by their authors. You will also learn just what it is that makes stories so interesting and enjoyable.

Each story in the book begins with an introduction. Be sure to read it. The purpose of the introduction is to help you understand more about the story you will read and about its author.

Lessons that follow the stories take you inside the author's head, in a manner of speaking. You will learn about the things that early people thought of as "magic" in the art of storytelling—how characters are created and used in the story, how the story is made to hold your interest, how the author makes you feel what he or she wants you to feel about the story and the characters, and how the author passes along ideas and influences your thinking.

Lesson exercises, writing activities, questions, discussion guides, and a final writing exercise round out each unit in the book. These will help sharpen your reading, reasoning, and writing skills.

As you become used to reading, thinking, and writing carefully, each story unit will be easier to work with than the one before it. So this may be the first textbook you've ever used that becomes easier instead of harder as you go along. And you will find that the skills you learn here will be useful throughout your life, not just for reading and writing, but in any situation in which you have to deal with people, their feelings, and their ideas.

Unit 1   The Short Story

First Confession
BY FRANK O'CONNOR

About the Illustration

How would you describe what is happening in this scene?
Point out some details in the drawing to support your
response.

Here are some questions to help you think about the
story:

◆ Where do you think this scene takes place?

◆ What are the children in the scene doing?

◆ Who do you think the main character is?

◆ What does the expression on the boy's face tell you
about how he feels? What details make you think that?

Unit 1

Introduction

About the Story

First communion is an important milestone in the religious life of young Catholics. This important event happens when the children are about seven or eight years old—old enough to know the difference between right and wrong. The occasion is a special one. The boys wear suits, the girls don fancy white dresses and white veils. Parents and grandparents take pictures. A special breakfast may be prepared for the children. Well-wishers present gifts of rosary beads, prayer books, and other religious objects. In church, on this special Sunday, the children are the center of attention as they march down the aisle, two by two, to receive communion for the first time.

First communion, however, comes only after the children have cleansed their souls by confessing their sins to the priest. Adults tend to remember their first communions and forget their first confessions.

But that first confession looms large in the mind of a small child. First of all, there's the shame of having to recite all of one's sins. Every child is sure his or her sins are worse than anyone else's. Equally worrisome is the thought of entering that dark, mysterious confession box for the first time.

The confessional, the cubicle in which the priest hears confessions, is divided into three compartments. The priest sits in the middle one. On either side of the priest's box is an adjoining compartment. A small screened opening covered with a sliding door connects each compartment to the priest's box. A Catholic wishing to confess his or her sins enters one compartment, kneels down, and waits for the priest to finish with the person in the compartment on the other side. When the little door finally slides back, the person begins his or her confession with these words: "Bless me, Father, for I have sinned. . . ." A child making a first confession goes on to say, "This is my first confession and these are my sins."

Confession sounds simple enough. But when you are a small child, the whole process can seem filled with complications. How do you know if the priest is in there? Is he *always* in there? What if you walk in on somebody else making a confession? What if somebody walks in on *you*? The chances of embarrassing oneself seem enormous.

Jackie, the small boy in Frank O'Connor's story "First Confession," finds himself in that awkward situation. He is hardly a little angel. At home he conducts running battles with his grandmother, whose country habits distress and embarrass him, and with his bossy older sister, Nora. Because of his feelings toward his grandmother and sister, Jackie figures he has broken all ten commandments.

Out of this minor childhood crisis, the author fashions an enjoyable, lighthearted story that will have you doubled over laughing.

Many of O'Connor's stories reflect the lives of small-town Irish people. So you will notice many Irish expressions in "First Confession." These give the story an Irish flavor. Imagine, if you can, the whole story told with an Irish accent—it adds to the fun.

Other short stories in this book have their own local flavors. One story is set in the Yukon. Another is set in Harlem. And a third is set in Poland during the last century. The words and expressions in each story help you picture people, places, and events.

You may be unfamiliar with some of the words that O'Connor uses in "First Confession." You can probably figure out the meanings of most of them yourself from the way they are used in the story.

a jug of porter. a dark brown ale

heart-scalded. heartsore or heartsick

half-crown. a British coin worth almost a dollar at the time the story takes place

dirty little caffler. a worthless fellow

begor. an Irish way of saying "by gosh!" The word is sometimes spelled *begorra*.

the screech of trams. trolley cars

Father gave me a flaking. See if you can figure that one out for yourself.

Frank O'Connor (1903–1966) wrote other humorous stories about Irish children. But his own childhood was far from funny. His real name was Michael O'Donovan. The son of very poor parents, he received almost no education, except what he could pick up on his own. Yet by the age of twelve he had turned out his first collection of writings, which included poems, biographies, and essays on history. "I was intended by God to be a painter," he once remarked, "but I was very poor and pencil and paper were the cheapest. . . . Literature is the poor man's art."

After reading "First Confession," you will probably want to read some other stories by Frank O'Connor. You can find his book *Collected Stories* in most libraries.

About the Lesson

The lesson that follows "First Confession" is about the short story as a form of literature. Like a novel, a short story has characters and a plot. It entertains the reader and explains an important idea. But unlike a novel, a short story is only a few pages long. Within that small space, the short-story writer must be precise and skillful. After you read "First Confession," you will learn how Frank O'Connor uses his writing skills to create an enjoyable story.

The following questions will help you notice some important elements in a short story. Try to keep these questions in mind as you read "First Confession":

◆ How does the author catch your interest right from the beginning of the story?

◆ How does the author make Jackie and his sister Nora seem real?

◆ How does the mood—the general feeling of the story—change as Jackie comes closer and closer to his moment of truth: his first confession?

◆ What is it about the ending of the story that leaves you with a satisfied feeling?

Develop Your Own Short Story

The very first step a writer has to take is to decide on an idea for the story. Use your writing notebook or a separate piece of paper and try the following suggestions:

1. "First Confession" is a humorous story about an experience the author had as a small boy. Think of a funny or embarrassing experience you had as a young child. To help you remember, talk to your friends about their experiences during childhood. Here are some ideas to help you get started.

   ☐ On my first visit to the dentist I screamed as though I were being murdered.

   ☐ My mother and father asked me to watch my sister for ten minutes. Instead of paying attention to her, I turned on the TV. I forgot all about her until I heard the cookie jar crash to the kitchen floor.

   ☐ I put on my mother's best dress for a make-believe tea party and got strawberry jam all over it.

2. Tell in just a few sentences what your story will be about.

First Confession

by Frank O'Connor

All the trouble began when my grandfather died and my grandmother—my father's mother—came to live with us. Relations in the one house are a strain at the best of times, but, to make matters worse, my grandmother was a real old countrywoman and quite unsuited to the life in town. She had a fat, wrinkled old face, and, to Mother's great indignation, went round the house in bare feet—the boots had her crippled, she said. For dinner she had a jug of porter and a pot of potatoes with—sometimes—a bit of salt fish, and she poured out the potatoes on the table and ate them slowly, with great relish, using her fingers by way of a fork.

Now, girls are supposed to be fastidious, but I was the one who suffered most from this. Nora, my sister, just sucked up to the old woman for the penny she got every Friday out of the old-age pension, a thing I could not do. I was too honest, that was my trouble; and when I was playing with Bill Connell, the sergeant-major's son, and saw my grandmother steering up the path with the jug of porter sticking out from beneath her shawl I was mortified. I made excuses not to let him come into the house, because I could never be sure what she would be up to when we went in.

When Mother was at work and my grandmother made the dinner I wouldn't touch it. Nora once tried to make me, but I hid under the table from her and took the bread-knife with me for protection. Nora let on to be very indignant (she wasn't, of course, but she knew Mother saw through her, so she sided with Gran) and came after me. I lashed out at her with the bread-knife, and after that she left me alone. I stayed there till Mother came in from work and made my dinner, but when Father came in later Nora said in a shocked voice: "Oh, Dadda, do you know what Jackie did at dinnertime?" Then, of course, it all came out; Father gave me a flaking; Mother interfered, and for days after that he didn't speak to me and Mother barely spoke to Nora. And all because of that old woman! God knows, I was heart-scalded.

Then, to crown my misfortunes, I had to make my first confession and communion. It was an old woman called Ryan who prepared us for these. She was about the one age with Gran; she was well-to-do, lived in a big house on Montenotte, wore a black cloak and bonnet, and came every day to school at three o'clock when we should have been going home, and talked to us of hell. She may have mentioned the other place as well, but that could only have been by accident, for hell had the first place in her heart.

She lit a candle, took out a new half-crown, and offered it to the first boy who would hold one finger—only one finger!—in the flame for five minutes by the school clock. Being always very ambitious I was tempted to volunteer, but I thought it might look greedy. Then she asked were we afraid of holding one finger—only one finger!—in a little candle flame for five minutes and not afraid of burning all over in roasting hot furnaces for all eternity. "All eternity! Just think of that! A whole lifetime goes by and it's nothing, not even a drop in the ocean of your sufferings." The woman was really interesting about hell, but my attention was all fixed on the half-crown. At the end of the lesson she put it back in her purse. It was a great disappointment; a religious woman like that, you wouldn't think she'd bother about a thing like a half-crown.

Another day she said she knew a priest who woke one night to find a fellow he didn't recognize leaning over the end of his bed. The priest was a bit frightened—naturally enough—but he asked the fellow what he wanted, and the fellow said in a deep, husky voice that he wanted to go to confession. The priest said it was an awkward time and wouldn't it do in the morning, but the fellow said that last time he went to confession, there was one sin he kept back, being ashamed to mention it, and now it was always on his mind. Then the priest knew it was a bad case, because the fellow was after making a bad confession and committing a mortal sin. He got up to dress, and just then the cock crew in the yard outside, and—lo and behold!—when the priest looked round there was no sign of the fellow, only a smell of burning timber, and when the priest looked at his bed didn't he see the print of two hands burned in it? That was because the fellow had made a bad confession. This story made a shocking impression on me.

But the worst of all was when she showed us how to examine our conscience. Did we take the name of the Lord, our God, in vain? Did we honor our father and our mother? (I asked her did this include grandmothers and she said it did.) Did we love our neighbors as ourselves? Did we covet our neighbor's goods? (I thought of the way I felt about the penny that Nora got every Friday.) I decided that, between one thing and another, I must have broken the whole ten commandments, all on account of that old woman, and so far as I could see, so long as she remained in the house I had no hope of ever doing anything else.

I was scared to death of confession. The day the whole class went I let on to have a toothache, hoping my absence wouldn't be noticed; but at three o'clock, just as I was feeling safe, along comes a chap with a message from Mrs. Ryan that I was to go to confession myself on Saturday and be at the chapel for communion with the rest. To make it worse, Mother couldn't come with me and sent Nora instead.

Now, that girl had ways of tormenting me that Mother never knew of. She held my hand as we went down the hill, smiling sadly and saying how sorry she was for me, as if she were bringing me to the hospital for an operation.

"Oh, God help us!" she moaned. "Isn't it a terrible pity you weren't a good boy? Oh, Jackie, my heart bleeds for you! How will you ever think of all your sins? Don't forget you have to tell him about the time you kicked Gran on the shin."

"Lemme go!" I said, trying to drag myself free of her. "I don't want to go to confession at all."

"But sure, you'll have to go to confession, Jackie," she replied in the same regretful tone. "Sure, if you didn't, the parish priest would be up to the house, looking for you. 'Tisn't, God knows, that I'm not sorry for you. Do you remember the time you tried to kill me with the bread-knife under the table? And the language you used to me? I don't know what he'll do with you at all, Jackie. He might have to send you up to the bishop."

I remember thinking bitterly that she didn't know the half of what I had to tell—if I told it. I knew I couldn't tell it, and understood perfectly why the fellow in Mrs. Ryan's story made a bad confession; it seemed to me a great shame that people wouldn't stop criticizing him. I remember that steep hill down to the church, and the sunlit hillsides beyond the valley of the river, which I saw in the gaps between the houses like Adam's last glimpse of Paradise.

Then, when she had manoeuvred me down the long flight of steps to the chapel yard, Nora suddenly changed her tone. She became the raging malicious devil she really was.

"There you are!" she said with a yelp of triumph, hurling me through the church door. "And I hope he'll give you the penitential psalms, you dirty little caffler."

I knew then I was lost, given up to eternal justice. The door with the colored-glass panels swung shut behind me, the sunlight went out and gave place to deep shadow, and the wind whistled outside so that the silence within seemed to crackle like ice under my feet. Nora sat in front of me by the confession box. There were a couple of old women ahead of her, and then a miserable-looking poor devil came and wedged me in at the other side, so that I couldn't escape even if I had the courage. He joined his hands and rolled his eyes in the direction of the roof, muttering aspirations in an anguished tone, and I wondered had he a grandmother too. Only a grandmother could account for a fellow behaving in that heartbroken way, but he was better off than I, for he at least could go and confess his sins; while I would make a bad confession and then die in the night and be continually coming back and burning people's furniture.

Nora's turn came, and I heard the sound of something slamming, and then her voice as if butter wouldn't melt in her mouth, and then another slam, and out she came. God, the hypocrisy of women! Her eyes were lowered, her head was bowed, and her hands were joined very low down on her stomach, and she walked up the aisle to the side altar looking like a saint. You never saw such an exhibition of devotion; and I remembered the devilish malice with which she had tormented me all the way from our door, and wondered were all religious people like that, really. It was my turn now. With the fear of damnation in my soul I went in, and the confessional door closed of itself behind me.

It was pitch-dark and I couldn't see priest or anything else. Then I really began to be frightened. In the darkness it was a matter between God and me, and He had all the odds. He knew what my intentions were before I even started; I had no chance. All I had ever been told about confession got mixed up in my mind, and I knelt to one wall and said: "Bless me, father, for I have sinned; this is my first confession." I waited for a few minutes, but nothing happened, so I tried it on the other wall. Nothing happened there either. He had me spotted all right.

It must have been then that I noticed the shelf at about one height with my head. It was really a place for grown-up people to rest their elbows, but in my distracted state I thought it was probably the place you were supposed to kneel. Of course, it was on the high side and not very deep, but I was always good at climbing and managed to get up all right. Staying up was the trouble. There was room only for my knees, and nothing you could get a grip on but a sort of wooden molding a bit above it. I held on to the molding and repeated the words a little louder, and this time something happened all right. A slide was slammed back; a little light entered the box, and a man's voice said: "Who's there?"

" 'Tis me, father," I said for fear he mightn't see me and go away again. I couldn't see him at all. The place the voice came from was under the molding, about level with my knees, so I took a good grip of the molding and swung myself down till I saw the astonished face of a young priest looking up at me. He had to put his head on one side to see me, and I had to put mine on one side to see him, so we were more or less talking to one another upside-down. It struck me as a queer way of hearing confessions, but I didn't feel it my place to criticize.

"Bless me, father, for I have sinned; this is my first confession," I rattled off in one breath, and swung myself down the least shade more to make it easier for him.

"What are you doing up there?" he shouted in an angry voice, and the strain the politeness was putting on my hold of the molding, and the shock of being addressed in such an uncivil tone, were too much for me. I lost my grip, tumbled, and hit the door an unmerciful wallop before I found myself flat on my back in the middle of the aisle. The people who had been waiting stood up with their mouths open. The priest opened the door of the middle box and came out, pushing his biretta back from his forehead; he looked something terrible. Then Nora came scampering down the aisle.

"Oh, you dirty little caffler!" she said. "I might have known you'd do it. I might have known you'd disgrace me.

I can't leave you out of my sight for one minute."

Before I could even get to my feet to defend myself she bent down and gave me a clip across the ear. This reminded me that I was so stunned I had even forgotten to cry, so that people might think I wasn't hurt at all, when in fact I was probably maimed for life. I gave a roar out of me.

"What's all this about?" the priest hissed, getting angrier than ever and pushing Nora off me. "How dare you hit the child like that, you little vixen?"

"But I can't do my penance with him, father," Nora cried, cocking an outraged eye up at him.

"Well, go and do it, or I'll give you some more to do," he said, giving me a hand up. "Was it coming to confession you were, my poor man?" he asked me.

" 'Twas, father," said I with a sob.

"Oh," he said respectfully, "a big hefty fellow like you must have terrible sins. Is this your first?"

" 'Tis, father," said I.

"Worse and worse," he said gloomily. "The crimes of a lifetime. I don't know will I get rid of you at all today. You'd better wait now till I'm finished with these old ones. You can see by the looks of them they haven't much to tell."

"I will, father," I said with something approaching joy.

The relief of it was really enormous. Nora stuck out her tongue at me from behind his back, but I couldn't even be bothered retorting. I knew from the very moment that man opened his mouth that he was intelligent above the ordinary. When I had time to think, I saw how right I was. It only stood to reason that a fellow confessing after seven years would have more to tell than people that went every week. The crimes of a lifetime, exactly as he said. It was only what he expected, and the rest was the cackle of old women and girls with their talk of hell, the bishop, and the penitential psalms. That was all they knew. I started to make my examination of conscience, and barring the one bad business of my grandmother it didn't seem so bad.

The next time, the priest steered me into the confession

box himself and left the shutter back the way I could see him get in and sit down at the further side of the grille from me.

"Well, now," he said, "what do they call you?"

"Jackie, father," said I.

"And what's a-trouble to you, Jackie?"

"Father," I said, feeling I might as well get it over while I had him in good humor, "I had it all arranged to kill my grandmother."

He seemed a bit shaken by that, all right, because he said nothing for quite a while.

"My goodness," he said at last, "that'd be a shocking thing to do. What put that into your head?"

"Father," I said, feeling very sorry for myself, "she's an awful woman."

"Is she?" he asked. "What way is she awful?"

"She takes porter, father," I said, knowing well from the way Mother talked of it that this was a mortal sin, and hoping it would make the priest take a more favorable view of my case.

"Oh, my!" he said, and I could see he was impressed.

"And snuff, father," said I.

"That's a bad case, sure enough, Jackie," he said.

"And she goes round in her bare feet, father," I went on in a rush of self-pity, "and she knows I don't like her, and she gives pennies to Nora and none to me, and my da sides with her and flakes me, and one night I was so heart-scalded I made up my mind I'd have to kill her."

"And what would you do with the body?" he asked with great interest.

"I was thinking I could chop that up and carry it away in a barrow I have," I said.

"Begor, Jackie," he said, "do you know you're a terrible child?"

"I know, father," I said, for I was just thinking the same thing myself. "I tried to kill Nora too with a bread-knife under the table, only I missed her."

"Is that the little girl that was beating you just now?" he asked.

" 'Tis, father."

"Someone will go for her with a bread-knife one day, and he won't miss her," he said rather cryptically. "You must have great courage. Between ourselves, there's a lot of people I'd like to do the same to but I'd never have the nerve. Hanging is an awful death."

"Is it, father?" I asked with the deepest interest—I was always very keen on hanging. "Did you ever see a fellow hanged?"

"Dozens of them," he said solemnly. "And they all died roaring."

"Jay!" I said.

"Oh, a horrible death!" he said with great satisfaction. "Lots of the fellows I saw killed their grandmothers too, but they all said 'twas never worth it."

He had me there for a full ten minutes talking, and then walked out the chapel yard with me. I was genuinely sorry to part with him, because he was the most entertaining character I'd ever met in the religious line. Outside, after the shadow of the church, the sunlight was like the roaring of waves on a beach; it dazzled me; and when the frozen silence melted and I heard the screech of trams on the road my heart soared. I knew now I wouldn't die in the night and come back, leaving marks on my mother's furniture. It would be a great worry to her, and the poor soul had enough.

Nora was sitting on the railing, waiting for me, and she put on a very sour puss when she saw the priest with me. She was mad jealous because a priest had never come out of the church with her.

"Well," she asked coldly, after he left me, "what did he give you?"

"Three Hail Marys," I said.

"Three Hail Marys," she repeated incredulously. "You mustn't have told him anything."

"I told him everything," I said confidently.

"About Gran and all?"

"About Gran and all."

(All she wanted was to be able to go home and say I'd made a bad confession.)

"Did you tell him you went for me with the bread-knife?" she asked with a frown.

"I did to be sure."

"And he only gave you three Hail Marys?"

"That's all."

She slowly got down from the railing with a baffled air. Clearly, this was beyond her. As we mounted the steps back to the main road she looked at me suspiciously.

"What are you sucking?" she asked.

"Bullseyes."

"Was it the priest gave them to you?"

" 'Twas."

"Lord God," she wailed bitterly, "some people have all the luck! 'Tis no advantage to anybody trying to be good. I might just as well be a sinner like you."

The Short Story

Just what it is that compels some people to make up stories and other people to read or listen to them is hard to pin down. Yet stories hold us spellbound. They always have and always will.

Myths are among the earliest stories ever told. They often explain natural events, such as the changing of the seasons, which ancient people did not understand. Greek, Roman, and Norse myths explain natural events by relating them to the behavior of the gods and goddesses, who were once believed to rule the earth and heavens. Powerful animals are important characters in African and native American myths. Many Asian myths include talking trees and rivers. In each culture, ancient people used myths to help them understand daily life. People believed that what the gods and goddesses did affected nature and the people on earth.

Fables and *parables* are other early forms of storytelling. Both kinds of stories teach a moral, or lesson. They set down rules of conduct and codes of behavior. They help people think about the difference between right and wrong.

The modern short story also helps readers think about right and wrong. Stories help us understand our thoughts and emotions. They make us laugh; sometimes they make us cry. An author's main purpose in writing a story is to share an important human experience.

Because a short story is *short,* it tells about a single situation or a single experience. There is one story, one plot line. The events in the story generally take place over a short period of time, and the author has room to create only one or two important, or main, characters.

Yet within a short space the author manages to recount an incident or an experience that strikes a common chord in every reader. And when you have finished the story, you feel as if you have shared an important moment in another person's life.

For the reader to experience powerful feelings when reading a story, the author must be careful and organized. A situation is presented, characters are introduced, things start happening. How an author organizes all those events is what this lesson, in fact this whole book, is about.

Let's look at Frank O'Connor's method of building a story in "First Confession." Along the way we'll mention some specific storytelling elements that will be the focus of later lessons. Right now, however, let's begin by looking at the story as a whole, from start to finish. Most short stories can be discussed by considering how the author has accomplished each of the following elements:

1 ♦ Beginning or setting up the story

2 ♦ Developing the characters

3 ♦ Building to a climax

4 ♦ Ending or winding down the story

1 ◆ Beginning the Story

The first few paragraphs of a story are very important because they must do several things. From the start, the author must set the mood, or frame of mind, he or she wishes the reader to share. Important characters must be introduced right away. The author must hint at the conflict, or struggle, to come. Most important, the author must catch your interest immediately to make sure that you don't stop reading.

Let's look at the opening paragraph of "First Confession" to see how Frank O'Connor begins his story. As you read it, ask yourself, "Who is talking? What am I learning about this character? What might happen next in this story?"

> All the trouble began when my grandfather died and my grandmother—my father's mother—came to live with us. Relations in the one house are a strain at the best of times, but, to make matters worse, my grandmother was a real old countrywoman and quite unsuited to the life in town. She had a fat, wrinkled old face, and, to Mother's great indignation, went round the house in bare feet—the boots had her crippled, she said. For dinner she had a jug of porter and a pot of potatoes with—sometimes—a bit of salt fish, and she poured out the potatoes on the table and ate them slowly, with great relish, using her fingers by way of a fork.

The speaker is a young child. (You learn in the next paragraph that it is a boy and later that he is seven years old.) He is the one who is telling the story. His voice says, "All the trouble began when my grandfather died and my grandmother . . . came to live with us." You are hearing the story as the boy sees it—from his *point of view*. Keep that fact in mind, because you may not want to take everything he says as the whole truth and nothing but. Other characters might see the situation in a different way. You can't be sure that the young boy is always correct or fair.

The little boy is clearly going to be an important character in the story. What have we already learned about him? We know two things: (1) he has a grievance against the newest member of the family—his grandmother—and (2) he feels "put upon." He feels he is being made to suffer by her presence in the house.

The first paragraph hints at the conflict to come: "Relations in the one house are a strain at the best of times," the boy tells you. His irritation gives us a reason to read on; it's interesting to read about other people's family squabbles.

Although you meet the grandmother in the first paragraph, she does not turn out to be a main character in the story. The author introduces her because he wants us to understand how the boy sees things. The grandmother is important because she affects the child's life. He is embarrassed because she behaves like a "real old countrywoman." Her manners, her clothes, and her habits probably haven't changed in fifty years. To the boy, she looks and acts differently and, therefore, she threatens his way of life. Like most young children, he has a limited point of view.

That different point of view, by the way, is what makes the story funny. The humor comes from the difference between a small boy's point of view and your own that makes you chuckle, even laugh out loud at times.

In Exercise A, you'll see Jackie's attitude toward another member of the family—his older sister Nora.

1 ✦ Exercise A

Read the following passage and answer the questions about it using what you have learned in this part of the lesson. Use your writing notebook or a separate piece of paper for your answers.

> When Mother was at work and my grandmother made the dinner I wouldn't touch it. Nora once tried to make me, but I hid under the table from her and took the bread-knife with me for protection. Nora let on to be very indignant (she wasn't, of course, but she knew Mother saw through her, so she sided with Gran) and came after me. I lashed out at her with the bread-knife, and after that she left me alone. I stayed there till Mother came in from work and made my dinner, but when Father came in later Nora said in a shocked voice: "Oh, Dadda, do you know what Jackie did at dinnertime?" Then, of course, it all came out; Father gave me a flaking; Mother interfered, and for days after that he didn't speak to me and Mother barely spoke to Nora. And all because of that old woman! God knows, I was heart-scalded.

1. Although several family members quarrel, Jackie thinks that one person is responsible for the trouble. Whom does he blame? How do you know?

2. Imagine that you are Jackie and that this incident happened in your family. As you think about the event, tell what you think is funny about it and what is not so funny.

Now check your answers using the suggestions in the Answer Key starting on page 457. Review this part of the lesson if you don't understand why an answer was wrong.

1♦Writing on Your Own

Look at the story idea you have written for Develop Your Own Short Story on page 26. Now do the following:

1. Write a paragraph or two that begins your story about a funny or embarrassing experience you had as a young child.

2. Try to set up the situation in your paragraphs and hint at the problem or trouble that is to come.

3. You may want to change and rewrite your paragraphs several times until they are just the way you want them.

2 ◆ Developing the Characters

As the story progresses, we get to know the main characters better. Like real people, they have public and private sides. Your public side is the part of you that strangers and people you're trying to impress see. When you are in public you are usually on your best behavior. Your private side is the part of you that your family, and maybe your closest friends, see—it reveals the personal things about you. Your private side can be sensitive, selfish, insecure, impatient, catty, or other things you may not be proud of. A good author tries to show both sides of main characters. That way the character seems rounded, or real.

Think about Jackie, for instance, the little boy telling the story in "First Confession." He would like you to believe that he is a splendid chap. According to him, his mistakes are always someone else's fault. Throughout the story, however, O'Connor lets you know that Jackie has real weaknesses. There are little hints about Jackie's true character.

In the following passage, Jackie tells us about Mrs. Ryan's little game with the half-crown (worth almost a dollar at the time this story takes place). How does Jackie explain *his* role in that short scene? How does the author show Jackie's deeper and truer feelings?

> She [Mrs. Ryan] lit a candle, took out a new half-crown, and offered it to the first boy who would hold one finger—only one finger!—in the flame for five minutes by the school clock. Being always very ambitious I was tempted to volunteer, but I thought it might look greedy. Then she asked were we afraid of holding one finger—only one finger!—in a little candle flame for five minutes and not afraid of burning all over in roasting hot furnaces for all eternity. . . . The woman was really interesting about hell, but my attention was all fixed on the half-crown. At the end of the lesson she put it back in her purse. It was a great disappointment; a religious woman like that, you wouldn't think she'd bother about a thing like a half-crown.

Remember, this small boy is always trying to make himself look as good as possible. He tells us that he decided not to hold his finger in the flame because he "thought it might look greedy." He is worried about outward appearances. But in fact, Jackie really *is* afraid to hold his finger in the flame, and he should be. But his excuse is the kind of little white lie that makes us smile.

It also becomes clear that, contrary to what he tells us, Jackie is very greedy indeed. Mrs. Ryan is using the coin to make a point about the terrors of hell. But Jackie couldn't care less about the point she is trying to make. As he says, "but my attention was all fixed on the half-crown." And Jackie is disappointed when Mrs. Ryan puts the coin away. By including that scene, the author reveals Jackie's private feelings.

Those little bits of information about Jackie's thoughts and feelings help round out his character. We see not only his public side but also his inner, private side. And the scene is realistic as well as funny. We have all behaved in ways similar to Jackie. By telling us about the incident and revealing Jackie's thoughts, the author has developed a character we can believe in.

There are two sides to Nora as well. See if you can spot them in Exercise B.

2 ♦ Exercise B

Read the following passage and answer the questions about it using what you have learned in this part of the lesson. Use your writing notebook or a separate piece of paper for your answers.

"Oh, God help us!" she moaned. "Isn't it a terrible pity you weren't a good boy? Oh, Jackie, my heart bleeds for you! How will you ever think of all your sins? Don't forget you have to tell him about the time you kicked Gran on the shin." . . .

Then, when she had manoeuvered me down the long flight of steps to the chapel yard, Nora suddenly changed her tone. She became the raging malicious devil she really was.

"There you are!" she said with a yelp of triumph, hurling me through the church door. "And I hope he'll give you the penitential psalms, you dirty little caffler."

1. In the last half of the passage, Nora does a complete turnabout. Now we see a side of Nora that she usually tries to hide. Is she the kind of person who enjoys seeing others get into trouble? What evidence can you find in the passage to support your answer?

2. Why do you think some people enjoy seeing others get into trouble?

Now check your answers using the suggestions in the Answer Key starting on page 457. Review this part of the lesson if you don't understand why an answer was wrong.

2 ◆ Writing on Your Own

Look at the story idea you have written for Develop Your Own Short Story on page 26. Now do the following:

1. Think of a person besides yourself who will be in your story. Show what this person is like by telling how he or she acts toward you.

2. You many want to change or rewrite your paragraphs several times until they are just the way you want them.

3 ◆ Building to a Climax

Jackie is worried about making his first confession. His sins are so dreadful (or so he imagines) that he is afraid to tell them to the priest. But if he holds anything back, he'll have made a bad confession, just like the poor man in Mrs. Ryan's story.

Jackie's situation—his fears—are an important part of the conflict, or struggle, in "First Confession." Every story contains conflict. Conflict gives the story a focus. When an author is writing a story, he or she concentrates on creating a conflict and then solving it. And when we are reading, we stay interested in a character's problems and look forward to seeing those problems solved. How the main character deals with his or her conflict, or problem, is what a story is all about.

Conflict creates suspense, and suspense keeps us wondering what will happen next. As the main character comes closer and closer to the heart of the problem, suspense builds. Finally, the character must solve the problem or be overwhelmed by it. This point of greatest suspense is called the *climax*. The climax, sometimes called a *crisis*, is also the turning point of the story.

In "First Confession" the climax approaches as Jackie enters the confession box. You can feel Jackie's tension as he steps inside:

> With the fear of damnation in my soul I went in, and the confessional door closed of itself behind me.
> It was pitch-dark and I couldn't see priest or anything else. Then I really began to be frightened. In the darkness it was a matter between God and me, and He had all the odds.

In the dark Jackie is scared and confused. He feels helpless. The reader shares his anxiety and sympathizes with his fears. Either Jackie is doomed to roast in the everlasting fires of hell, or he will be forgiven for his sins. One way or another something must change, because the crisis is always a turning point in the story. But there is also humor in the situation. The humor comes from knowing that things are hardly as bad as Jackie imagines. Frank O'Connor creates tension and humor at the same time.

In Exercise C Jackie finally meets the priest through the little sliding window of the confessional.

Read the following passage and answer questions about it using what you have learned in this part of the lesson. Use your writing notebook or a separate piece of paper for your answers.

> The place the voice came from was under the molding, about level with my knees, so I took a good grip of the molding and swung myself down till I saw the astonished face of a young priest looking up at me. He had to put his head on one side to see me, and I had to put mine on one side to see him, so we were more or less talking to one another upside-down. It struck me as a queer way of hearing confessions, but I didn't feel it my place to criticize.
>
> "Bless me, father, for I have sinned; this is my first confession," I rattled off in one breath. . . .
>
> "What are you doing up there?" he shouted in an angry voice, and the strain the politeness was putting on my hold of the molding, and the shock of being addressed in such an uncivil tone, were too much for me. I lost my grip, tumbled, and hit the door an unmerciful wallop before I found myself flat on my back in the middle of the aisle.

1. In an adventure story the climax is usually the most exciting part. In a humorous story the climax is often the funniest part. A number of events are funny in this passage. Why do you think this is the climax, or turning point, of the story?

2. In this passage the priest seems angry with Jackie. Later they become good friends. That change in a relationship happens all the time in real life. Parents or teachers may become angry with a child, but later they may laugh about the incident that made them angry. Why do you think people react that way?

Now check your answers using the suggestions in the Answer Key starting on page 457. Review this part of the lesson if you don't understand why an answer was wrong.

3♦Writing on Your Own

Look at the story idea you have written for Develop Your Own Short Story on page 26. Now do the following:

1. Describe the funny or embarrassing experience you had as a young child.

2. Stop writing when you get to the worst or the funniest part of the experience.

3. You may want to change or rewrite your paragraphs several times until they are just the way you want them.

4 ◆ Ending the Story

Finally, after building the conflict to a funny climax, O'Connor has to wind down the action and end the story. The conclusion of the story, and the end of the conflict, is called the *resolution*. The feeling of suspense has passed. The conflict has been worked out, and the crisis is over. Now the author has to create a quick, neat ending.

A good short story leaves you with a sense of completion. You get a final glimpse of the main characters. Have they changed at all? Have they learned something as a result of their experiences? What is the real point of the story?

If you can answer those questions, then you have found the *theme,* or main idea, of the story. The theme is similar to the moral that appears at the end of a fable. It is the point of the story; the lesson we have learned.

Read the following passage, taken from the last part of "First Confession." What mood do you sense? Does Jackie seem a little bit different—a little older or more mature—than when you first met him?

> He [the priest] had me there for a full ten minutes talking, and then walked out the chapel yard with me. I was genuinely sorry to part with him, because he was the most entertaining character I'd ever met in the religious line. Outside, after the shadow of the church, the sunlight was like the roaring of waves on a beach; it dazzled me; and when the frozen silence melted and I heard the screech of trams on the road my heart soared. I knew now I wouldn't die in the night and come back, leaving marks on my mother's furniture. It would be a great worry to her, and the poor soul had enough.

You can almost hear a big sigh of relief from Jackie; the mood is one of relief. "My heart soared," says Jackie as he comes out of the church. The ordeal is behind him, and the experience wasn't so bad after all.

But Jackie has also learned a lesson. "I knew now I wouldn't die in the night and come back, leaving marks on my mother's furniture," he says. In the space of an afternoon he has outgrown Mrs. Ryan's and Nora's limited idea of religion. The young priest has shown Jackie that religion should not frighten a person into being good.

As we leave Jackie, we feel that we have shared an important experience in his life. The author's ability to make us feel we have been involved in the events of the story is the essence of a good short story.

But there's more to "First Confession." O'Connor adds a humorous twist to the ending. The twist involves Nora, who has been self-righteous and cruel to Jackie. Go on to Exercise D now, and savor with Jackie his moment of triumph.

4 ◆ Exercise D

Read the following passage and answer the questions about it using what you have learned in this part of the lesson. Use your writing notebook or a separate piece of paper for your answers.

> "What are you sucking?" she [Nora] asked.
> "Bullseyes."
> "Was it the priest gave them to you?"
> " 'Twas."
> "Lord God," she wailed bitterly, "some people have all the luck! 'Tis no advantage to anybody trying to be good. I might just as well be a sinner like you."

1. Do you think this is a good ending for the story? Are you pleased or sorry at Nora's disappointment? Why?

2. Suppose the priest had told Jackie that he was a sinner and a "dirty little caffler" who was headed for an eternity in hell. Why would that be a poor ending for the story?

Now check your answers using the suggestions in the Answer Key starting on page 457. Review this part of the lesson if you don't understand why an answer was wrong.

4♦Writing on Your Own

Look at the story idea you have written for Develop Your Own Short Story on page 26. Now do the following:

1. Finish telling about your funny or embarrassing experience as a young child.

2. The paragraphs you are writing now should start to wind down your story and bring it to an end.

3. You may want to change or rewrite your paragraphs several times until they are just the way you want them.

Now go on to Reviewing and Interpreting the Story.

Reviewing and Interpreting the Story

Answer these questions without looking back at the story. Choose the best answer to each question and put an *x* in the box beside it, or write your answer on a separate piece of paper.

Remembering Facts

1. According to Jackie, who was responsible for all the trouble in his household?

   ☐ a. Nora

   ☐ b. his father

   ☐ c. his mother

   ☐ d. his grandmother

2. When Jackie falls out of the confession box and into the aisle, Nora

   ☐ a. helps him up.

   ☐ b. leaves the church.

   ☐ c. slaps his head.

   ☐ d. pretends not to know him.

Following the Order of Events

3. Jackie hid under the table

   ☐ a. to keep from eating dinner.

   ☐ b. to stab Nora with a knife.

   ☐ c. because he knew he was a sinner.

   ☐ d. to avoid getting a flaking.

4. How did Mrs. Ryan prepare the children for their first confession and communion?

☐ a. She frightened them about sin.

☐ b. She bribed them with money.

☐ c. She had Nora help her.

☐ d. Jackie held his finger in a candle.

5. Jackie says, "When I was playing with Bill Connell . . . and saw my grandmother steering up the path with the jug of porter sticking out from underneath her shawl I was <u>mortified</u>. The prefix *mort-* means "death." The word *mortified* is a good word choice because it means that Jackie felt

☐ a. frightened to death.

☐ b. a deadly hatred.

☐ c. embarrassed to death.

☐ d. deathly ill.

6. Jackie's father gave him a <u>flaking</u> for threatening Nora with a knife. You won't find that word in the dictionary because it's an Irish slang. But you can figure out from the way it is used in the story that *flaking* means a

☐ a. walloping or beating.

☐ b. good talking to.

☐ c. bitter argument.

☐ d. warning.

7. How does Jackie feel about making his first
   confession?

   ☐ a. He is looking forward to it.

   ☐ b. It is a big joke to him.

   ☐ c. He dreads it.

   ☐ d. It means nothing to him.

8. The priest spent more time with Jackie because he

   ☐ a. wanted Jackie to realize his sinful ways.

   ☐ b. felt he had to keep Jackie from killing his
        grandmother.

   ☐ c. wanted to help Jackie feel better about himself.

   ☐ d. was really having fun at Jackie's expense.

9. Author Frank O'Connor talks about sin and
   hellfire. The way he tells the story you understand
   that he thinks

   ☐ a. children are terrible sinners.

   ☐ b. Jackie and Nora have not done anything
        wrong.

   ☐ c. first communion should be abolished.

   ☐ d. small children really don't understand the
        nature of sin.

10. "First Confession" could be considered a good
    lesson in

    ☐ a. religion.

    ☐ b. child psychology.

    ☐ c. criminal justice.

    ☐ d. the history of Ireland.

11. A "first-person narrator" is a character the
author uses to tell the story. Who is the first-
person narrator in "First Confession"?

☐ a. Frank O'Connor

☐ b. Jackie

☐ c. Nora

☐ d. the priest

12. There is only one character in the story who is
made to look mean, self-important, and spiteful.
Who is that person?

☐ a. Father

☐ b. the priest

☐ c. Grandmother

☐ d. Nora

13. When Jackie enters the church, the setting is
described as: "The door . . . swung shut behind
me, the sunlight went out and gave place to deep
shadow, and the wind whistled outside so that the
silence within seemed to crackle like ice under my
feet." The way the setting is described gives a
feeling of

☐ a. warmth.

☐ b. religious awe.

☐ c. cold fear.

☐ d. cool refreshment.

14. Jackie says, "Outside, after the shadow of the church, the sunlight was like the roaring of waves on the beach; it dazzled me; and when the frozen silence melted, and I heard the screech of trams on the road my heart soared." From the way that setting is described, Jackie seems to go from

☐ a. death to life.

☐ b. a bad situation to a worse one.

☐ c. badness to goodness.

☐ d. childhood to adulthood.

Understanding Feelings

15. For the most part, the story portrays the feelings of

☐ a. most people who go to confession.

☐ b. a sister toward her brother.

☐ c. a small boy.

☐ d. a family in trouble.

16. At the end of the story, Nora feels bitter and disappointed that Jackie got off so easily. How are the readers made to feel?

☐ a. satisfied that Nora gets what she deserves

☐ b. disappointed the priest was so nice to Jackie

☐ c. sorry for Jackie's grandmother

☐ d. bitterly angry with Nora

Now check your answers using the Answer Key starting on page 457. Make no mark for right answers. <u>Correct</u> any wrong answers you may have by putting a check mark (✓) in the box next to the right answer. Count the number of questions you answered correctly and plot the total on the Comprehension Scores graph on page 468.

Next, look at the questions you answered incorrectly. What types of questions were they? Count the number you got wrong of each type and enter the numbers in the spaces below.

Remembering Facts _____

Following the Order of Events _____

Understanding Word Choices _____

Understanding Important Ideas _____

Understanding Levels of Meaning _____

Understanding Character _____

Understanding Setting _____

Understanding Feelings _____

Now use these numbers to fill in the Comprehension Skills Profile on page 469.

Discussion Guides

The questions below will help you to think about the story and the lesson you have just read. If you don't discuss these questions in class, try to think about them or discuss them with your classmates. Perhaps you will want to write a few paragraphs in answer to the questions.

Discussing Short Stories

1. This story is told from Jackie's point of view; we see everything through Jackie's eyes. Should we believe everything he tells us? Find something in the story that might be only half true.

2. Dialect is a manner of speaking that marks a person as coming from a particular area or background. What are some examples of Irish dialect in "First Confession"? What do they add to the story?

3. Suppose the story ended when Jackie came out of the church feeling relieved. What is gained by including that last little exchange with Nora?

Discussing the Story

4. In your opinion, did Mrs. Ryan do a good job of preparing the children to make their first confession? Explain your answer.

5. What are some things the priest does and says that make Jackie feel better? If Mrs. Ryan had been the priest, how might she have handled the same confession?

6. The presence of Jackie's grandmother is felt throughout much of the story. Yet we never meet her. Why do you think the author never introduces her? If we *were* to meet her, is it possible she would not prove to be the old witch Jackie claims she is? Give reasons for your opinion.

Discussing the Author's Work

7. Frank O'Connor is famous for writing simple stories about simple people. But it is said that through his stories he dealt with important and complicated problems of life. What important and complicated problems of living does the author deal with in "First Confession"?

8. Frank O'Connor wanted to write stories that were purely Irish. He wanted to make the Irish people aware and proud of their heritage. How does he achieve his goals in "First Confession"?

9. "First Confession" is a very Irish story. Why do you think people who aren't Irish or who aren't Catholics enjoy the story just as much as Irish Catholics do?

Writing Exercise

Read all the instructions before you begin writing. If you have any questions about how to begin the writing assignment, review Using the Writing Process beginning on page 445, or confer with your writing coach.

1. At the beginning of the unit you were asked to think of a funny or embarrassing experience you had as a young child. If you haven't done that yet, read the instructions for Develop Your Own Short Story on page 26, and make your list now. Follow the instructions in the four lesson exercises called Writing on Your Own.

2. If you are just beginning your story, here is a review of the instructions:

   ◆ Think of a funny or embarrassing experience you had as a young child. Tell in a few sentences what the story will be about.

   ◆ Write a paragraph or two that begins your story. Try to set up the situation in these paragraphs and hint at the problem or trouble to come.

   ◆ Tell how a person in the story acted toward you.

   ◆ Describe the funny or embarrassing experience.

   ◆ Write a paragraph that winds down the story and brings it to an end.

3. Now you will have a rough draft that tells what your story will be when it is finished. Now do this:

   a. Make a list or outline that shows what parts of your story you want to come first, second, third, and so on.

b. Rewrite your story. If you want to get a feel for how a short story about childhood might sound, reread "First Confession" to see how Frank O'Connor builds his story.

c. Reread your story once again. Make changes and corrections. You may want a friend, teacher, or your writing coach to make suggestions at this point.

d. Write your story in its final form. Some authors write a final draft two or three times until they get the story just the way they want it.

Unit 2 Character

Raymond's Run

BY TONI CADE BAMBARA

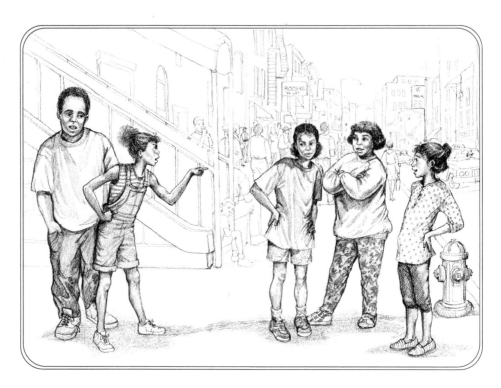

About the Illustration

What can you tell about the characters in this illustration? Point out some details in the drawing to support your response.

Here are some questions to help you think about the story:

◆ What are the girls doing? What is the boy doing?

◆ What is the girl who is standing next to the boy doing? What do you think she is saying to the girls?

◆ What is special about the boy's appearance?

◆ How do the girls who are looking over at the boy seem to feel about him?

Unit 2

Introduction

About the Story

Hazel Elizabeth Deborah Parker, also known as Squeaky, is a young girl growing up in New York City's Harlem district. She is a runner and proud of it. "The big kids call me Mercury," she says, "because I'm the swiftest thing in the neighborhood."

It is Squeaky's responsibility to look after her brother Raymond when they are outdoors. Raymond is older and bigger than Squeaky, but he is mentally retarded. Unfortunately, Raymond is often taunted by the neighborhood kids, at least that used to be the case when his brother George was taking care of him. But now that Squeaky is in charge, things are very different. If anybody has anything to say to Raymond, "they have to come by me," she announces.

Squeaky won't stand for any nonsense from anyone. And she has no patience for things she considers stupid, dishonest, phony, or disloyal. She is both independent and feisty, that is short-tempered, quarrelsome, and defensive. People don't cross her without hearing about it, and they had better be ready to fight if they push her too far.

You will undoubtedly admire Squeaky for her self-confidence, for the way she cares for Raymond, and for her fierce independence. But you may wonder if she isn't just a bit too proud. Even her defense of Raymond seems to stem more from a desire to protect her own reputation than from concern for her brother's feelings.

The story builds toward a race that Squeaky is sure she will win. The race is the climax of the story, and it brings about a change in Squeaky. You will want to watch for that change. But if the story leads to a race that features Squeaky, why is the title of the story "Raymond's Run"? Try to discover the answer to that question as you read.

Toni Cade Bambara was born in New York City and attended Queens College there. Before turning to teaching and writing, Ms. Bambara studied drama and dancing in Italy, France, and at the well-known Katherine Dunham Dance Studio in New York. She has lectured, given readings, taught, and taken an active role in raising African-American consciousness. She is now writer-in-residence at Spelman College in Atlanta.

After reading "Raymond's Run," you may want to read other stories by Toni Bambara, which are collected in the books titled *Gorilla, My Love* and *The Sea Birds Are Still Alive*. Or you may wish to read her novel *The Salt Eaters,* published by Random House, 1980.

About the Lesson

The lesson following the reading selection is about character. People, as well as animals and other creatures, are the characters you find in stories. But the word *character* has another, more important meaning. Character is the sum total of a person—what that person is like. Character is how a person looks, acts, and feels—his or her personality.

For a story to be believable, to have a true-to-life ring to it, the characters must be realistic and believable. The technique an author uses to breathe life into make-believe characters is called *characterization*. The lesson will focus on some of the ways an author creates believable, real characters.

The following questions will help you focus on how characters are developed in "Raymond's Run." Read the story carefully and try to answer these questions as you go along:

◆ Can you get to know Squeaky, Raymond, and the other characters in the story from what Squeaky tells you?

◆ What do you learn about the characters in the story from the way they talk to one another and from the way they behave toward one another?

◆ The author tries to make you like Squeaky and dislike the other girls in the story. How does she do that?

◆ How does the change that takes place in Squeaky at the end of the story help you understand her better?

Develop Your Own Character

Creating realistic, believable characters is one of the most important elements when writing a story. Use your writing notebook or a separate piece of paper and try the following suggestions:

1. To make a story believable, the characters themselves must first be believable. Imagine you are creating a character for a short story of your own. What type of character would you create? Here are some ideas to get you started:

   □ Create a character who reminds you of your best friend, someone who enjoys the same activities you do.

   □ Create a character you despise, perhaps a bully or a show-off.

   □ You could also choose to use yourself as your character.

   Write a few sentences describing the character's physical appearance. Is the character male or female, young or old, tall or short? Write a complete description of what that character looks like.

2. Looks often play an important role in how a person feels. If a person is unhappy about his or her looks, chances are he or she will have a low self-image. Even a very attractive person may feel ugly and lack self-esteem. Consider how your character feels about his or her

looks. Does your character's feelings determine his or her moods? Describe in a few sentences how your character feels about his or her looks. How is the character influenced as a result of those feelings, if at all?

3. Does your character seem realistic to you? Share your sentences with your classmates. Are their characters any more believable? Why?

Raymond's Run

by Toni Cade Bambara

I don't have much work to do around the house like some girls. My mother does that. And I don't have to earn my pocket money by hustling; George runs errands for the big boys and sells Christmas cards. And anything else that's got to get done, my father does. All I have to do in life is mind my brother Raymond, which is enough.

Sometimes I slip and say my little brother Raymond. But as any fool can see he's much bigger and he's older too. But a lot of people call him my little brother cause he needs looking after cause he's not quite right. And a lot of smart mouths got lots to say about that too, especially when George was minding him. But now, if anybody has anything to say to Raymond, anything to say about his big head, they have to come by me. And I don't play the dozens or believe in standing around with somebody in my face doing a lot of talking. I much rather just knock you down and take my chances even if I am a little girl with skinny arms and a squeaky voice, which is how I got the name Squeaky. And if things get too rough, I run. And as anybody can tell you, I'm the fastest thing on two feet.

There is no track meet that I don't win the first place medal. I use to win the twenty-yard dash when I was a little kid in kindergarten. Nowadays it's the fifty-yard dash. And tomorrow I'm subject to run the quarter-mile relay all by myself and come in first, second, and third. The big kids call me Mercury cause I'm the swiftest thing in the neighborhood. Everybody knows that—except two people who know better, my father and me.

He can beat me to Amsterdam Avenue with me having a two fire-hydrant headstart and him running with his hands in his pockets and whistling. But that's private information. Cause can you imagine some thirty-five-year-old man stuffing himself into PAL shorts to race little kids? So as far as everyone's concerned, I'm the fastest and that goes for Gretchen, too, who has put out the tale that she is going to win the first place medal this year. Ridiculous. In the second place, she's got short legs. In the third place, she's got freckles. In the first place, no one can beat me and that's all there is to it.

I'm standing on the corner admiring the weather and about to take a stroll down Broadway so I can practice my breathing exercises, and I've got Raymond walking on the inside close to the buildings cause he's subject to fits of fantasy and starts thinking he's a circus performer and that the curb is a tightrope strung high in the air. And sometimes after a rain, he likes to step down off his tightrope right into the gutter and slosh around getting his shoes and cuffs wet. Then I get hit when I get home. Or sometimes if you don't watch him, he'll dash across traffic to the island in the middle of Broadway and give the pigeons a fit. Then I have to go behind him apologizing to all the old people sitting around trying to get some sun and getting all upset with the pigeons fluttering around them, scattering their newspapers and upsetting the wax-paper lunches in their laps. So I keep Raymond on the inside of me, and he plays like he's driving a stage coach which is O.K. by me so long as he doesn't run me over or interrupt my breathing exercises, which I have to do on account of I'm serious about my running and don't care who knows it.

Now some people like to act like things come easy to them, won't let on that they practice. Not me. I'll high prance down 34th Street like a rodeo pony to keep my knees strong even if it does get my mother uptight so that she walks ahead like she's not with me, don't know me, is all by herself on a shopping trip, and I am somebody else's crazy child.

Now you take Cynthia Procter for instance. She's just the opposite. If there's a test tomorrow, she'll say something like, "Oh I guess I'll play handball this afternoon and watch television tonight," just to let you know she ain't thinking about the test. Or like last week when she won the spelling bee for the millionth time, "A good thing you got 'receive,' Squeaky, cause I would have got it wrong. I completely forgot about the spelling bee." And she'll clutch the lace on her blouse like it was a narrow escape. Oh, brother.

But of course when I pass her house on my early morning trots around the block, she is practicing the scales on the piano over and over and over and over. Then in music class, she always lets herself get bumped around so she falls accidently on purpose onto the piano stool and is so surprised to find herself sitting there, and so decides just for fun to try out the ole keys and what do you know— Chopin's waltzes just spring out of her fingertips and she's the most surprised thing in the world. A regular prodigy. I could kill people like that.

I stay up all night studying the words for the spelling bee. And you can see me anytime of day practicing running. I never walk if I can trot and shame on Raymond if he can't keep up. But of course he does, cause if he hangs back someone's liable to walk up to him and get smart, or take his allowance from him, or ask him where he got that great big pumpkin head. People are so stupid sometimes.

So I'm strolling down Broadway breathing out and breathing in on counts of seven, which is my lucky number, and here comes Gretchen and her sidekicks—Mary Louise who used to be a friend of mine when she first moved to Harlem from Baltimore and got beat up by everybody till I took up for her on account of her mother and my mother used to sing in the same choir when they were young girls, but people ain't grateful, so now she hangs out with the new girl Gretchen and talks about me like a dog; and Rosie who is as fat as I am skinny and has a big mouth where Raymond is concerned and is too stupid to know that there is not a big deal of difference between herself and Raymond and that she can't afford to throw stones. So they are steady coming up Broadway and I see right away that it's going to be one of those Dodge City scenes cause the street ain't that big and they're close to the buildings just as we are. First I think I'll step into the candy store and look over the new comics and let them pass. But that's chicken and I've got a reputation to consider. So then I think I'll just walk straight on through them or over them if necessary. But as they get to me, they slow down. I'm ready to fight, cause like I said I don't feature a whole lot of chitchat, I much prefer to just knock you down right from the jump and save everybody a lotta precious time.

"You signing up for the May Day Races?" smiles Mary Louise, only it's not a smile at all.

A dumb question like that doesn't deserve an answer. Besides, there's just me and Gretchen standing there really, so no use wasting my breath talking to shadows.

"I don't think you're going to win this time," says Rosie, trying to signify with her hands on her hips all salty, completely forgetting that I have whupped her behind many times for less salt than that.

"I always win cause I'm the best," I say straight at Gretchen who is, as far as I'm concerned, the only one talking in this ventriloquist-dummy routine.

Gretchen smiles but it's not a smile and I'm thinking that girls never really smile at each other because they don't know how and don't want to know how and there's probably no one to teach us how cause grown-up girls don't know either. Then they all look at Raymond who has just brought his mule team to a standstill. And they're about to see what trouble they can get into through him.

"What grade you in now, Raymond?"

"You got anything to say to my brother, you say it to me, Mary Louise Williams of Raggedy Town, Baltimore."

"What are you, his mother?" sasses Rosie.

"That's right, Fatso. And the next word out of anybody and I'll be their mother too." So they just stand there and Gretchen shifts from one leg to the other and so do they. Then Gretchen puts her hands on her hips and is about to say something with her freckle-face self but doesn't. Then she walks around me looking me up and down but keeps walking up Broadway, and her sidekicks follow her. So me and Raymond smile at each other and he says, "Gidyap" to his team and I continue with my breathing exercises, strolling down Broadway toward the icey man on 145th with not a care in the world cause I am Miss Quicksilver herself.

I take my time getting to the park on May Day because the track meet is the last thing on the program. The biggest thing on the program is the May Pole dancing which I can do without, thank you, even if my mother thinks it's a shame I don't take part and act like a girl for a change. You'd think my mother'd be grateful not to have to make me a white organdy dress with a big satin sash and buy me new white baby-doll shoes that can't be taken out of the box till the big day. You'd think she'd be glad her daughter ain't out there prancing around a May Pole getting the new clothes all dirty and sweaty and trying to act like a fairy or a flower or whatever you're supposed to be when you should be trying to be yourself, whatever that is, which is, as far as I am concerned, a poor Black girl who really can't afford to buy shoes and a new dress you only wear once a lifetime cause it won't fit next year.

I was once a strawberry in a Hansel and Gretel pageant when I was in nursery school and didn't have no better sense than to dance on tiptoe with my arms in a circle over my head doing umbrella steps and being a perfect fool just so my mother and father could come dressed up and clap.

You'd think they'd know better than to encourage that kind of nonsense. I am not a strawberry. I do not dance on my toes. I run. That is what I am all about. So I always come late to the May Day program, just in time to get my number pinned on and lay in the grass till they announce the fifty-yard dash.

I put Raymond in the little swings, which is a tight squeeze this year and will be impossible next year. Then I look around for Mr. Pearson who pins the numbers on. I'm really looking for Gretchen if you want to know the truth, but she's not around. The park is jam-packed. Parents in hats and corsages and breast-pocket handkerchiefs peeking up. Kids in white dresses and light blue suits. The parkees unfolding chairs and chasing the rowdy kids from Lenox as if they had no right to be there. The big guys with their caps on backwards, leaning against the fence swirling the basketballs on the tips of their fingers waiting for all these crazy people to clear out the park so they can play. Most of the kids in my class are carrying bass drums and glockenspiels and flutes. You'd think they'd put in a few bongos or something for real like that.

Then here comes Mr. Pearson with his clipboard and his cards and pencils and whistles and safety pins and fifty million other things he's always dropping all over the place with his clumsy self. He sticks out in a crowd cause he's on stilts. We used to call him Jack and the Beanstalk to get him mad. But I'm the only one that can outrun him and get away, and I'm too grown for that silliness now.

"Well, Squeaky," he says checking my name off the list and handing me number seven and two pins. And I'm thinking he's got no right to call me Squeaky, if I can't call him Beanstalk.

"Hazel Elizabeth Deborah Parker," I correct him and tell him to write it down on his board.

"Well, Hazel Elizabeth Deborah Parker, going to give someone else a break this year?" I squint at him real hard to see if he is seriously thinking I should lose the race on purpose just to give someone else a break.

"Only six girls running this time," he continues, shaking his head sadly like it's my fault all of New York didn't turn out in sneakers. "That new girl should give you a run for your money." He looks around the park for Gretchen like a periscope in a submarine movie. "Wouldn't it be a nice gesture if you were . . . to ahhh . . ."

I give him such a look he couldn't finish putting that idea into words. Grownups got a lot of nerve sometimes. I pin number seven to myself and stomp away—I'm so burnt. And I go straight for the track and stretch out on the grass while the band winds up with "Oh the Monkey Wrapped His Tail Around the Flag Pole," which my teacher calls by some other name. The man on the loudspeaker is calling everyone over to the track and I'm on my back looking at the sky trying to pretend I'm in the country, but I can't, because even grass in the city feels hard as sidewalk and there's just no pretending you are anywhere but in a "concrete jungle" as my grandfather says.

The twenty-yard dash takes all of the two minutes cause most of the little kids don't know no better than to run off the track or run the wrong way or run smack into the fence and fall down and cry. One little kid though has got the good sense to run straight for the white ribbon up ahead so he wins. Then the second graders line up for the thirty-yard dash and I don't even bother to turn my head to watch cause Raphael Perez always wins. He wins before he even begins by psyching the runners, telling them they're going to trip on their shoelaces and fall on their faces or lose their shorts or something, which he doesn't really have to do since he is very fast, almost as fast as I am. After that is the forty-yard dash which I use to run when I was in first grade. Raymond is hollering from the swings cause he knows I'm about to do my thing cause the man on the loudspeaker has just announced the fifty-yard dash, although he might just as well be giving a recipe for Angel Food cake cause you can hardly make out what he's saying for the static. I get up and slip off my sweat pants and then I see Gretchen standing at the starting line kicking her legs out like a pro. Then as I get into place I see that ole Raymond is in line on the other side of the fence, bending down with his fingers on the ground just like he knew what he was doing. I was going to yell at him but then I didn't. It burns up your energy to holler.

Every time, just before I take off in a race, I always feel like I'm in a dream, the kind of dream you have when you're sick with fever and feel all hot and weightless. I dream I'm flying over a sandy beach in the early morning sun, kissing the leaves of the trees as I fly by. And there's always the smell of apples, just like in the country when I was little and use to think I was a choo-choo train, running through the fields of corn and chugging up the hill to the orchard. And all the time I'm dreaming this, I get lighter and lighter until I'm flying over the beach again, getting blown through the sky like a feather that weighs nothing at all. But once I spread my fingers in the dirt and crouch over for the Get on Your Mark, the dream goes and I am solid again and am telling myself, Squeaky you must win, you must win, you are the fastest thing in the world, you can even beat your father up Amsterdam if you really try. And then I feel my weight coming back just behind my knees then down to my feet then into the earth and the pistol shot explodes in my blood and I am off and weightless again, flying past the other runners, my arms pumping up and down and the whole world is quiet except for the crunch as I zoom over the gravel in the track. I glance to my left and there is no one. To the right a blurred Gretchen who's got her chin jutting out as if it would win the race all by itself. And on the other side of the fence is Raymond with his arms down to his side and the palms tucked up behind him, running in his very own style and the first time I ever saw that and I almost stopped to watch my brother Raymond on his first run. But the white ribbon is bouncing toward me and I tear past it racing into the distance till my feet with a mind of their own start digging up footfuls of dirt and brake me short. Then all the kids standing on the side pile on me, banging me on the back and slapping my head with their May Day programs, for I have won again and everybody on 151st Street can walk tall for another year.

"In first place . . ." the man on the loudspeaker is clear as a bell now. But then he pauses and the loudspeaker starts to whine. Then static. And I lean down to catch my breath and here comes Gretchen walking back for she's overshot the finish line too, huffing and puffing with her hands on her hips taking it slow, breathing in steady time like a real pro and I sort of like her a little for the first time. "In first place . . ." and then three or four voices get all mixed up on the loudspeaker and I dig my sneaker into the grass and stare at Gretchen who's staring back, we both wondering just who did win. I can hear old Beanstalk arguing with the man on the loudspeaker and then a few others running their mouths about what the stop watches say.

Then I hear Raymond yanking at the fence to call me and I wave to shush him, but he keeps rattling the fence like a gorilla in a cage like in them gorilla movies, but then like a dancer or something he starts climbing up nice and easy but very fast. And it occurs to me, watching how smoothly he climbs hand over hand and remembering how he looked running with his arms down to his side and with the wind pulling his mouth back and his teeth showing and all, it occurred to me that Raymond would make a very fine runner. Doesn't he always keep up with me on my trots? And he surely knows how to breathe in counts of seven cause he's always doing it at the dinner table, which drives my brother George up the wall. And I'm smiling to beat the band cause if I've lost this race, or if me and Gretchen tied, or even if I've won, I can always retire as a runner and begin a whole new career as a coach with Raymond as my champion. After all, with a little more study I can beat Cynthia and her phony self at the spelling bee. And if I bugged my mother, I could get piano lessons and become a star. And I have a big rep as the baddest thing around. And I've got a roomful of ribbons and medals and awards. But what has Raymond got to call his own?

So I stand there with my new plan, laughing out loud by this time as Raymond jumps down from the fence and runs over with his teeth showing and his arms down to the side which no one before him has quite mastered as a running style. And by the time he comes over I'm jumping up and down so glad to see him—my brother Raymond, a great runner in the family tradition. But of course everyone thinks I'm jumping up and down because the men on the loudspeaker have finally gotten themselves together and compared notes and are announcing "In first place— Miss Hazel Elizabeth Deborah Parker." (Dig that.) "In second place—Miss Gretchen P. Lewis." And I look over at Gretchen wondering what the P stands for. And I smile. Cause she's good, no doubt about it. Maybe she'd like to help me coach Raymond; she obviously is serious about running, as any fool can see. And she nods to congratulate me and then she smiles. And I smile. We stand there with this big smile of respect between us. It's about as real a smile as girls can do for each other, considering we don't practice real smiling every day you know, cause maybe we too busy being flowers or fairies or strawberries instead of something honest and worthy of respect . . . you know . . . like being people.

Character

The best authors are those who create characters you can truly believe in. We all know that characters in stories are not real people. But when an author's imagination and a reader's imagination work together, characters simply come alive! When this happens, the author has succeeded in making the characters *believable*.

In "Raymond's Run," Toni Cade Bambara has given life to Hazel Elizabeth Deborah Parker—Squeaky—who lives at some unknown address in the vicinity of Broadway and 145th Street in New York City's district of Harlem. You are led to believe that Squeaky is a real person because you are told what she looks like, what she thinks, and how she feels. As you read, you come to see Squeaky's world through her eyes. You see the characters in her world as she sees them. And you come to feel much the same way about them as she does. You can *identify* with Squeaky. And because you can identify with her, you also believe in her brother Raymond and all the other characters that you see through her eyes.

Getting to know the characters in a story is one of the great joys of reading. Rarely do you get to know as much about the personal thoughts and feelings of a person as you do about the characters from the stories and novels you read. Characters in a story are presented, described, and explained to you by the author. That kind of in-depth introduction is a service you don't have when you meet a new person at school. This "service" that a writer provides is the process known as *characterization*.

Characterization is controlled by the author. It is like a paintbrush in the hands of an artist. By adding a line here and there, an artist can make a person look beautiful or ugly. A subtle shading around the eyes can make a person appear mean or kind, sad or cheerful. In the same way, with a word or two, a description or an action, an author can make you like or dislike a character. Depending on how the author wants you to feel, you may sympathize with one character and wish the worst for another. As you will see in the lesson, understanding the characters in a story is not something you have to work very hard at. In the hands of a good author, characters clearly identify and explain themselves.

In this lesson we will look at four ways in which author Toni Bambara creates characters whom you can understand and believe in:

1 ♦ The characters are described by the author.

2 ♦ The author shows you the characters in action.

3 ♦ The author explains how the characters feel.

4 ♦ By showing you different aspects of the personalities of the characters, the author helps you analyze and understand them.

1 ◆ Character and Description

Many different qualities make up a person's character. The most obvious part of any person, of course, is what he or she looks like. Is he tall or short? Is she dark or fair? Age, dress, facial expressions, and many other details all influence your first impression of any new person you meet.

After you have known someone awhile, you know a lot more about that person's character. You know whether the person is clever or dull, friendly or distant, nervous and self-conscious, or cool and self-assured. Now you are getting past outward appearances to the person's true inner nature.

When you meet a character in a story, the more you learn about the character the more interesting the character becomes. Authors realize this and go to great lengths to acquaint you with their characters. Writers spark your interest in the main characters in a story.

The easiest way to present a character is with a description. Because Bambara has planned her characters very carefully, she is able to describe both their outer and inner characters at any point in the story. Sometimes an author describes a character right away. Other times, though, an author will describe a character slowly, letting you in on important details as the story progresses. Author Toni Bambara gets right to it in the following early paragraph from "Raymond's Run." Notice how much you learn about both the "outer" and "inner" Squeaky from the author's description. And you learn a good bit about Raymond, too.

(Like Frank O'Connor's story "First Confession," this story is told in the *first person*. This means the story is told as if one of the characters is speaking directly to you. In this case, Squeaky is speaking to the reader. Keep in mind, however, that it is really the *author* speaking to you *through* the character Squeaky.)

> Sometimes I slip and say my little brother Raymond. But as any fool can see he's much bigger and he's older too. But a lot of people call him my little brother cause he needs looking after cause he's not quite right. And a lot of smart mouths got lots to say about that too, especially when George was minding him. But now, if anybody has anything to say to Raymond, anything to say about his big head, they have to come by me. And I don't play the

dozens or believe in standing around with somebody in my face doing a lot of talking. I much rather just knock you down and take my chances even if I am a little girl with skinny arms and a squeaky voice, which is how I got the name Squeaky. And if things get too rough, I run. And as anybody can tell you, I'm the fastest thing on two feet.

First Squeaky describes Raymond to you. Because of Raymond's mental retardation, he is not very attractive. His head is too big, and sometimes other kids pick on him. But Squeaky is fiercely loyal to her brother. No one picks on Raymond and gets away with it.

As she describes herself, you learn a great deal about both the outer and inner Squeaky. Outwardly, she is small and skinny and has a squeaky voice. But what she lacks in size she makes up for in courage and "street smarts." Not one to waste words on people who cross her, she prefers to fight rather than stand around trading insults (playing "the dozens"). And she is smart enough to know when it's time to run, being that she is "the fastest thing on two feet."

In the passage in Exercise A, see how much you can learn about the girls Squeaky meets on Broadway from the author's (Squeaky's) description.

1 ◆ Exercise A

Read the following passage and answer the questions about it using what you have learned in this part of the lesson. Use your writing notebook or a separate piece of paper for your answers.

So I'm strolling down Broadway . . . and here comes Gretchen and her sidekicks—Mary Louise who used to be a friend of mine when she first moved to Harlem from Baltimore and got beat up by everybody till I took up for her . . . , but people ain't grateful, so now she hangs out with the new girl Gretchen and talks about me like a dog; and Rosie who is as fat as I am skinny and has a big mouth where Raymond is concerned and is too stupid to know that there is not a big deal of difference between herself and Raymond. . . .

1. In the passage Squeaky describes Rosie exactly as she sees her. What type of description is it? What words in the story support your answer?

2. Squeaky and Mary Louise were once friends. Now, however, they are on opposing sides. How does Squeaky feel about Mary Louise now? Why does she feel that way? Be specific.

Now check your answers using the suggestions in the Answer Key starting on page 457. Review this part of the lesson if you don't understand why an answer was wrong.

1♦Writing on Your Own

Look at the sentences you have written for Develop Your Own Character on page 65. Now do the following:

1. Expand on the sentences you wrote earlier by writing a short paragraph describing your character. You can use *third-person point of view* (you as the author describe your character) or *first-person point of view* (your character describes himself or herself).

2. Now write a short paragraph in which your character describes someone he or she knows. Will your character be generous or selfish? Sympathetic or insensitive?

3. You may want to change and rewrite your paragraphs several times until you get them just the way you want them.

2 ◆ Character and Action

We judge people not only by their appearance but also by how they behave. A person may be beautifully dressed yet act nasty and cruel. Another person may look reserved and quiet but is really carefree and fun-loving. It is only after you get to know someone well that a complete picture of character finally emerges.

An author, then, in addition to describing characters to you, develops them through their actions. Developing a character through description is called *exposition*. The author *exposes* the character to you. Developing a character through his or her actions is called *characterization by dramatic action*.

The action in plays, movies, or on television is dramatic action. It may consist of anything from a wild, out-of-control fistfight to a quiet conversation. Most dramatic action, in fact, is conversation—usually called *dialogue*. In the following passage you get a good idea of what Cynthia Procter is like, both from what she says and from what she does:

> Now you take Cynthia Procter for instance. She's just the opposite [of me]. If there's a test tomorrow, she'll say something like, "Oh I guess I'll play handball this afternoon and watch television tonight," just to let you know she ain't thinking about the test. Or like last week when she won the spelling bee for the millionth time, "A good thing you got 'receive,' Squeaky, cause I would have got it wrong. I completely forgot about the spelling bee." And she'll clutch the lace on her blouse like it was a narrow escape. Oh, brother.

From her words and actions, Cynthia shows herself to be a bit of a phony. She would like everyone to think that all things come very easily for her when, in fact, she has to work very hard. In the next paragraph Squeaky describes how Cynthia practices the piano for hours on end. Then in music class she sits down to play and acts as if the music just springs from her fingertips through sheer genius.

Cynthia Procter's actions in the story have another purpose that you should be aware of. Her character is used to help you get to know Squeaky better. Cynthia is the *opposite* of Squeaky. Squeaky is straightforward. She has to work hard for the things she does well, and she doesn't care who knows it. In fact, she's very proud of her hard work. Cynthia's phoniness and Squeaky's feelings about Cynthia serve to emphasize Squeaky's directness.

2 ✦ Exercise B

Read the following passage and answer the questions about it using what you have learned in this part of the lesson. Use your writing notebook or a separate piece of paper for your answers.

> [Mary Louise asks Raymond a question and Squeaky answers for him.]
> "What grade you in now, Raymond?"
> "You got anything to say to my brother, you say it to me, Mary Louise Williams of Raggedy Town, Baltimore."
> "What are you, his mother?" sasses Rosie.
> "That's right, Fatso. And the next word out of anybody and I'll be their mother too." So they just stand there and Gretchen shifts from one leg to the other and so do they. Then Gretchen puts her hands on her hips and is about to say something with her freckle-face self but doesn't. Then she walks around me looking me up and down but keeps walking up Broadway, and her sidekicks follow her. So me and Raymond smile at each other and he says, "Gidyap" to his team and I continue with my breathing exercises, strolling down Broadway toward the icey man on 145th with not a care in the world cause I am Miss Quicksilver herself.

1. Squeaky has a lot of confidence in herself. In a few short sentences, describe how Squeaky shows this confidence. Do you admire her for the way she acts? Why or why not?

2. Mary Louise, Rosie, and Gretchen act as a group. They go along with one another without argument. Compare their actions to Squeaky's actions. How are their actions similar and different?

Now check your answers using the suggestions in the Answer Key starting on page 457. Review this part of the lesson if you don't understand why an answer was wrong.

2♦Writing on Your Own

Look at the sentences you have written for Develop Your Own Character on page 65. Now do the following:

1. Two people will usually see the same situation quite differently, especially when there is a confrontation involved. Think about a problem you may have had with a classmate. There is no doubt that the story would be told differently depending on who is telling it. It is part of human nature to see our own side of a confrontation as truth.

   From your character's point of view, create a confrontation with another character. Consider how your character would act and how your character sees the reactions of the other person. Write a few paragraphs of dialogue between the two characters.

2. In a short paragraph, point out how the confrontation is one-sided. How might the confrontation be seen by the other character?

3. You may want to change and rewrite your paragraphs several times until you get them just the way you want them.

3 ◆ Character and Feeling

Each person you know affects you differently. You *feel* differently about different people. You love members of your family, but you may love a boyfriend or girlfriend in a very different way. Some people may annoy you, while others may be downright scary. There are still others whom you admire, and some who make you uneasy for reasons you can't explain. There is no limit to the range of feelings you can have toward people.

Authors see to it that you develop certain feelings about the characters you meet in their stories. The *tone* used by the author creates these feelings, as you will see in a lesson further on in this book. For example, you can tell by the way Squeaky describes Mary Louise and Rosie that she doesn't like them. The author passes that tone or attitude on to you through Squeaky, and you come to feel the same way as Squeaky does about the girls because you sympathize with her.

> "You signing up for the May Day races?" smiles Mary Louise, only it's not a smile at all. . . .
>
> "I don't think you're going to win this time," says Rosie, trying to signify with her hands on her hips all salty, completely forgetting that I have whupped her behind many times for less salt than that.
>
> "I always win cause I'm the best," I say straight at Gretchen who is, as far as I'm concerned, the only one talking in this ventriloquist-dummy routine.
>
> Gretchen smiles but it's not a smile and I'm thinking that girls never really smile at each other because they don't know how. . . .

From the very beginning of the story, the author has put you on Squeaky's side. The author wants you to have a feeling of sympathy for the main character. If you stop to think about it, though, you might not be especially fond of Squeaky if she were a real person. She thinks an awful lot of herself—she's very proud—and doesn't seem to get along well with other people. She has a chip on her shoulder. And she does not tolerate common faults in anyone, even though she has some of her own.

The author destroyed any sympathetic feelings you might have had for Mary Louise and Rosie a few paragraphs back. You know just how to feel about them. Now the author adds to your feelings of dislike. Mary Louise asks a "dumb question" and Squeaky ignores her. Rosie, who has been described as fat and stupid, is now pictured as sassy and prissy. At this point you would just love to see Squeaky whup her as she says she has done before.

3 ✦ Exercise C

Read the following passage and answer the questions about it using what you have learned in this part of the lesson. Use your writing notebook or a separate piece of paper for your answers.

> Then here comes Mr. Pearson with his clipboard and his cards and pencils and whistles and safety pins and fifty million other things he's always dropping all over the place with his clumsy self. He sticks out in a crowd cause he's on stilts. We used to call him Jack and the Beanstalk to get him mad. . . .
>
> "Well, Hazel Elizabeth Deborah Parker, going to give someone else a break this year?" I squint at him real hard to see if he is seriously thinking I should lose the race on purpose just to give someone else a break. . . .
>
> "That new girl should give you a run for your money. . . . Wouldn't it be a nice gesture if you were . . . to ahhh . . ."
>
> I give him such a look he couldn't finish putting that idea into words. Grownups got a lot of nerve sometimes. I pin number seven to myself and stomp away—I'm so burnt.

1. Briefly, in your own words, describe Mr. Pearson. Does your description match one that Squeaky might give? Why or why not?

2. How does Squeaky feel toward Mr. Pearson after he hints that she should lose the race on purpose? How would you feel if you were Squeaky?

Now check your answers using the suggestions in the Answer Key starting on page 457. Review this part of the lesson if you don't understand why an answer was wrong.

3♦Writing on Your Own

Look at the sentences you have written for Develop Your Own Character on page 65 that tell about your own character. Now do the following:

1. Have your character describe his or her feelings about something important. Perhaps your character feels he or she has been treated unfairly by a teacher or a classmate. Or maybe there is a social issue he or she feels strongly about. Write a few sentences describing your character's feelings.

2. In a short paragraph, have your character justify his or her feelings about the important issue. Why does your character feel he or she is right in feeling that way?

3. You may want to change and rewrite you paragraphs several times until you get them just the way you want them.

4 ◆ Understanding Character

One of the many advantages of reading is that it helps you develop your ability to understand people. And that is one of life's most important skills. People who don't understand others, who can't figure out their natures and true intentions, are doomed to make very serious mistakes in their relationships with others.

Reading stories and novels opens up a whole world of characters you might otherwise never have known. Readers in California, for example, might never have known a girl from Harlem if they hadn't met Squeaky. But, most important, authors provide readers with the opportunity to think very carefully about various types of characters. You don't often get a chance to focus as closely on a person in real life as you do on a character in a story. You especially don't get the chance to look *inside* a person, at their very thoughts, as you do with Squeaky.

Thinking about characters and discussing them with other people is called *character analysis*. Character analysis is an effort to understand a character by putting together the facts and feelings about them that an author provides. Once you feel you understand a character, you usually make judgments about him or her.

We will analyze Squeaky's character a bit in the passage that follows. Then you can do your own analysis in Exercise D.

> . . . it occurred to me that Raymond would make a very fine runner. Doesn't he always keep up with me on my trots? And he surely knows how to breathe in counts of seven. . . . And I'm smiling to beat the band cause if I've lost this race, or if me and Gretchen tied, or even if I've won, I can always retire as a runner and begin a whole new career as a coach with Raymond as my champion. After all, with a little more study I can beat Cynthia and her phony self at the spelling bee. And if I bugged my mother, I could get piano lessons and become a star. . . . And I've got a roomful of ribbons and medals and awards. But what has Raymond got to call his own? . . .
>
> . . . and by the time he comes over I'm jumping up and down so glad to see him—my brother Raymond, a great runner in the family tradition.

This passage should cause you to stop and take a new look at Squeaky. A change has come over her. Not only do you see her in a new light, but you also see her actions and feelings.

This is the first time you've seen Squeaky really happy. Oh, she's been proud of herself, but she has not felt the happiness of pride in another person. This is also the first time she has thought about someone else being a winner besides herself. And the thought doesn't upset her.

You have to feel sympathetic toward the old Squeaky who hates phonies and is always ready for a fight. Good old self-confident Squeaky. But now, through your analysis of her, you can probably see that Squeaky was awful to other people. She didn't get along very well with people. She demanded too much. And her thoughts were almost entirely related to herself.

Now, for the first time, Squeaky is thinking about others. And she finds she is happier for it.

4 ♦ Exercise D

Read the following passage and answer the questions about it using what you have learned in this part of the lesson. Use your writing notebook or a separate piece of paper for your answers.

> "In first place—Miss Hazel Elizabeth Deborah Parker." (Dig that.) "In second place—Miss Gretchen P. Lewis." And I look over at Gretchen wondering what the P stands for. And I smile. Cause she's good, no doubt about it. Maybe she'd like to help me coach Raymond; she obviously is serious about running, as any fool can see. And she nods to congratulate me and then she smiles. And I smile. We stand there with this big smile of respect between us. It's about as real a smile as girls can do for each other. . . .

1. Certainly a change has come about in Squeaky. For the first time she finds happiness in the achievements of others. Describe the change in Squeaky. When compared to the Squeaky in the beginning of the story, how has she changed?

2. Throughout most of the story Squeaky speaks out against people. Now, however, she is seeing others in an entirely different light. What brought about this change in Squeaky? How do you think she will change as a result?

Now check your answers using the suggestions in the Answer Key starting on page 457. Review this part of the lesson if you don't understand why an answer was wrong.

4♦Writing on Your Own

Look at the sentences you have written for Develop Your Own Character on page 65. Now do the following:

1. In a few sentences, describe a change in your character. Perhaps your character comes to understand the feelings of another. Or maybe your character sees a situation from a more mature point of view. Compare your character's new feelings to those he or she held before.

2. How will your character be different as a result of this change of heart? Will he or she be more understanding and accepting of others? Write a short paragraph explaining the changes in your character.

3. You may want to change and rewrite your paragraphs several times until you get them just the way you want them.

Now go on to Reviewing and Interpreting the Story.

Reviewing and Interpreting the Story

Answer these questions without looking back at the story. Choose the best answer to each question and put an *x* in the box beside it, or write your answer on a separate piece of paper.

Remembering Facts

1. Squeaky has one very important responsibility. What is it?

   ☐ a. running errands

   ☐ b. watching Raymond

   ☐ c. cooking dinner

   ☐ d. practicing the piano

2. Raymond is often the butt of neighborhood jokes because of his

   ☐ a. imaginary games.

   ☐ b. big mouth.

   ☐ c. small body.

   ☐ d. large head.

Following the Order of Events

3. Three of the events below did not occur at the time of the story. Choose the event that *did* occur during the story.

   ☐ a. Raymond races along side of Squeaky, Gretchen, and the other runners.

   ☐ b. George gets angry with Raymond for breathing in counts of seven at the dinner table.

   ☐ c. Squeaky races her father down Amsterdam Ave. and loses.

   ☐ d. Raymond chases the pigeons in the park.

4. Squeaky decides to coach Raymond because

☐ a. he is able to keep up with her on her daily runs.

☐ b. he has a running style all his own.

☐ c. she realizes that Raymond deserves to be a winner.

☐ d. she wants to become friends with Gretchen.

Understanding Word Choices

5. Cynthia Procter wants others to think that she is a naturally gifted pianist—a <u>prodigy.</u> The word *prodigy* means

☐ a. a great talent.

☐ b. a show-off.

☐ c. good at only one thing.

☐ d. a female pianist.

6. Squeaky says of Rosie, ". . . there is not a big deal of difference between herself and Raymond and . . . she can't afford <u>to throw stones.</u>" That expression means Rosie shouldn't

☐ a. throw stones at Raymond because he can't defend himself.

☐ b. make fun of Raymond because of his mental retardation.

☐ c. make mean remarks about Raymond because she is far from perfect herself.

☐ d. throw stones at Raymond because she will have to answer to Squeaky.

7. One thing bothers Squeaky more than anything
else. What is it?

☐ a. people who make fun of Raymond

☐ b. people who brag about their
accomplishments

☐ c. people who are afraid to stand up for
themselves

☐ d. people who are phonies

8. A change happens in Squeaky at the end of the
story. What is it?

☐ a. Squeaky no longer cares about running.

☐ b. Squeaky realizes the importance of other
people.

☐ c. Squeaky thinks Gretchen could be an asset
to Raymond's training.

☐ d. Squeaky decides to concentrate on spelling
and the piano.

9. Consider the change that happens in Squeaky.
Choose one of the words below to describe this
change.

☐ a. respect

☐ b. honesty

☐ c. trust

☐ d. growth

10. Squeaky experiences a change when she realizes how important Raymond's feelings are. What does she realize about Raymond that she hadn't really known before?

☐ a. She learns that Raymond will always have limits in life while she'll be free to strive and achieve.

☐ b. She feels bad for Raymond since he cannot participate in the race.

☐ c. Squeaky realizes how cruel the other kids are to make fun of Raymond.

☐ d. She knows she will not always be around to watch over Raymond.

Understanding Character

11. Squeaky says of Mary Louise, ". . . who used to be a friend of mine . . . [she] now hangs out with the new girl Gretchen and talks about me like a dog. . . ." In Squeaky's eyes, Mary Louise is a

☐ a. snob.

☐ b. traitor.

☐ c. coward.

☐ d. follower.

12. Throughout most of the story, which phrase best describes Squeaky's attitude?

☐ a. serious and mean

☐ b. proud and defensive

☐ c. clever and witty

☐ d. serious and smart

13. Squeaky says of the local park, ". . . there's just no pretending you are anywhere but in a 'concrete jungle' as my grandfather says." What does that sentence tell you about Squeaky's world?

   ☐ a. There are still a few beautiful places left in New York City.

   ☐ b. Squeaky is grateful that there are still a few grassy areas where kids can play.

   ☐ c. The park is a badly needed oasis in the middle of the big city.

   ☐ d. A little grass cannot change the fact that she lives in a noisy, dirty city.

14. Just before a race Squeaky dreams she is, "flying over a sandy beach in the early morning sun, kissing the leaves of the trees. . . . there's always a smell of apples, just like in the country." Why do you think Squeaky imagines these things?

   ☐ a. She imagines that she is running to reach this place.

   ☐ b. The image helps her clear her mind of her troubles before every race.

   ☐ c. These thoughts allow her to forget about Raymond.

   ☐ d. She would rather live in the country.

15. By the end of the story, Squeaky has undergone a major change. Which word describes Squeaky's new attitude?

   ☐ a. distant

   ☐ b. negative

   ☐ c. troubled

   ☐ d. positive

16. How do you think Gretchen's feelings about Squeaky will change after the race?

☐ a. She will share a feeling of respect with Squeaky.

☐ b. She will continue to dislike Squeaky.

☐ c. Feelings of jealousy will develop because she lost to Squeaky.

☐ d. She will try to be like the old Squeaky.

Now check your answers using the Answer Key starting on page 457. Make no mark for right answers. Correct any wrong answers you may have by putting a check mark (✓) in the box next to the right answer. Count the number of questions you answered correctly and plot the total on the Comprehension Scores graph on page 468.

Next, look at the questions you answered incorrectly. What types of questions were they? Count the number you got wrong of each type and enter the numbers in the spaces below.

Remembering Facts	_____
Following the Order of Events	_____
Understanding Word Choices	_____
Understanding Important Ideas	_____
Understanding Levels of Meaning	_____
Understanding Character	_____
Understanding Setting	_____
Understanding Feelings	_____

Now use these numbers to fill in the Comprehension Skills Profile on page 469.

Discussion Guides

The questions below will help you to think about the story and the lesson you have just read. If you don't discuss these questions in class, try to think about them or discuss them with your classmates. Perhaps you will want to write a few paragraphs in answer to the questions.

Discussing Characterization

1. Squeaky is the main character (sometimes called the *protagonist*) of the story. Of all the characters in a story, readers usually feel the most sympathy for the protagonist. In "Raymond's Run" you sympathize with Squeaky. But how would you feel about Squeaky if she were in your class at school? Give reasons for the way you feel.

2. Some characters in a story are not very important. They are used as background or setting. Which people described in the story are used that way?

3. When you only see one side of a character in a story—only a good side, or only a bad side—the character is said to be a *flat* character. If you can see many different traits in a character—both good and bad—the character is a *round* character. Who are flat characters and who are round characters in "Raymond's Run"? Try to give reasons for your choices.

Discussing the Story

4. Why do you think the story is called "Raymond's Run" instead of "Squeaky's Run"?

5. If you belonged to a group whose job it was to defend the rights of children with mental retardation, how would you judge the story "Raymond's Run"?

6. One of the great things about reading short stories and novels is that you can learn important lessons about life and living from the experiences of the characters. What did you learn about life and living from this story?

Discussing the Author's Work

7. Toni Cade Bambara is a black author writing about black people in

"Raymond's Run." Frank O'Connor was Irish and wrote about Irish people in "First Confession." Most authors of short stories and novels write about what they know. Why do you think that is so?

8. If you don't live in New York City, some things in the story may not mean much to you. For example, "I continue . . . strolling down Broadway toward the icey man on 145th. . . ." Here's another: ". . . can you imagine some thirty-five-year-old man stuffing himself into PAL shorts. . . ?" (PAL stands for Police Athletic League, an athletic association.) Why do you think the author includes references that will not be familiar to all her readers? Is the story more or less interesting as a result? Give examples and reasons for your opinion.

9. In addition to being a writer, Toni Bambara has a background in acting and dancing. At one time she was director of recreation for a New York City mental hospital. What evidence of these experiences can you find in the story?

Writing Exercise

Read all the instructions before you begin writing. If you have any questions about how to begin the writing assignment, review Using the Writing Process beginning on page 445, or confer with your writing coach.

1. At the beginning of the unit you were asked to create your own character. If you haven't done that yet, read the instructions for Develop Your Own Character on page 65, and write these descriptions now.

   Develop the character by following the instructions in the four Writing on Your Own exercises.

2. Write a short story about the character you have developed. In your story create a conflict or crisis that your character must face. Consider how your character will respond to the crisis and what steps he or she will take to reach a solution.

3. You may use first-person point of view or third-person point of view. Include dialogue if your character's conflict is with another person.

4. Write, revise, correct, and rewrite your story until you are sure you have got it just the way you want it.

Unit 3   Plot

To Build a Fire
BY JACK LONDON

About the Illustration

What do you think is happening in this scene? Point out some details in the drawing to support your response.

Here are some questions to help you think about the story:

◆ Where do you think this scene takes place? How cold do you think it is? Why?

◆ What is the man doing?

◆ How would you describe the feeling of this entire scene? Is it frightening? sad? cheerful? What details do you think give the scene that feeling?

Unit 3

Introduction

About the Story

The story takes place near the Alaskan border, in Canada's Yukon Territory. It is winter, about 1898. For several years, ever since the discovery of gold in this wilderness not far from the Arctic Circle, adventurers had been rushing north to seek their fortunes. These men from the south were called *cheechakos* (chi-CHAHK-ohs), which is the Chinook Indian word for *newcomer*.

Because they were newcomers to this wild country, the cheechakos were not used to its ways and its weather. They could not imagine how cold it could become in winter. And they found it hard to believe that such beautiful country could be so dangerous to travel in.

The newcomer that Jack London tells about in "To Build a Fire" has ventured out alone in the coldest part of the winter. The sun has not shone above the horizon for many days. Daylight is no more than a gray gloom. When we meet the cheechako, he is heading for a mining camp, to join his friends. He is traveling with a dog and has decided to take a roundabout route to camp in order to check out the bends and turns of the Yukon River. The men are planning to cut timber in the spring and float the logs down the river. It is extremely cold, but the man knows that camp is only a few hours away, and he is sure he will have no trouble getting there.

He has heard stories about the bitter cold, and he has been warned of its dangers by some of the old-timers. But he laughs at the stories and only half believes the warnings. He is strong, clever in the wilderness, for a newcomer, and he is confident of his ability to survive. But, being new to the land, he doesn't understand the fierce treachery of the northern wilderness. His journey becomes a life-and-death struggle with the forces of nature.

Many readers consider "To Build a Fire" one of Jack London's finest short stories. It is just the kind of story he wrote best, in which a man and a half-wild dog engage in a bitter contest with the forces of the wilderness. From beginning to end, you will find yourself shivering from the bitter cold and the spine-tingling suspense. And when you have finished reading, you will know that you have read a story that is impossible to forget.

Jack London (1876–1916) was an adventurer, a self-taught writer, and a natural yarn spinner. When he was twenty-one, he went north to seek his fortune in the gold fields of Alaska and the Yukon. He returned a year later sick and penniless but with a head full of stories that were to make him famous. After reading "To Build a Fire," you may want to read one of Jack London's exciting novels: *The Call of the Wild, White Fang,* or *The Sea-Wolf.*

If you want to know more about Jack London's life, one of the best-known biographies is *Sailor on Horseback* by Irving Stone.

About the Lesson

The lesson that follows the story is about plot—how an author plans a story so that it moves along smoothly and holds your interest.

You have probably noticed that as you read a story, the author moves you from one action, or event, to another. This change in action is the movement of the plot. Each action causes something new to happen, which keeps the story going in an orderly way. It is the plot that keeps you reading a story from beginning to end.

The following questions will help you focus on elements of the plot in Jack London's story "To Build a Fire." Read the story carefully and try to answer these questions as you go along:

◆ At the beginning of the story, what do you find out about the weather that could give the man trouble later on?

◆ The author tells about bubbling springs of water from the hillsides that are hidden under the snow. How do these springs contribute to the battle, or conflict, between the man and the Arctic wilderness?

◆ The man accidentally falls into a hidden spring. Why is that event a turning point in the story?

◆ Near the end of the story, the man is seized by fear and panic. That scene is a high point in the action of the story. After that event, what is said in the story that tells you that the action is starting to calm down?

Develop Your Plot Outline

You can understand how important a plot is when you think of how a story of your own might go. Use your writing notebook or a separate piece of paper and try the following suggestions:

1. Choose one of the following ideas for a story, or think of an idea of your own.

   ☐ You are on a camping trip with your parents and become lost in the woods. Think of a story that tells what happens.

   ☐ While fishing from the shore of a lake, you see a canoe tip over and three people cry for help. Tell a story about what happens next.

   ☐ You are walking your dog before bedtime when you see red and green lights approaching out of the sky. Tell a story about how you feel and what you do.

2. Make a list of ideas, people, places, and events that will be in your story. Your list should include

   ☐ who is in the story

☐ where the story takes place

☐ some events that will happen in the story

3. Rewrite your list and try to put the events in the order in which you think they will happen in your story. You should rewrite your list several times until you get the order just the way you want it.

To Build a Fire

by Jack London

ay had broken cold and gray, exceedingly cold and gray, when the man turned aside from the main Yukon trail and climbed the high earth-bank, where a dim and little-traveled trail led eastward through the fat spruce timberland. It was a steep bank, and he paused for breath at the top, excusing the act to himself by looking at his watch. It was nine o'clock. There was no sun nor hint of sun, though there was not a cloud in the sky. It was a clear day, and yet there seemed an intangible pall over the face of things, a subtle gloom that made the day dark, and that was due to the absence of sun. This fact did not worry the man. He was used to the lack of sun. It had been days since he had seen the sun, and he knew that a few more days must pass before that cheerful orb, due south, would just peep above the skyline and dip immediately from view.

The man flung a look back along the way he had come. The Yukon lay a mile wide and hidden under three feet of ice. On top of this ice were as many feet of snow. It was all pure white, rolling in gentle undulations where the ice-jams of the freeze-up had formed. North and south, as far as his eye could see, it was unbroken white, save for a dark hairline that curved and twisted from around the spruce-covered island to the south, and that curved and twisted away into the north, where it disappeared behind another spruce-covered island. This dark hairline was the trail—the main trail—that led south five hundred miles to the Chilcoot Pass, Dyea, and salt water; and that led north seventy miles to Dawson, and still on to the north a thousand miles to Nulato, and finally to St. Michael on Bering Sea, a thousand miles and half a thousand more.

But all this—the mysterious, far-reaching hairline trail, the absence of sun from the sky, the tremendous cold, and the strangeness and weirdness of it all—made no impression on the man. It was not because he was long used to it. He was a newcomer in the land, a *Cheechako,* and this was his first winter. The trouble with him was that he was without imagination. He was quick and alert in the things of life, but only in the things, and not in the significances. Fifty degrees below zero meant eighty-odd degrees of frost. Such fact impressed him as being cold and uncomfortable, and that was all. It did not lead him to meditate upon his frailty as a creature of temperature, and upon man's frailty in general, able only to live within certain narrow limits of heat and cold; and from there on it did not lead him to the conjectural field of immortality and man's place in the universe. Fifty degrees below zero stood for a bite of frost that hurt and that must be guarded against by the use of mittens, ear-flaps, warm moccasins, and thick socks. Fifty degrees below zero was to him just precisely fifty degrees below zero. That there should be anything more to it than that was a thought that never entered his head.

As he turned to go on, he spat speculatively. There was a sharp, explosive crackle that startled him. He spat again. And again, in the air, before it could fall to the snow, the spittle crackled. He knew that at fifty below spittle crackled on the snow, but this spittle had crackled in the air. Undoubtedly it was colder than fifty below—how much colder he did not know. But the temperature did not matter. He was bound for the old claim on the left fork of Henderson Creek, where the boys were already. They had come over across the divide from the Indian Creek country, while he had come the round-about way to take a look at the possibilities of getting out logs in the spring from the islands in the Yukon. He would be in to camp by six o'clock; a bit after dark, it was true, but the boys would be there, a fire would be going, and a hot supper would be ready. As for lunch, he pressed his hand against the protruding bundle under his jacket. It was also under his shirt, wrapped up in a handkerchief and lying against the naked skin. It was the only way to keep the biscuits from freezing. He smiled agreeably to himself as he thought of those biscuits, each cut open and sopped in bacon grease, and each enclosing a generous slice of fried bacon.

He plunged in among the big spruce trees. The trail was faint. A foot of snow had fallen since the last sled had passed over, and he was glad he was without a sled, traveling light. In fact, he carried nothing but the lunch wrapped in the handkerchief. He was surprised, however, at the cold. It certainly was cold, he concluded, as he rubbed his numb nose and cheekbones with his mittened hand. He was a warm-whiskered man, but the hair on his face did not protect the high cheekbones and the eager nose that thrust itself aggressively into the frosty air.

At the man's heels trotted a dog, a big native husky, the proper wolf-dog, gray-coated and without any visible or temperamental difference from its brother, the wild wolf. The animal was depressed by the tremendous cold. It knew that it was no time for traveling. Its instinct told it a truer tale than was told to the man by the man's judgment. In reality, it was not merely colder than fifty below zero; it was colder than sixty below, than seventy below. It was seventy-five below zero. Since the freezing point is thirty-two above zero, it meant that one hundred and seven degrees of frost obtained. The dog did not know anything about thermometers. Possibly in its brain there was no sharp consciousness of a condition of very cold such as was in the man's brain. But the brute had its instinct. It experienced a vague but menacing apprehension that subdued it and made it slink along at the man's heels, and that made it question eagerly every unwonted movement of the man as if expecting him to go into camp or to seek shelter somewhere and build a fire. The dog had learned fire, and it wanted fire, or else to burrow under the snow and cuddle its warmth away from the air.

The frozen moisture of its breathing had settled on its fur in a fine powder of frost, and especially were its jowls, muzzle, and eyelashes whitened by its crystalled breath. The man's red beard and mustache were likewise frosted, but more solidly, the deposit taking the form of ice and increasing with every warm, moist breath he exhaled. Also, the man was chewing tobacco, and the muzzle of ice held his lips so rigidly that he was unable to clear his chin when he expelled the juice. The result was that a crystal beard of the color and solidity of amber was increasing its length on his chin. If he fell down it would shatter itself, like glass, into brittle fragments. But he did not mind the appendage. It was the penalty all tobacco-chewers paid in that country, and he had been out before in two cold snaps. They had not been so cold as this, he knew, but by the spirit thermometer at Sixty Mile he knew they had been registered at fifty below and at fifty-five.

He held on through the level stretch of woods for several miles, crossed a wide flat of niggerheads, and dropped down a bank to the frozen bed of a small stream. This was Henderson Creek, and he knew he was ten miles from the forks. He looked at his watch. It was ten o'clock. He was making four miles an hour, and he calculated that he would arrive at the forks at half-past twelve. He decided to celebrate that event by eating his lunch there.

The dog dropped in again at his heels, with a tail drooping discouragement, as the man swung along the creek-bed. The furrow of the old sled-trail was plainly visible, but a dozen inches of snow covered the marks of the last runners. In a month no man had come up or down that silent creek. The man held steadily on. He was not much given to thinking, and just then particularly he had nothing to think about save that he would eat lunch at the forks and that at six o'clock he would be in camp with the boys. There was nobody to talk to; and, had there been, speech would have been impossible because of the ice-muzzle on his mouth. So he continued monotonously to chew tobacco and to increase the length of his amber beard.

Once in a while the thought reiterated itself that it was very cold and that he had never experienced such cold. As he walked along he rubbed his cheekbones and nose with the back of his mittened hand. He did this automatically, now and again changing hands. But rub as he would, the instant he stopped his cheekbones went numb, and the following instant the end of his nose went numb. He was sure to frost his cheeks; he knew that, and experienced a pang of regret that he had not devised a nose-strap of the sort Bud wore in cold snaps. Such a strap passed across the cheeks, as well, and saved them. But it didn't matter much, after all. What were frosted cheeks? A bit painful, that was all; they were never serious.

Empty as the man's mind was of thoughts, he was keenly observant, and he noticed the changes in the creek, the curves and bends and timber-jams, and always he sharply noted where he placed his feet. Once, coming around a bend, he shied abruptly, like a startled horse, curved away from the place where he had been walking, and retreated several paces back along the trail. The creek he knew was frozen clear to the bottom,—no creek could contain water in that arctic winter,—but he knew also that there were springs that bubbled out from the hillsides and ran along under the snow and on top the ice of the creek. He knew that the coldest snaps never froze these springs, and he knew likewise their danger. They were traps. They hid pools of water under the snow that might be three inches deep, or three feet. Sometimes a skin of ice half an inch thick covered them, and in turn was covered by the snow. Sometimes there were alternate layers of water and ice-skin, so that when one broke through he kept on breaking through for a while, sometimes wetting himself to the waist.

That was why he had shied in such panic. He had felt the give under his feet and heard the crackle of a snow-hidden ice-skin. And to get his feet wet in such a temperature meant trouble and danger. At the very least it meant delay, for he would be forced to stop and build a fire, and under its protection to bare his feet while he dried his socks and moccasins. He stood and studied the creek-bed and its banks, and decided that the flow of water came from the right. He reflected a while, rubbing his nose and cheeks, then skirted to the left, stepping gingerly and testing the footing for each step. Once clear of the danger, he took a fresh chew of tobacco and swung along at his four-mile gait.

In the course of the next two hours he came upon several similar traps. Usually the snow above the hidden pools had a sunken, candied appearance that advertised the danger. Once again, however, he had a close call; and once, suspecting danger, he compelled the dog to go on in front. The dog did not want to go. It hung back until the man shoved it forward, and then it went quickly across the white, unbroken surface. Suddenly it broke through, floundered to one side, and got away to firmer footing. It had wet its forefeet and legs, and almost immediately the water that clung to it turned to ice. It made quick efforts to lick the ice off its legs, then dropped down in the snow and began to bite out the ice that had formed between the toes. This was a matter of instinct. To permit the ice to remain would mean sore feet. It did not know this, it merely obeyed the mysterious prompting that arose from the deep crypts of its being. But the man knew, having achieved a judgment on the subject, and he removed the mitten from his right hand and helped tear out the ice-particles. He did not expose his fingers more than a minute, and was astonished at the swift numbness that smote them. It certainly was cold. He pulled on the mitten hastily, and beat the hand savagely across his chest.

At twelve o'clock the day was at its brightest. Yet the sun

was too far south on its winter journey to clear the horizon. The bulge of the earth intervened between it and Henderson Creek, where the man walked under a clear sky at noon and cast no shadow. At half-past twelve, to the minute, he arrived at the forks of the creek. He was pleased at the speed he had made. If he kept it up, he would certainly be with the boys by six. He unbuttoned his jacket and shirt and drew forth his lunch. The action consumed no more than a quarter of a minute, yet in that brief moment the numbness laid hold of the exposed fingers. He did not put the mitten on, but, instead, struck the fingers a dozen sharp smashes against his leg. Then he sat down on a snow-covered log to eat. The sting that followed upon the striking of his fingers against his leg ceased so quickly that he was startled. He had had no chance to take a bite of biscuit. He struck the fingers repeatedly and returned them to the mitten, baring the other hand for the purpose of eating. He tried to take a mouthful, but the ice-muzzle prevented. He had forgotten to build a fire and thaw out. He chuckled at his foolishness, and as he chuckled he noted the numbness creeping into the exposed fingers. Also, he noted that the stinging which had first come to his toes when he sat down was already passing away. He wondered whether the toes were warm or numb. He moved them inside the moccasins and decided that they were numb.

He pulled the mitten on hurriedly and stood up. He was a bit frightened. He stamped up and down until the stinging returned into the feet. It certainly was cold, was his thought. That man from Sulphur Creek had spoken the truth when telling how cold it sometimes got in the country. And he had laughed at him at the time! That showed one must not be too sure of things. There was no mistake about it, it *was* cold. He strode up and down, stamping his feet and threshing his arms, until reassured by the returning warmth. Then he got out matches and proceeded to make a fire. From the undergrowth, where high water of the previous spring had lodged a supply of seasoned twigs, he got his firewood. Working carefully from a small beginning, he soon had a roaring fire, over which he thawed the ice from his face and in the protection of which he ate his biscuits. For the moment the cold of space was outwitted. The dog took satisfaction in the fire, stretching out close enough for warmth and far enough away to escape being singed.

When the man had finished, he filled his pipe and took his comfortable time over a smoke. Then he pulled on his mittens, settled the earflaps of his cap firmly about his ears, and took the creek trail up the left fork. The dog was disappointed and yearned back toward the fire. This man did not know cold. Possibly all the generations of his ancestry had been ignorant of cold, of real cold, of cold one hundred and seven degrees below freezing point. But the dog knew; all its ancestry knew, and it had inherited the knowledge. And it knew that it was not good to walk abroad in such fearful cold. It was the time to lie snug in the hole in the snow and wait for a curtain of cloud to be drawn across the face of outer space whence this cold came. On the other hand, there was no keen intimacy between the dog and the man. The one was the toil-slave of the other, and the only caresses it had ever received were the caresses of the whiplash and of harsh and menacing throat-sounds that threatened the whiplash. So the dog made no effort to communicate its apprehension to the man. It was not concerned in the welfare of the man; it was for its own sake that it yearned back toward the fire. But the man whistled, and spoke to it with the sound of whiplashes, and the dog swung in at the man's heel and followed after.

The man took a chew of tobacco and proceeded to start a new amber beard. Also, his moist breath quickly powdered with white his mustache, eyebrows, and lashes. There did not seem to be so many springs on the left fork of the Henderson, and for half an hour the man saw no signs of any. And then it happened. At a place where there were no signs, where the soft, unbroken snow seemed to advertise solidity beneath, the man broke through. It was not deep. He wet himself halfway to the knees before he floundered out to the firm crust.

He was angry, and cursed his luck aloud. He had hoped to get into camp with the boys at six o'clock, and this would delay him an hour, for he would have to build a fire and dry out his foot-gear. This was imperative at that low temperature—he knew that much; and he turned aside to the bank, which he climbed. On top, tangled in the underbrush about the trunks of several small spruce trees, was a high-water deposit of dry firewood—sticks and twigs, principally, but also larger portions of seasoned branches and fine, dry, last-year's grasses. He threw down several large pieces on top of the snow. This served for a foundation and prevented the young flame from drowning itself in the snow it otherwise would melt. The flame he got by touching a match to a small shred of birch bark that he took from his pocket. This burned more readily than paper. Placing it on the foundation, he fed the young flame with wisps of dry grass and with the tiniest dry twigs.

He worked slowly and carefully, keenly aware of his danger. Gradually, as the flame grew stronger, he increased the size of the twigs with which he fed it. He squatted in the snow, pulling the twigs out from their entanglement in the brush and feeding directly to the flame. He knew there must be no failure. When it is seventy-five below zero, a man must not fail in his first attempt to build a fire—that is, if his feet are wet. If his feet are dry, and he fails, he can run along the trail for half a mile and restore his circulation. But the circulation of wet and freezing feet cannot be restored by running when it is seventy-five below. No matter how fast he runs, the wet feet will freeze the harder.

All this the man knew. The old-timer on Sulphur Creek had told him about it the previous fall, and now he was appreciating the advice. Already all sensation had gone

out of his feet. To build the fire he had been forced to remove his mittens, and the fingers had quickly gone numb.
His pace of four miles an hour had kept his heart pumping
blood to the surface of his body and to all the extremities.
But the instant he stopped, the action of the pump eased
down. The cold of space smote the unprotected tip of the
planet, and he, being on that unprotected tip, received
the full force of the blow. The blood of his body recoiled
before it. The blood was alive, like the dog, and like the dog
it wanted to hide away and cover itself up from the fearful
cold. So long as he walked four miles an hour, he pumped
that blood, willy-nilly, to the surface; but now it ebbed
away and sank down into the recesses of his body. The
extremities were the first to feel its absence. His wet feet
froze the faster, and his exposed fingers numbed the
faster, though they had not yet begun to freeze. Nose and
cheeks were already freezing, while the skin of all his
body chilled as it lost its blood.

But he was safe. Toes and nose and cheeks would be only
touched by the frost, for the fire was beginning to burn
with strength. He was feeding it with twigs the size of his
finger. In another minute he would be able to feed it with
branches the size of his wrist, and then he could remove
his wet footgear, and, while it dried, he could keep his
naked feet warm by the fire, rubbing them at first, of
course, with snow. The fire was a success. He was safe. He
remembered the advice of the old-timer on Sulphur Creek,
and smiled. The old-timer had been very serious in laying
down the law that no man must travel alone in the
Klondike after fifty below. Well, here he was; he had had
the accident; he was alone; and he had saved himself.
Those old-timers were rather womanish, some of them, he
thought. All a man had to do was to keep his head; and
he was all right. Any man who was a man could travel
alone. But it was surprising, the rapidity with which his
cheeks and nose were freezing. And he had not thought
his fingers could go lifeless in so short a time. Lifeless

they were, for he could scarcely make them move together to grip a twig, and they seemed remote from his body and from him. When he touched a twig, he had to look and see whether or not he had hold of it. The wires were pretty well down between him and his finger-ends.

All of which counted for little. There was the fire, snapping and crackling and promising life with every dancing flame. He started to untie his moccasins. They were coated with ice; the thick German socks were like sheaths of iron halfway to the knees; and the moccasin strings were like rods of steel all twisted and knotted as by some conflagration. For a moment he tugged with his numb fingers, then, realizing the folly of it, he drew his sheath-knife.

But before he could cut the strings, it happened. It was his own fault or, rather, his mistake. He should not have built the fire under the spruce tree. He should have built it in the open. But it had been easier to pull the twigs from the brush and drop them directly on the fire. Now the tree under which he had done this carried a weight of snow on its boughs. No wind had blown for weeks, and each bough was fully freighted. Each time he had pulled a twig he had communicated a slight agitation to the tree—an imperceptible agitation, so far as he was concerned, but an agitation sufficient to bring about the disaster. High up in the tree one bough capsized its load of snow. This fell on the boughs beneath, capsizing them. This process continued, spreading out and involving the whole tree. It grew like an avalanche, and it descended without warning upon the man and the fire, and the fire was blotted out! Where it had burned was a mantle of fresh and disordered snow.

The man was shocked. It was as though he had just heard his own sentence of death. For a moment he sat and stared at the spot where the fire had been. Then he grew very calm. Perhaps the old-timer on Sulphur Creek was right. If he had only had a trail-mate he would have been in no danger now. The trail-mate could have built the fire. Well, it was up to him to build the fire over again, and this second time there must be no failure. Even if he succeeded, he would most likely lose some toes. His feet must be badly frozen by now, and there would be some time before the second fire was ready.

Such were his thoughts, but he did not sit and think them. He was busy all the time they were passing through his mind. He made a new foundation for a fire, this time in the open, where no treacherous tree could blot it out. Next, he gathered dry grasses and tiny twigs from the high-water flotsam. He could not bring his fingers together to pull them out, but he was able to gather them by the handful. In this way he got many rotten twigs and bits of green moss that were undesirable, but it was the best he could do. He worked methodically, even collecting an armful of the larger branches to be used later when the fire gathered strength. And all the while the dog sat and watched him, a certain yearning wistfulness in its eyes, for it looked upon him as the fire-provider, and the fire was slow in coming.

When all was ready, the man reached in his pocket for a second piece of birch bark. He knew the bark was there, and, though he could not feel it with his fingers, he could hear its crisp rustling as he fumbled for it. Try as he would, he could not clutch hold of it. And all the time, in his consciousness, was the knowledge that each instant his feet were freezing. This thought tended to put him in a panic, but he fought against it and kept calm. He pulled on his mittens with his teeth, and threshed his arms back and forth, beating his hands with all his might against his sides. He did this sitting down, and he stood up to do it; and all the while the dog sat in the snow, its wolf-brush of a tail curled around warmly over its forefeet, its sharp wolf-ears pricked forward intently as it watched the man. And the man, as he beat and threshed with his arms and hands, felt a great surge of envy as he regarded the creature that was warm and secure in its natural covering.

After a time he was aware of the first far-away signals

of sensation in his beaten fingers. The faint tingling grew stronger till it evolved into a stinging ache that was excruciating, but which the man hailed with satisfaction. He stripped the mitten from his right hand and fetched forth the birch bark. The exposed fingers were quickly going numb again. Next he brought out his bunch of sulphur matches. But the tremendous cold had already driven the life out of his fingers. In his effort to separate one match from the others, the whole bunch fell in the snow. He tried to pick it out of the snow, but failed. The dead fingers could neither touch nor clutch. He was very careful. He drove the thought of his freezing feet, and nose, and cheeks, out of his mind, devoting his whole soul to the matches. He watched, using the sense of vision in place of touch, and when he saw his fingers on each side the bunch, he closed them—that is, he willed to close them, for the wires were down, and the fingers did not obey. He pulled the mitten on the right hand, and beat it fiercely against his knee. Then, with both mittened hands, he scooped the bunch of matches, along with much snow, into his lap. Yet he was no better off.

After some manipulation he managed to get the bunch between the heels of his mittened hands. In this fashion he carried it to his mouth. The ice crackled and snapped when by a violent effort he opened his mouth. He drew the lower jaw in, curled the upper lip out of the way, and scraped the bunch with his upper teeth in order to separate a match. He succeeded in getting one, which he dropped on his lap. He was no better off. He could not pick it up. Then he devised a way. He picked it up in his teeth and scratched it on his leg. Twenty times he scratched before he succeeded in lighting it. As it flamed he held it with his teeth to the birch bark. But the burning brimstone went up his nostrils and into his lungs, causing him to cough spasmodically. The match fell into the snow and went out.

The old-timer on Sulphur Creek was right, he thought in the moment of controlled despair that ensued: after fifty below, a man should travel with a partner. He beat his hands, but failed in exciting any sensation. Suddenly he bared both hands, removing the mittens with his teeth. He caught the whole bunch between the heels of his hands. His arm-muscles not being frozen enabled him to press the hand-heels tightly against the matches. Then he scratched the bunch along his leg. It flared into flame, seventy sulphur matches at once! There was no wind to blow them out. He kept his head to one side to escape the strangling fumes, and held the blazing bunch to the birch bark. As he so held it, he became aware of sensation in his hand. His flesh was burning. He could smell it. Deep down below the surface he could feel it. The sensation developed into pain that grew acute. And still he endured it, holding the flame of the matches clumsily to the bark that would not light readily because his own burning hands were in the way, absorbing most of the flame.

At last, when he could endure no more, he jerked his hands apart. The blazing matches fell sizzling into the snow, but the birch bark was alight. He began laying dry grasses and the tiniest twigs on the flame. He could not pick and choose, for he had to lift the fuel between the heels of his hands. Small pieces of rotten wood and green moss clung to the twigs, and he bit them off as well as he could with his teeth. He cherished the flame carefully and awkwardly. It meant life, and it must not perish. The withdrawal of blood from the surface of his body now made him begin to shiver, and he grew more awkward. A large piece of green moss fell squarely on the little fire. He tried to poke it out with his fingers, but his shivering frame made him poke too far, and he disrupted the nucleus of the little fire, the burning grasses and tiny twigs separating and scattering. He tried to poke them together again, but in spite of the tenseness of the effort, his shivering got away with him, and the twigs were hopelessly scattered. Each twig gushed a puff of smoke and went out. The fire provider had failed. As he looked apathetically about him, his eyes chanced on the dog, sitting across the ruins of the fire from him, in the snow, making restless, hunching movements, slightly lifting one forefoot and then the other, shifting its weight back and forth on them with wistful eagerness.

The sight of the dog put a wild idea into his head. He remembered the tale of the man, caught in a blizzard, who killed a steer and crawled inside the carcass, and so was saved. He would kill the dog and bury his hands in the warm body until the numbness went out of them. Then he could build another fire. He spoke to the dog, calling it to him; but in his voice was a strange note of fear that frightened the animal, who had never known the man to speak in such way before. Something was the matter, and its suspicious nature sensed danger—it knew not what danger, but somewhere, somehow, in its brain arose an apprehension of the man. It flattened its ears down at the sound of the man's voice, and its restless, hunching movements and the liftings and shiftings of its forefeet became more pronounced; but it would not come to the man. He got on his hands and knees and crawled toward the dog. This unusual posture again excited suspicion, and the animal sidled mincingly away.

The man sat up in the snow for a moment and struggled for calmness. Then he pulled on his mittens, by means of his teeth, and got upon his feet. He glanced down at first in order to assure himself that he was really standing up, for the absence of sensation in his feet left him unrelated to the earth. His erect position in itself started to drive the webs of suspicion from the dog's mind; and when he spoke peremptorily, with the sound of whiplashes in his voice, the dog rendered its customary allegiance and came to him. As it came within reaching distance, the man lost his control. His arms flashed out to the dog, and he experienced genuine surprise when he discovered that his hands could not clutch, that there was neither bend nor feeling in the fingers. He had forgotten for the moment that they were frozen and that they were freezing more and more. All this happened quickly, and before the animal could get away, he encircled its body with his arms. He sat down in the snow, and in this fashion held the dog, while it snarled and whined and struggled.

But it was all he could do, hold its body encircled in his arms and sit there. He realized that he could not kill the dog. There was no way to do it. With his helpless hands he could neither draw nor hold his sheath-knife nor throttle the animal. He released it, and it plunged wildly away, with tail between its legs, and still snarling. It halted forty feet away and surveyed him curiously, with ears sharply pricked forward. The man looked down at his hands in order to locate them, and found them hanging on the ends of his arms. It struck him as curious that one should have to use his eyes in order to find out where his hands were. He began threshing his arms back and forth, beating the mittened hands against his sides. He did this for five minutes, violently, and his heart pumped enough blood up to the surface to put a stop to his shivering. But no sensation was aroused in the hands. He had an impression that they hung like weights on the ends of his arms, but when he tried to run the impression down, he could not find it.

A certain fear of death, dull and oppressive, came to him. This fear quickly became poignant as he realized that it was no longer a mere matter of freezing his fingers and toes, or of losing his hands and feet, but that it was a matter of life and death with the chances against him. This threw him into a panic, and he turned and ran up the creek-bed along the old, dim trail. The dog joined in behind and kept up with him. He ran blindly, without intention, in fear such as he had never known in his life. Slowly, as he plowed and floundered through the snow, he began to see things again,—the banks of the creeks, the old timber-jams, the leafless aspens, and the sky. The running made him feel better. He did not shiver. Maybe, if he ran on, his feet would thaw out; and, anyway, if he ran far enough, he would reach camp and the boys. Without doubt he would lose some fingers and toes and some of his face; but the boys would take care of him, and save the rest of him when he got there. And at the same time there was another thought in his mind that said he would never get to the camp and the boys; that it was too many miles away, that the freezing had too great a start on him, and that he would soon be stiff and dead. This thought he kept in the background and refused to consider. Sometimes it pushed itself forward and demanded to be heard, but he thrust it back and strove to think of other things.

It struck him as curious that he could run at all on feet so frozen that he could not feel them when they struck the earth and took the weight of his body. He seemed to himself to skim along above the surface, and to have no connection with the earth. Somewhere he had once seen a winged Mercury, and he wondered if Mercury felt as he felt when skimming over the earth.

His theory of running until he reached camp and the boys had one flaw in it: he lacked the endurance. Several times he stumbled, and finally he tottered, crumpled up, and fell. When he tried to rise, he failed. He must sit and rest, he decided, and next time he would merely walk and keep on going. As he sat and regained his breath, he noted that he was feeling quite warm and comfortable. He was not shivering, and it even seemed that a warm glow had come to his chest and trunk. And yet, when he touched his nose or cheeks, there was no sensation. Running would not thaw them out. Nor would it thaw out his hands and feet. Then the thought came to him that the frozen portions of his body must be extending. He tried to keep this thought down, to forget it, to think of something else; he was aware of the panicky feeling that it caused, and he was afraid of the panic. But the thought asserted itself, and persisted, until it produced a vision of his body totally frozen. This was too much, and he made another wild run along the trail. Once he slowed down to a walk, but the thought of the freezing extending itself made him run again.

And all the time the dog ran with him, at his heels. When he fell down a second time, it curled its tail over its forefeet and sat in front of him, facing him, curiously eager and intent. The warmth and security of the animal angered him, and he cursed it till it flattened down its ears appeasingly. This time the shivering came more quickly upon the man. He was losing in his battle with the frost. It was creeping into his body from all sides. The thought of it drove him on, but he ran no more than a hundred feet, when he staggered and pitched headlong. It was his last panic. When he had recovered his breath and control, he sat up and entertained in his mind the conception of meeting death with dignity. However, the conception did not come to him in such terms. His idea of it was that he had been making a fool of himself, running around like a chicken with its head cut off—such was the simile that occurred to him. Well, he was bound to freeze anyway, and he might as well take it decently. With this newfound peace of mind came the first glimmerings of drowsiness. A good idea, he thought, to sleep off to death. It was like taking an anaesthetic. Freezing was not so bad as people thought. There were lots worse ways to die.

He pictured the boys finding his body next day. Suddenly he found himself with them, coming along the trail and looking for himself. And, still with them, he came around a turn in the trail and found himself lying in the snow. He did not belong with himself any more, for even then he was out of himself, standing with the boys and looking at himself in the snow. It certainly was cold, was his thought. When he got back to the States he could tell the folks what real cold was. He drifted on from this to a vision of the old-timer on Sulphur Creek. He could see him quite clearly, warm and comfortable, and smoking a pipe.

"You were right, old hoss; you were right," the man mumbled to the old-timer of Sulphur Creek.

Then the man drowsed off into what seemed to him the

most comfortable and satisfying sleep he had ever known. The dog sat facing him and waiting. The brief day drew to a close in a long, slow twilight. There were no signs of a fire to be made, and, besides, never in the dog's experience had it known a man to sit like that in the snow and make no fire.

As the twilight drew on, its eager yearning for the fire mastered it, and with a great lifting and shifting of fore-feet, it whined softly, then flattened its ears down in anticipation of being chidden by the man. But the man remained silent. Later, the dog whined loudly. And still later it crept close to the man and caught the scent of death. This made the animal bristle and back away. A little longer it delayed, howling under the stars that leaped and danced and shone brightly in the cold sky. Then it turned and trotted up the trail in the direction of the camp it knew, where were the other food providers and fire providers.

Plot

Think about the situation described in the following scene. It is one you have surely come across before in a number of stories and movies:

> The enemy is closing in on the fort. Surrounded and outnumbered, the gallant defenders have sent a messenger for help. If someone can blow up the bridge that spans the river, the enemy will be slowed down. Then, perhaps, help will arrive in time. Captain Braveheart volunteers for the dangerous job.

At that point in the story you can't wait for the answers to a dozen questions that spring to mind. Can Captain Braveheart succeed? Will help arrive in time? What will happen next?

The built-in question, What will happen next? is what keeps a story moving and keeps you interested in reading it. When your curiosity is aroused, when you must know what will happen, the author has got you hooked on the plot of the story. You are led from one problem to another and from one kind of action to another, from the beginning of the story to the end.

An author plans, or *plots,* a story so that one action leads to another. Problems or conflicts arise and must be solved: If the fort is surrounded or the bridge must be blown up, a character in the story, Captain Braveheart, must take action to deal with the problem. But the action always creates a new problem. Perhaps Captain Braveheart is wounded. What will he do now?

Actions are related by cause and effect. A problem arises—creating a cause for action. The effect of the action causes a new problem. And so the story—the plot—goes from problem to action to a new problem and a new action.

If there are just a series of actions, there is no story: Paul went to the store, came home, watched TV, and went to bed. There is no story because there are no problems or conflicts to lead the story from one action to another.

But if Paul went to the store, witnessed a murder, watched TV to pretend he hadn't been out, and then pretended to be asleep when a strange car pulled into the driveway, you'd have a plot and a story.

Plot is the backbone or framework of a story. Some stories have stronger plots than others. But there must always be some sort of plot to hold a story together and to take you from the beginning to the end.

In this lesson, we will look at four ways in which author Jack London develops the plot of "To Build a Fire":

1 ✦ The author uses exposition to prepare the reader for the conflicts and actions to come.

2 ✦ The author uses conflicts and complications to move the story along.

3 ✦ The conflicts and complications are used to lead the plot to a crisis and a climax.

4 ✦ The author gives the plot a beginning, a middle, and an end.

1 ◆ Exposition

Before you can understand what is going on in a story, there are some things you have to know. You have to know who the characters are and a little bit about them. You have to know the setting of the story—where and when the story takes place. And you have to know what is going on at the point at which the story begins.

An author reveals, or exposes, all those facts to the reader in what is called the *exposition*. The exposition is the part of the plot in which important background information is given, the characters are introduced, and the author gives hints of the problems to come. It is those hints that arouse your curiosity and make you want to find out what the problems are and how they are dealt with. In other words, the author uses the exposition to tempt you and lead you into the story.

Jack London provides many important facts in the opening paragraphs of "To Build a Fire." He also hints broadly at the cause of trouble to come.

> Day had broken cold and gray, exceedingly cold and gray, when the man turned aside from the main Yukon trail and climbed the high earth-bank, where a dim and little-traveled trail led eastward through the fat spruce timberland. It was a steep bank, and he paused for breath at the top, excusing the act to himself by looking at his watch. It was nine o'clock. There was no sun nor hint of sun, though there was not a cloud in the sky. It was a clear day, and yet there seemed an intangible pall over the face of things, a subtle gloom that made the day dark, and that was due to the absence of sun. This fact did not worry the man. He was used to the lack of sun. It had been days since he had seen the sun, and he knew that a few more days must pass before that cheerful orb, due south, would just peep above the skyline and dip immediately from view.

The first thing you learn about in the exposition is the cold: "Day had broken cold and gray, exceedingly cold and gray. . . ." The author emphasizes the cold to be sure that you pay attention to this fact. The cold is the main fact on which the story turns. It also provides the main conflict, the man's major problem.

The main character of the story is "the man." You never learn his name, but that is not important to the story. What is important is that he is a man, a kind of creature that cannot get along very well in severe cold.

You find out that he is on a trail in the Yukon. The author goes on to explain that the sun has not shone that day, even though the sky has been clear. That fact emphasizes the cold once again. It is the middle of the Arctic winter, when the sun doesn't rise above the horizon.

The author says that there is a pall and gloom over the face of things. Those words make you feel in your bones that something is about to happen. You are instantly curious to know what will happen in such a place, and you read on.

1 ✦ Exercise A

Read the following passage and answer the questions about it using what you have learned in this part of the lesson. Use your writing notebook or a separate piece of paper for your answers.

> But all this—the mysterious, far-reaching hairline trail, the absence of sun from the sky, the tremendous cold, and the strangeness and weirdness of it all—made no impression on the man. It was not because he was long used to it. He was a newcomer in the land, a *cheechako,* and this was his first winter. The trouble with him was that he was without imagination. He was quick and alert in the things of life, but only in the things, and not in the significances. Fifty degrees below zero meant eighty-odd degrees of frost. Such fact impressed him as being cold and uncomfortable, and that was all. It did not lead him to meditate upon his frailty as a creature of temperature, and upon man's frailty in general, able only to live within certain narrow limits of heat and cold. . . .

1. In this part of the exposition, the author tells the reader something about human beings and temperature, something that the man in the story does not think about. What fact does the man fail to consider that will become the main problem for him and cause the major crisis of the story? Write a few sentences to explain your answer.

2. The author makes an important point about the strangeness of the country, the extreme cold, and the man's attitude. It is a hint of trouble to come. Explain the point that the author makes about the cold and strangeness of the country and the man's thoughts about them.

Now check your answers using the suggestions in the Answer Key starting on page 457. Review this part of the lesson if you don't understand why an answer was wrong.

1◆Writing on Your Own

Look at the list you have written for Develop Your Plot Outline on page 105 that tells about your own story idea. Now do the following:

1. Select the items from your list that tell where the story takes place and who the most important person in the story is.

2. Write a short paragraph that could be a beginning for your story. As you write your paragraph, try to give a hint to your readers about a problem that the main character may face.

3. You may want to change and rewrite your paragraph several times until you get it just the way you like it.

2 ♦ Conflicts and Complications

You probably know from your own experience that one problem can lead to another. Sometimes when you have a problem, what you do to solve that problem only complicates matters. Consider this situation: Myra has a conflict with a teacher in school. She decides to tell her parents about it. But that only complicates matters by creating a new problem: Myra's parents side with the teacher and ground Myra for a week. Feeling she has been treated unfairly, Myra decides that she will teach her parents a lesson. She sneaks out and goes joyriding in the family car. Finding the car gone and thinking it is stolen, Myra's mother calls the police. The police spot Myra in the car and signal her to stop. Myra speeds off in a panic, with the police in pursuit.

As you can see, Myra's small problem at school was complicated by a series of new conflicts and new actions. And the conflicts and actions were all related. Each led to another.

That is how plots are built. In "To Build a Fire" a man is planning to earn some money by cutting timber and selling it. He wants to float the logs down the Yukon River in the spring. Figuring out how to do that is a small problem. To solve his problem he decides to check out the bends and curves in the river to see how much trouble he can expect with the job. But the man's action—traveling alone—puts him in conflict with the great forces of nature. The severe cold is a complication that calls for another action. The man's new actions cause still more conflicts.

In general, there are four kinds of conflict that a character in a story may face:

1. **Conflict with other characters.** At one point, the man is in conflict with the dog. He tries to kill it.

2. **Conflict with nature.** The man's fight against the cold is clearly a conflict with nature.

3. **Conflict within oneself.** This is often called inner conflict. The man in the story experiences an inner conflict when he feels fear and panic rising within him but knows he must stay calm if he is to act to save himself.

4. **Conflicts with society.** Someone who has been arrested and is

facing a court trial is in conflict with society. Someone who speaks out against, or protests, something that most people think is good is in conflict with society. There is no real conflict with society in this story.

If the man in the story had traveled quietly and safely to camp, there would have been no story. There may have been an interesting description of life in the Arctic wilderness, but no story. It is the conflicts and the actions they trigger, together with the resulting complications, that make a story. The rule is *conflict creates plot*.

Watch for the gradually rising conflict in this passage from "To Build a Fire":

> Empty as the man's mind was of thoughts, he was keenly observant, and he noticed the changes in the creek, the curves and bends and timber-jams, and always he sharply noted where he placed his feet. Once, coming around a bend, he shied abruptly, like a startled horse, curved away from the place where he had been walking, and retreated several paces back along the trail. The creek he knew was frozen clear to the bottom,—no creek could contain water in that arctic winter,—but he knew also that there were springs that bubbled out from the hillsides and ran along under the snow and on top the ice of the creek. He knew that the coldest snaps never froze these springs, and he knew likewise their danger. They were traps. They hid pools of water under the snow that might be three inches deep, or three feet. . . .
>
> That was why he had shied in such panic. He had felt the give under his feet and heard the crackle of a snow-hidden ice-skin.

What Jack London is describing in that passage is the beginning of the man's conflict with nature. The Arctic wilderness has laid "traps" for the man. The traps are springs of water hidden under the snow. To avoid falling into these springs and getting wet, with the accompanying danger of freezing his feet, the man must be alert and observant. He treads across the snow with great care.

At this point in the story, several possible complications have been suggested. It is extremely cold, even for the Arctic. The man is traveling alone, which he shouldn't be doing. And there is danger from hidden springs of water. These things are controlling the man's actions and creating new problems as the story goes along. You can see how the plot is progressing from conflict to action to complication to new problems and new actions.

2 ◆ Exercise B

Read the following passage and answer the questions about it using what you have learned in this part of the lesson. Use your writing notebook or a separate piece of paper for your answers.

> He unbuttoned his jacket and shirt and drew forth his lunch. The action consumed no more than a quarter of a minute, yet in that brief moment the numbness laid hold of the exposed fingers. He did not put the mitten on, but, instead, struck the fingers a dozen sharp smashes against his leg. Then he sat down on a snow-covered log to eat. The sting that followed upon the striking of his fingers against his leg ceased so quickly that he was startled. He had had no chance to take a bite of biscuit. He struck the fingers repeatedly and returned them to the mitten, baring the other hand for the purpose of eating. He tried to take a mouthful, but the ice-muzzle prevented. He had forgotten to build a fire and thaw out. He chuckled at his foolishness, and as he chuckled he noted the numbness creeping into the exposed fingers. Also, he noted that the stinging which had first come to his toes when he sat down was already passing away. He wondered whether the toes were warm or numb. He moved them inside the moccasins and decided that they were numb.

1. The man forgot to do something when he stopped for lunch. This mistake is causing new problems for him. What was the first thing he should have done when he stopped to eat? Why?

2. In a few sentences explain what major complication you are told about in the passage.

Now check your answers using the suggestions in the Answer Key starting on page 457. Review this part of the lesson if you don't understand why an answer was wrong.

2◆Writing on Your Own

Look at the list you have written for Develop Your Plot Outline on page 105 that tells about your own story idea. Now do the following:

1. Select an item from your list that tells about an event that creates a problem or difficulty for the most important character. (Examples: You are frightened by dark shapes in the woods. People may drown and you don't know what to do. Lights approach out of the sky and your dog suddenly disappears.)

2. Write a short paragraph telling what happens and how the character feels.

3. You may want to change and rewrite your paragraph several times until you get it just the way you like it.

3 ◆ Crisis and Climax

In a tug of war, each team pulls and strains against the other. First one side and then the other seems to be winning as the conflict continues. Finally, one team makes its greatest effort. All the team members strain with all the strength and determination they have against the force of the other team. This moment is the high point of the action for them. With this effort they will win or lose. That high point is the *climax* of the conflict.

The climax of an action is also a turning point. All the strength of the people and all their emotional reserves have been put into their effort. At this point, something has to give. Because they have no more strength or energy for the conflict, they must either push to victory or accept defeat.

That turning point, that moment of decision, in a conflict is called the *crisis*. For instance, when news reporters speak of a crisis, they mean a turning point in some event; some sort of conflict that has been going on has reached a point at which an important change will occur.

In a story, as one conflict leads to another, the suspense grows. The emotions of both the characters in the story and of the reader mount to a high point. This is the climax of the story. The climax may occupy several chapters in a novel, or just a few paragraphs in a short story. Then an event, or a series of events, that can be seen as a turning point in the fortunes of the main characters will take place. From that point on things will either improve or move toward some tragic or unhappy conclusion.

As you have seen, "To Build a Fire" tells of a conflict between a man and the forces of nature. The emotional excitement of the story begins to build from the moment you learn that it is seventy-five degrees below zero. Who can imagine such cold! And here is a man struggling against it. The conflict and the fearful excitement grow as the man makes one mistake after another. Each time he tries to build a fire there is hope that he will win the struggle. And each time he fails you catch your breath.

Finally, he makes his final and greatest effort to save himself. The emotions of both the man in the story and the reader are at their highest point. That moment is the climax of the story. At the end of his effort, when he fails to build a fire, the man gives in to the idea of death. This scene is the turning point, the crisis, of the story.

The climax of the story takes place over several paragraphs. One of these paragraphs follows:

> Then the thought came to him that the frozen portions of his body must be extending. He tried to keep this thought down, to forget it, to think of something else; he was aware of the panicky feeling that it caused, and he was afraid of the panic. But the thought asserted itself, and persisted, until it produced a vision of his body totally frozen. This was too much, and he made another wild run along the trail. Once he slowed down to a walk, but the thought of the freezing extending itself made him run again.

The man's first shock (and the reader's, as well) came when he fell into the hidden spring. The man knew the springs were dangerous, but he did not think it was serious. Then his beautiful fire was smothered by falling snow. He begins to sense the danger of his situation as he tries to start a fire with his frozen fingers.

Now the man is at the end of his rope. He has reached his limit of endurance, and he gives in to panic and runs. We are at the highest point of the climax. The climax actually began some paragraphs before at the point when the man finally realizes that it is "a matter of life and death with the chances against him."

3 ◆ Exercise C

Read the following passage and answer the questions about it using what you have learned in this part of the lesson. Use your writing notebook or a separate piece of paper for your answers.

> And all the time the dog ran with him, at his heels. When he fell down a second time, it curled its tail over its forefeet and sat in front of him, facing him, curiously eager and intent. The warmth and security of the animal angered him, and he cursed it till it flattened down its ears appeasingly. This time the shivering came more quickly upon the man. He was losing in his battle with the frost. It was creeping into his body from all sides. The thought of it drove him on, but he ran no more than a hundred feet, when he staggered and pitched headlong. It was his last

panic. When he had recovered his breath and control, he sat up and entertained in his mind the conception of meeting death with dignity.

1. The man has been running in panic and fear. But suddenly his panic and fear is over. Why has his attitude changed? Explain your answer.

2. Since a crisis is a turning point, it is followed by an important change. How do the man's feelings change in the passage you just read?

Now check your answers using the suggestions in the Answer Key starting on page 457. Review this part of the lesson if you don't understand why an answer was wrong.

3 ✦ Writing on Your Own

Look at the list you have written for Develop a Plot Outline on page 105 that tells about your own story idea. Now do the following:

1. Select an item from your list that tells the most exciting event of the story—something that will be important in deciding how the story will come out. (Examples: A sudden storm forces you into a cave. You reach the drowning people using an old, leaky rowboat. You throw your coat over one of the mysterious lights and capture it.)

2. Write a short paragraph telling about that event. Try to tell how the character feels about what is happening.

3. You may want to change and rewrite your paragraph several times until you get it just the way you like it.

4 ◆ A Beginning, a Middle, and an End

In ancient Greece, more than two thousand years ago, drama was the most important form of storytelling. At that time, the great philosopher Aristotle proposed some "rules" for writing plays. One thing that is important, he said, is that the story have a beginning, a middle, and an end.

At first glance, this seems like pretty simple stuff for a great philosopher. Everything has a beginning and an end, you might say. And somewhere in between there must be a middle.

Indeed, it does *seem* simple until you try it. Think of some of the compositions you yourself have written. Did you find it easy to start writing? More writers fail because they cannot write beginnings than for any other reason. If you wanted to write about your vacation, for instance, where would you start? Would you begin with the packing, with the auto trip, or with your arrival at the lake?

You would have the same questions and problems with what to put in the middle. If you were to try to include everything that happened on your vacation, you'd have the dullest story ever told. How, then, do you pick and choose among all the activities and events? And where do you stop? A story can't go on forever. But *how* to stop can be a problem. Many good stories fall flat at the end, leaving the reader dissatisfied and angry.

So you can see why a story must have a beginning, a middle, and an end. But what Aristotle was really getting at was that it is important that the beginning, the middle, and the end of a story work together. They must all be connected.

Let's see how London handled these problems in "To Build a Fire."

The Beginning. You recall that there has to be an exposition at the beginning of a story. This provides the *who, what, when, where,* and *why* of the story. But in the exposition the author tells you only what you need to know to get into the story. The only details he provides are those that are necessary for you to understand what is about to happen.

The author connects the beginning of a story to the middle by introducing in the beginning things that relate to the conflicts and actions that will take place in the middle.

> . . . the tremendous cold, and the strangeness and weird-
> ness of it all—made no impression on the man.

That information prepares you for the conflict between the man and the cold that occupies the middle of the story.

> As he turned to go on, he spat speculatively. There was
> a sharp, explosive crackle that startled him.

Of all the things the author can tell you, why does he dwell on the man spitting? It is to show just how cold it is, of course. And that leads you to the middle of the story.

The Middle. Conflicts, complications, and actions occupy the middle of the story. And, as you have seen, these things lead you through the story to the climax, or high point of interest and excitement.

Suppose the story had been written like this: At the beginning, the man is out checking the bends and turns of a river. After telling you how cold it is, the author describes plans for cutting and shipping timber. Suddenly, the man falls in a spring and begins to freeze. The trouble with this story is that there is no connection between the beginning and the middle. The conflicts don't develop, they are simply dropped on you. A plot must *develop*. Conflicts and actions must grow out of the beginning and then proceed to develop from one another.

The End. There is an old joke among writers that the easiest way to end a story is to skip a line and write THE END. That may end the story, but it does leave the reader hanging.

Suppose Jack London had never told you whether the man lived or died? Did he reach camp or not? Many good stories end just that way. They leave readers to figure out their own endings. But that kind of ending leaves most readers a bit uneasy. Some readers even get angry because they feel the author has wasted their time by giving them a story without an end.

Suppose London had not connected the end of the story to the beginning and the middle—if when the character was close to death, he had been rescued by a member of the Royal Canadian Mounted Police who happened to be passing by? That would be worse than no ending at all! While it's nice to have a happy ending, a sudden rescue in *this* story would have nothing to do with all the conflict that has gone before.

There is usually one other thing that happens in an ending. In most stories, an author will bring the reader down gently from the high point of excitement—the climax. The problems in the story are solved or concluded in some way. This conclusion, or ending, to the story is called the *resolution*. In a detective mystery, for example, the author answers all the questions about how the crime was committed and "whodunit" in the resolution.

The following paragraph from "To Build a Fire" comes immediately after the climax of the story. How does it help bring you down from the climax?

> When he had recovered his breath and control, he sat up and entertained in his mind the conception of meeting death with dignity. However, the conception did not come to him in such terms. His idea of it was that he had been making a fool of himself, running around like a chicken with its head cut off—such was the simile that occurred to him. Well, he was bound to freeze anyway, and he might as well take it decently. With this newfound peace of mind came the first glimmerings of drowsiness. A good idea, he thought, to sleep off to death. It was like taking an anaesthetic. Freezing was not so bad as people thought.

The man has gone from complete panic to quiet control. This change in his behavior relieves the tension. The conflict is over and the man accepts the fact that he has lost, "Well . . . he might as well take it decently. . . . Freezing was not so bad as people thought."

Notice how the ending is related to the middle of the story and to the beginning. The main conflict all along has been between the man and the cold. The action has led the man from what seemed, at first, a simple journey to certain death on the trail.

With the conflict between the man and the cold resolved, the author turns to the smaller conflict between the man and the dog. This is resolved in the paragraph you will work with in Exercise D.

4 ◆ Exercise D

Read the following passage and answer the questions about it using what you have learned in this part of the lesson. Use your writing notebook or a separate piece of paper for your answers.

> The brief day drew to a close in a long, slow twilight. There were no signs of a fire to be made, and, besides, never in the dog's experience had it known a man to sit like that

in the snow and make no fire. As the twilight drew on, its eager yearning for the fire mastered it, and with a great lifting and shifting of forefeet, it whined softly, then flattened its ears down in anticipation of being chidden by the man. But the man remained silent. Later, the dog whined loudly. And still later it crept close to the man and caught the scent of death. . . . Then it turned and trotted up the trail in the direction of the camp it knew, where were the other food providers and fire providers.

1. In the passage, the brief day in the life of the man draws to a close. His conflict with nature is over. He did not realize the power of nature, and that lack of understanding has killed him. At what point in the story were you sure of the outcome? Is it a satisfactory outcome?

2. The dog has also experienced many conflicts. How does the dog finally resolve its problems?

Now check your answers using the suggestions in the Answer Key starting on page 457. Review this part of the lesson if you don't understand why an answer was wrong.

4♦Writing on Your Own

Look at the list you have written for Develop Your Plot Outline on page 105 that tells about your own story idea. Now do the following:

1. Select an item from your list that can provide a good ending for your story. (Examples: You are found in a cave by a large animal that turns out to be a search-and-rescue dog. You rescue the drowning people and return to shore just as your leaky boat sinks. You make a deal with the alien you have captured.)

2. Write a short paragraph that tells how your story ends.

3. You may want to change and rewrite your paragraph several times until you get it just the way you like it.

Now go on to Reviewing and Interpreting the Story.

Answer these questions without looking back at the story. Choose the best answer to each question and put an *x* in the box beside it, or write your answer on a separate piece of paper.

Remembering
Facts

1. How cold was it?

   ☐ a. It was seventy-five degrees below zero.

   ☐ b. It was about fifty degrees below zero.

   ☐ c. There was eighty degrees of frost.

   ☐ d. There was no way of telling how cold it was.

2. What are referred to as "traps" in the story?

   ☐ a. the Arctic cold and ice

   ☐ b. heavy snow on the trees

   ☐ c. pools of water under the snow

   ☐ d. snares set by hunters

Following the
Order of Events

3. The first time the man is frightened by the cold is when he

   ☐ a. stops for lunch and realizes his feet are numb.

   ☐ b. starts out on the journey and his face gets cold.

   ☐ c. realizes he is traveling alone.

   ☐ d. falls into a pool of water hidden beneath the snow.

4. The man has trouble trying to build a fire the third time because he

☐ a. panics.

☐ b. drops the matches in the snow.

☐ c. can't find any birch bark.

☐ d. can't move his frozen fingers.

Understanding
Word Choices
5. As the dog follows the man, it experiences a vague but <u>menacing apprehension</u> about the extreme cold. That phrase means the dog felt

☐ a. comfortable with the cold.

☐ b. nervous and cold.

☐ c. a threatening sense of danger.

☐ d. concerned about the man.

6. "Once in a while the thought <u>reiterated</u> itself that it was very cold and that he had never experienced such cold." In this context *reiterated* means the thought was

☐ a. repeated again about the cold.

☐ b. blocked from his mind.

☐ c. nothing to worry about.

☐ d. that he would make it to camp.

Understanding
Important Ideas
7. What did the dog know by instinct that the man did not know by using his judgment?

☐ a. The trip was longer than the man thought.

☐ b. They would become lost in the snow.

☐ c. The dog knew the man couldn't make a fire.

☐ d. It was too cold to be traveling anywhere.

8. The most important point the author makes about the man is that he

☐ a. didn't think enough about the cold.

☐ b. was an old-timer in the Arctic.

☐ c. was safe traveling with the dog.

☐ d. wasn't sure he was on the right trail.

Understanding
Levels of
Meaning
9. We know the man is far away from any town. That fact is important because it tells you the man is

☐ a. probably lonesome.

☐ b. lost.

☐ c. very frightened.

☐ d. alone in the wilderness.

10. "He knew that at fifty below spittle crackled on the snow, but this spittle had crackled in the air. Undoubtedly it was colder than fifty below—how much colder he did not know." The author included that description to

☐ a. make the scene more interesting and exciting.

☐ b. show that the man still doesn't realize how serious his situation is.

☐ c. add humor to the story.

☐ d. show that the man chewed tobacco.

Understanding
Character
11. Which adjective best describes the man's attitude toward the extreme cold?

☐ a. alert

☐ b. cautious

☐ c. unconcerned

☐ d. desperate

12. At the end of the story the man mumbles to the old-timer, "You were right, old hoss; you were right." The man discovered too late that he

   ☐ a. should have listened to and learned from the old-timer.

   ☐ b. wasn't going to make it to camp by dinnertime.

   ☐ c. never should have believed the old-timer.

   ☐ d. should not have traveled with the old-timer.

Understanding Setting

13. The story begins, "Day had broken cold and gray, exceedingly cold and gray. . . ." The author stresses the cold in the beginning because it

   ☐ a. is a problem for the dog.

   ☐ b. is important to the old-timer.

   ☐ c. becomes the conflict the man struggles with.

   ☐ d. will become less important at the end of the story.

14. "There was the fire, snapping and crackling and promising life with every dancing flame." The way the setting is described gives a feeling of

   ☐ a. warmth and security.

   ☐ b. fear and danger.

   ☐ c. coldness and dampness.

   ☐ d. sadness and uncertainty.

Understanding Feelings

15. In the story the dog is one of the characters. Which description best explains the relationship between the dog and the man?

   ☐ a. trusting and confident

   ☐ b. content and happy

☐ c. suspicious and unsure

☐ d. terrified and vicious

16. Very little is actually said about the man, yet we feel we know him. Even though he seems confident, we know that the author feels the man is

☐ a. able to take care of himself.

☐ b. frightened by the environment.

☐ c. careful about the cold.

☐ d. foolish to underestimate the power of nature.

Now check your answers using the Answer Key starting on page 457. Make no mark for right answers. Correct any wrong answers you may have by putting a check mark (✓) in the box next to the right answer. Count the number of questions you answered correctly and plot the total on the Comprehension Scores graph on page 468.

Next, look at the questions you answered incorrectly. What types of questions were they? Count the number you got wrong of each type and enter the numbers in the spaces below.

Remembering Facts   _____

Following the Order of Events   _____

Understanding Word Choices   _____

Understanding Important Ideas   _____

Understanding Levels of Meaning   _____

Understanding Character   _____

Understanding Setting   _____

Understanding Feelings   _____

Now use these numbers to fill in the Comprehension Skills Profile on page 469.

Discussion Guides

The questions below will help you think about the story and the lesson you have just read. If you don't discuss these questions in class, try to think about them or discuss them with your classmates. Perhaps you will want to write a few paragraphs in answer to the questions.

Discussing Plot

1. The author often uses a common theme, or idea, in a story to tie the plot together from beginning to end. It is sometimes called a "thread" that runs through the story. Cold and fire are used that way in "To Build a Fire." How are they threads that run through the story?

2. One kind of conflict is conflict between people. The dog in the story isn't a person, but it is a character. What kinds of conflict does the dog experience?

3. In a way, each new problem in a story brings a new turning point or crisis. How was falling in the water a crisis? Was the snow falling on the fire also a turning point?

Discussing the Story

4. There is an old saying, Fools rush in where angels fear to tread. Early in the story, Jack London says of the man, "The trouble with him was that he was without imagination." How are those two statements alike?

5. In many of his short stories and novels, Jack London points out that people are frail creatures. How is the man in the story frail?

6. In the story, the man dies and the dog lives. Does that mean the dog is smarter than the man? Or is there some other reason why the dog survives while the man does not?

Discussing the Author's Work

7. A good storyteller captures your interest at once. Review the first two paragraphs of the story. What do you find there that captures your interest?

8. Many of Jack London's stories end with someone's death. Is the man's death a good ending for this story? Would you have ended the story some other way? Explain your opinions.

9. How does Jack London use the old-timer from Sulphur Creek as a character in the story, even though the old-timer never appears on the scene?

Writing Exercise

Read all the instructions before you begin writing. If you have any questions about how to begin the writing assignment, review Using the Writing Process beginning on page 445, or confer with your writing coach.

1. At the beginning of the unit you were asked to think of an idea for a story and to make a list of people, places, and events that would become part of your story. If you haven't done that yet, read the instructions for Develop Your Plot Outline on page 105, and make your list now.

2. Write a short story based on your idea and the list you have made. The story should have the plot elements you learned about in this unit:

   ◆ **An Exposition:** Describe where the story takes place; who the main characters are; how the story begins; something that shows there are problems coming.

   ◆ **Conflicts and Complications:** These are the problems that arise in the story and reactions and feeling of the characters to these problems.

   ◆ **Crisis and Climax:** This tells about the events that are most exciting and that will lead to how the story turns out.

   ◆ **A Beginning, a Middle, and an End:** The story should move along in a regular order so that your readers can easily follow and understand what's going on.

3. If you have written the paragraphs suggested in the four lesson exercises called Writing on Your Own, you may use those to help write your story.

4. Write, revise, correct, and rewrite your story until you are sure you have got it just the way you want it.

Unit 4 Setting

Marigolds
BY EUGENIA COLLIER

About the Illustration

How would you describe the setting in which this scene is taking place? Point to some details in the drawing to support your response.

Here are some questions to help you think about the story:

◆ Where do you think this scene takes place? Are the people rich or poor? What details about the place lead you to those conclusions?

◆ What is the woman in the picture doing?

◆ What do you think the woman is thinking about?

Unit 4

Introduction

About the Story

Miss Lottie's yellow marigolds really catch your eye. Unlike the rest of the poor shabby town, the marigolds glow with life, color, and warmth. That's why Miss Lottie loves them.

But Lizabeth, the girl who tells the story, has a hard time understanding the significance of Miss Lottie's marigolds. Their bright color seems to emphasize how ugly everything else is. Poor and uneducated, Lizabeth can see no hope for the future. She is angry and frustrated with life. So she takes out her anger on Miss Lottie's marigolds.

But even though Lizabeth makes some bad decisions, she does learn from her actions. She discovers something about Miss Lottie, and she also learns something about herself. She's not happy with her behavior, but she begins to understand why she behaved the way she did. In the end, those yellow marigolds become an important part of her growing up.

Like Lizabeth in "Marigolds," author Eugenia Collier grew up in Maryland during the Depression. After getting degrees from Howard University and Columbia University, Collier took a job as a case-worker for the Baltimore Department of Public Welfare in Maryland. But before long, she decided to go into teaching. Today she is a professor at Morgan State College in Baltimore.

In addition to teaching, Collier has published many stories, poems, and books of nonfiction. When asked about her writing, she once said, "The fact of my blackness is the core and center of my creativity. . . . I discovered the richness, the diversity, the beauty of my black heritage." As you will see, that commitment to her black heritage is one of the important themes in her award-winning story "Marigolds."

About the Lesson

The lesson that follows the story is about setting. The setting of a story is the backdrop for the events that take place. It includes many things—the time, the place, the scenery, and even the people themselves. Sights, sounds, and smells can all be part of the setting of a story.

The setting helps readers keep track of where a story is taking place and of what is going on. But the best settings take you one step further. They help you understand how the characters feel about the places in which they find themselves. A good setting helps you share more fully in the experience of the story.

The following questions will help you see how Eugenia Collier develops the setting in "Marigolds." Read the story carefully and try to answer these questions as you go along:

◆ At the beginning of the story you learn about Lizabeth's memories of her hometown. How does her picture of the town prepare you for events in the story?

◆ What words does the author use to make the marigolds stand out? How does she make them different from anything else in the story?

◆ How do the author's descriptions of people contribute to the setting?

◆ Toward the end of the story, when Lizabeth returns to the garden, the author includes details of sound and smell. Why?

Develop Your Own Setting

You can understand the importance of setting when you think about writing your own story. Use your writing notebook or a separate piece of paper and try the following suggestions:

1. Choose one of the following ideas for a story, or think of an idea of your own.

   ☐ You're traveling in a car on a hot day. You feel like you've never been so hot in your life. Then the car stalls on the highway.

   ☐ You're in a crowded store trying to avoid a person you don't want to see. You look everywhere, but you can't find the exit.

   ☐ You're standing in a field watching some horses. In the distance you hear a roll of thunder, and the horses begin to get jumpy and nervous. Soon they start to run.

2. Make a list of details that show the setting of your story. Your list should include the following:

   ☐ Time (What's the time of day or time of year? Are you in the past or in the present?)

   ☐ Place (Where is the story taking place?)

   ☐ Sights (What do you see around you?)

   ☐ Smells (What do you smell?)

   ☐ Sounds (What do you hear?)

3. Rewrite your list, trying to add as many details as you can. Even if you don't end up using every detail in your story, your ideas will help you get a feeling for the place you are writing about.

Marigolds

by Eugenia Collier

When I think of the home town of my youth, all that I seem to remember is dust—the brown, crumbly dust of late summer—arid, sterile dust that gets into the eyes and makes them water, gets into the throat and between the toes of bare brown feet. I don't know why I should remember only the dust. Surely there must have been lush green lawns and paved streets under leafy shade trees somewhere in town; but memory is an abstract painting—it does not present things as they are, but rather as they *feel*. And so, when I think of that time and that place, I remember only the dry September of the dirt roads and grassless yards of the shanty-town where I lived. And one other thing I remember, another incongruency of memory—a brilliant splash of sunny yellow against the dust—Miss Lottie's marigolds.

Whenever the memory of those marigolds flashes across my mind, a strange nostalgia comes with it and remains long after the picture has faded. I feel again the chaotic emotions of adolescence, illusive as smoke, yet as real as the potted geranium before me now. Joy and rage and wild animal gladness and shame become tangled together in the multicolored skein of 14-going-on-15 as I recall that devastating moment when I was suddenly more woman than child, years ago in Miss Lottie's yard. I think of those marigolds at the strangest times; I remember them vividly now as I desperately pass away the time waiting for you, who will not come.

I suppose that futile waiting was the sorrowful background

music of our impoverished little community when I was young. The Depression that gripped the nation was no new thing to us, for the black workers of rural Maryland had always been depressed. I don't know what it was that we were waiting for; certainly not for the prosperity that was "just around the corner," for those were white folks' words, which we *never* believed. Nor did we wait for hard work and thrift to pay off in shining success as the American Dream promised, for we knew better than that, too. Perhaps we waited for a miracle, amorphous in concept but necessary if one were to have the grit to rise before dawn each day and labor in the white man's vineyard until after dark, or to wander about in the September dust offering one's sweat in return for some meager share of bread. But God was chary with miracles in those days, and so we waited—and waited.

We children, of course, were only vaguely aware of the extent of our poverty. Having no radios, few newspapers, and no magazines, we were somewhat unaware of the world outside our community. Nowadays we would be called "culturally deprived" and people would write books and hold conferences about us. In those days everybody we knew was just as hungry and ill-clad as we were. Poverty was the cage in which we all were trapped, and our hatred of it was still the vague, undirected restlessness of the zoo-bred flamingo who knows that nature created him to fly free.

As I think of those days I feel most poignantly the tag-end of summer, the bright dry times when we began to have a sense of shortening days and the imminence of the cold.

By the time I was 14 my brother Joey and I were the only children left at our house, the older ones having left home for early marriage or the lure of the city, and the two babies having been sent to relatives who might care for them better than we. Joey was three years younger than I, and a boy, and therefore vastly inferior. Each morning our mother and father trudged wearily down the dirt road and around the bend, she to her domestic job, he to his daily unsuccessful quest for work. After our few chores around the tumble-down shanty, Joey and I were free to run wild in the sun with other children similarly situated.

For the most part, those days are ill-defined in my memory, running together and combining like a fresh water-color painting left out in the rain. I remember squatting in the road drawing a picture in the dust, a picture which Joey gleefully erased with one sweep of his dirty foot. I remember fishing for minnows in a muddy creek and watching sadly as they eluded my cupped hands, while Joey laughed uproariously. And I remember, that year, a strange restlessness of body and of spirit, a feeling that something old and familiar was ending, and something unknown and therefore terrifying was beginning.

One day returns to me with special clarity for some reason, perhaps because it was the beginning of the experience that in some inexplicable way marked the end of innocence. I was loafing under the great oak tree in our yard, deep in some reverie which I have now forgotten except that it involved some secret, secret thoughts of one of the Harris boys across the yard. Joey and a bunch of kids were bored now with the old tire suspended from an oak limb which had kept them entertained for awhile.

"Hey, Lizabeth," Joey yelled. He never talked when he could yell. "Hey, Lizabeth, let's us go somewhere."

I came reluctantly from my private world. "Where at, Joey?"

The truth was that we were becoming tired of the formlessness of our summer days. The idleness whose prospect had seemed so beautiful during the busy days of spring now had degenerated to an almost desperate effort to fill up the empty midday hours.

"Let's go see can we find us some locusts on the hill," someone suggested.

Joey was scornful. "Ain't no more locusts there. Y'all got 'em all while they was still green."

The argument that followed was brief and not really

worth the effort. Hunting locust trees wasn't fun any more by now.

"Tell you what," said Joey finally, his eyes sparkling. "Let's us go over to Miss Lottie's."

The idea caught on at once, for annoying Miss Lottie was always fun. I was still child enough to scamper along with the group over rickety fences and through bushes that tore our already raggedy clothes, back to where Miss Lottie lived. I think now that we must have made a tragicomic spectacle, five or six kids of different ages, each of us clad in only one garment—the girls in faded dresses that were too long or too short, the boys in patchy pants, their sweaty brown chests gleaming in the hot sun. A little cloud of dust followed our thin legs and bare feet as we tramped over the barren land.

When Miss Lottie's house came into view we stopped, ostensibly to plan our strategy, but actually to reinforce our courage. Miss Lottie's house was the most ramshackle of all our ramshackle homes. The sun and rain had long since faded its rickety frame siding from white to a sullen gray. The boards themselves seemed to remain upright not from being nailed together but rather from leaning together like a house that a child might have constructed from cards. A brisk wind might have blown it down, and the fact that it was still standing implied a kind of enchantment that was stronger than the elements. There it stood, and as far as I know is standing yet—a gray rotting thing with no porch, no shutters, no steps, set on a cramped lot with no grass, not even any weeds—a monument to decay.

In front of the house in a squeaky rocking chair sat Miss Lottie's son, John Burke, completing the impression of decay. John Burke was what was known as "queer-headed." Black and ageless, he sat, rocking day in and day out in a mindless stupor, lulled by the monotonous squeak-squawk of the chair. A battered hat atop his shaggy head shaded him from the sun. Usually John Burke was totally unaware of everything outside his quiet dream world.

But if you disturbed him, if you intruded upon his fantasies, he would become enraged, strike out at you, and curse at you in some strange enchanted language which only he could understand. We children made a game of thinking of ways to disturb John Burke and then to elude his violent retribution.

But our real fun and our real fear lay in Miss Lottie herself. Miss Lottie seemed to be at least a hundred years old. Her big frame still held traces of the tall, powerful woman she must have been in youth, although it was bent and drawn. Her smooth skin was a dark reddish-brown, and her face had Indian-like features and the stern stoicism that one associates with Indian faces. Miss Lottie didn't like intruders either, especially children. She never left her yard, and nobody ever visited her. We never knew how she managed those necessities which depend on human interaction—how she ate, for example, or even whether she ate. When we were tiny children, we thought Miss Lottie was a witch and we made up tales, that we half believed ourselves, about her exploits. We were far too sophisticated now, of course, to believe the witch-nonsense. But old fears have a way of clinging like cobwebs, and so when we sighted the tumble-down shack, we had to stop to reinforce our nerves.

"Look, there she is," I whispered, forgetting that Miss Lottie could not possibly have heard me from that distance. "She's fooling with them crazy flowers."

"Yeh, look at 'er."

Miss Lottie's marigolds were perhaps the strangest part of the picture. Certainly they did not fit in with the crumbling decay of the rest of her yard. Beyond the dusty brown yard, in front of the sorry gray house, rose suddenly and shockingly a dazzling strip of bright blossoms, clumped together in enormous mounds, warm and passionate and sun-golden. The old black witch-woman worked on them all summer, every summer, down on her creaky knees, weeding and cultivating and arranging, while the house crumbled and John Burke rocked. For some perverse reason, we children hated those marigolds. They interfered with the perfect ugliness of the place; they were too beautiful; they said too much that we could not understand; they did not make sense. There was something in the vigor with which the old woman destroyed the weeds that intimidated us. It should have been a comical sight—the old woman with the man's hat on her cropped white head, leaning over the bright mounds, her big backside in the air—but it wasn't comical, it was something we could not name. We had to annoy her by whizzing a pebble into her flowers or by yelling a dirty word, then dancing away from her rage, revelling in our youth and mocking her age. Actually, I think it was the flowers we wanted to destroy, but nobody had the nerve to try it, not even Joey, who was usually fool enough to try anything.

"Y'all git some stones," commanded Joey now, and was met with instant giggling obedience as everyone except me began to gather pebbles from the dusty ground. "Come on, Lizabeth."

I just stood there peering through the bushes, torn between wanting to join the fun and feeling that it was all a bit silly.

"You scared, Lizabeth?"

I cursed and spat on the ground—my favorite gesture of phony bravado. "Y'all children get the stones, I'll show you how to use 'em."

I said before that we children were not consciously aware of how thick were the bars of our cage. I wonder now, though, whether we were not more aware of it than I thought. Perhaps we had some dim notion of what we were, and how little chance we had of being anything else. Otherwise, why would we have been so preoccupied with destruction? Anyway, the pebbles were collected quickly, and everybody looked at me to begin the fun.

"Come on, y'all."

We crept to the edge of the bushes that bordered the narrow road in front of Miss Lottie's place. She was working placidly, kneeling over the flowers, her dark hand plunged into the golden mound. Suddenly "zing"—an expertly-aimed stone cut the head off one of the blossoms.

"Who out there?" Miss Lottie's backside came down and her head came up as her sharp eyes searched the bushes. "You better git!"

We had crouched down out of sight in the bushes, where we stifled the giggles that insisted on coming. Miss Lottie gazed warily across the road for a moment, then cautiously returned to her weeding. "Zing"—Joey sent a pebble into the blooms, and another marigold was beheaded.

Miss Lottie was enraged now. She began struggling to her feet, leaning on a rickety cane and shouting, "Y'all git! Go on home!" Then the rest of the kids let loose with their pebbles, storming the flowers and laughing wildly and senselessly at Miss Lottie's impotent rage. She shook her stick at us and started shakily toward the road crying, "Black bastards, git 'long! John Burke! John Burke, come help!"

Then I lost my head entirely, mad with the power of inciting such rage, and ran out of the bushes in the storm of pebbles, straight toward Miss Lottie chanting madly, "Old witch, fell in a ditch, picked up a penny and thought she was rich!" The children screamed with delight, dropped their pebbles and joined the crazy dance, swarming around Miss Lottie like bees and chanting, "Old lady witch!" while she screamed curses at us. The madness lasted only a moment, for John Burke, startled at last, lurched out of his chair, and we dashed for the bushes just as Miss Lottie's cane went whizzing at my head.

I did not join the merriment when the kids gathered again under the oak in our bare yard. Suddenly I was ashamed, and I did not like being ashamed. The child in me sulked and said it was all in fun, but the woman in me flinched at the thought of the malicious attack that I had led. The mood lasted all afternoon. When we ate the beans and rice that was supper that night, I did not notice my father's silence, for he was always silent these days, nor did I notice my mother's absence, for she always worked until well into evening. Joey and I had a particularly bitter argument after supper; his exuberance got on my nerves. Finally I stretched out upon the palette in the room we shared and fell into a fitful doze.

When I awoke, somewhere in the middle of the night, my mother had returned, and I vaguely listened to the conversation that was audible through the thin walls that separated our rooms. At first I heard no words, only voices. My mother's voice was like a cool, dark room in summer—peaceful, soothing, quiet. I loved to listen to it; it made things seem alright somehow. But my father's voice cut through hers, shattering the peace.

"Twenty-two years, Maybelle, 22 years," he was saying, "and I got nothing for you, nothing, nothing."

"It's all right, honey, you'll get something. Everybody out of work now, you know that."

"It ain't right. Ain't no man ought to eat his woman's food year in and year out, and see his children running wild. Ain't nothing right about that."

"Honey, you took good care of us when you had it. Ain't nobody got nothing nowadays."

"I ain't talking about nobody else, I'm talking about *me*. God knows I try." My mother said something I could not hear, and my father cried out louder, "What must a man do, tell me that?"

"Look, we ain't starving. I git paid every week, and Mrs. Ellis is real nice about giving me things. She gonna let me have Mr. Ellis' old coat for you this winter—"

"God damn Mr. Ellis' coat! And God damn his money! You think I want white folks' leavings? God damn, Maybelle"—and suddenly he sobbed, loudly and painfully, and cried helplessly and hopelessly in the dark night. I had never heard a man cry before. I did not know men ever cried. I covered my ears with my hands but could not cut off the sound of my father's harsh, painful, despairing sobs. My father was a strong man who would whisk a child upon his shoulders and go singing through the house. My father whittled toys for us and laughed so loud that the great oak seemed to laugh with him, and taught us how to fish and hunt rabbits. How could it be that my father was crying? But the sobs went on, unstifled, finally quieting until I could hear my mother's voice, deep and rich, humming softly as she used to hum to a frightened child.

The world had lost its boundary lines. My mother, who was small and soft, was now the strength of the family; my father, who was the rock on which the family had been built, was sobbing like the tiniest child. Everything was suddenly out of tune, like a broken accordion. Where did I fit into this crazy picture? I do not now remember my thoughts, only a feeling of great bewilderment and fear.

Long after the sobbing and the humming had stopped, I lay on the palette, still as stone with my hands over my ears, wishing that I could cry and be comforted. The night was silent now except for the sound of the crickets and of Joey's soft breathing. But the room was too crowded with fear to allow me to sleep, and finally, feeling the terrible aloneness of 4 A.M., I decided to awaken Joey.

"Ouch! What's the matter with you? What you want?" he demanded disagreeably when I had pinched and slapped him awake.

"Come on, wake up."

"What for? Go 'way."

I was lost for a reasonable reply. I could not say, "I'm scared and I don't want to be alone," so I merely said, "I'm going out. If you want to come, come on."

The promise of adventure awoke him. "Going out now? Where at, Lizabeth? What you going to do?"

I was pulling my dress over my head. Until now I had not thought of going out. "Just come on," I replied tersely.

I was out the window and halfway down the road before Joey caught up with me.

"Wait, Lizabeth, where you going?"

I was running as if the furies were after me, as perhaps they were—running silently and furiously until I came to where I had half-known I was headed: to Miss Lottie's yard.

The half-dawn light was more eerie than complete darkness, and in it the old house was like the ruin that my world had become—foul and crumbling, a grotesque caricature. It looked haunted, but I was not afraid because I was haunted too.

"Lizabeth, you lost your mind?" panted Joey.

I had indeed lost my mind, for all the smoldering emotions of that summer swelled in me and burst—the great need for my mother who was never there, the hopelessness of our poverty and degradation, the bewilderment of being neither child nor woman and yet both at once, the fear unleashed by my father's tears. And these feelings combined in one great impulse toward destruction.

"Lizabeth!"

I leaped furiously into the mounds of marigolds and pulled madly, trampling and pulling and destroying the perfect yellow blooms. The fresh smell of early morning and of dew-soaked marigolds spurred me on as I went tearing and mangling and sobbing while Joey tugged my dress or my waist crying, "Lizabeth, stop, please stop!"

And then I was sitting in the ruined little garden among the uprooted and ruined flowers, crying and crying, and it was too late to undo what I had done. Joey was sitting beside me, silent and frightened, not knowing what to say. Then, "Lizabeth, look."

I opened my swollen eyes and saw in front of me a pair of large calloused feet; my gaze lifted to the swollen legs, the age-distorted body clad in a tight cotton night dress, and then the shadowed Indian face surrounded by stubby white hair. And there was no rage in the face now, now that the garden was destroyed and there was nothing any longer to be protected.

"M-miss Lottie!" I scrambled to my feet and just stood there and stared at her, and that was the moment when childhood faded and womanhood began. That violent, crazy act was the last act of childhood. For as I gazed at the immobile face with the sad, weary eyes, I gazed upon a kind of reality which is hidden to childhood. The witch was no longer a witch but only a broken old woman who had dared to create beauty in the midst of ugliness and sterility. She had been born in squalor and lived in it all her life. Now at the end of that life she had nothing except a falling-down hut, a wrecked body, and John Burke, the mindless son of her passion. Whatever verve there was left in her, whatever was of love and beauty and joy that had not been squeezed out by life, had been there in the marigolds she had so tenderly cared for.

Of course I could not express the things that I knew about Miss Lottie as I stood there awkward and ashamed. The years have put words to the things I knew in that moment, and as I looked back upon it, I know that the moment marked the end of innocence. Innocence involves an unseeing acceptance of things at face value, an ignorance of the area below the surface. In that humiliating moment I looked beyond myself and into the depths of another person. This was the beginning of compassion, and one cannot have both compassion and innocence.

The years have taken me worlds away from that time and that place, from the dust and squalor of our lives and from the bright thing that I destroyed in a blind childish striking out at God-knows-what. Miss Lottie died long ago and many years have passed since I last saw her hut, completely barren at last, for despite my wild contrition she never planted marigolds again. Yet, there are times when the image of those passionate yellow mounds returns with a painful poignancy. For one does not have to be ignorant and poor to find that his life is barren as the dusty yards of our town. And I too have planted marigolds.

Setting

Every story has three major elements: plot, character, and setting. Of the three, setting is the least obvious. Unlike vivid characters and exciting plots, settings tend to slip into the background, which is where they belong. But you would miss them if they were left out. Think back to the story "To Build a Fire." Imagine how different it would be if Jack London left out those details about the Yukon's terrible cold. And what if he changed his mind and decided to set the story in a desert?

Setting works hand in hand with the other elements of a story. Characters are shaped by their surroundings. Plots spring naturally out of a certain setting and move forward as scenes change. Important ideas are reinforced by the settings. And last but not least, feelings—yours and the characters'—are influenced by the many details of an author's carefully prepared setting.

Setting consists of many things, including the place and time of the story, sights, sounds, smells, tastes, objects, and weather. Even minor characters, when they are just hovering in the background, can be thought about as part of the setting.

Authors do not spell out every last detail of every setting. If they did, the story would become bogged down in endless description. Instead they pick and choose, presenting the reader with only those details that are important to the story.

In this lesson we will look at four important ways in which Eugenia Collier uses setting to enhance her story "Marigolds":

1♦ The author uses setting to suggest the kind of action that might take place.

2♦ She uses setting to influence the way characters feel—and the way you feel.

3♦ She uses setting to help you picture the story in your mind. She helps you feel you are really there.

4♦ She uses setting to reinforce important ideas, or themes, that she wants you to understand.

1 ♦ Setting and Action

An author creates a setting to match the plot. He or she uses setting to support what's going on in the story. In many cases, settings actually help create the actions that occur.

For example, the story "First Confession," which you read earlier in this book, is set in a town in Ireland where most of the people are Catholics. The story is about an Irish boy taking part in a Catholic ceremony. The setting of "Raymond's Run" is in Harlem, a district in New York City, and the story is about a girl dealing with life in a city neighborhood. Each of these stories could only have happened in the settings the authors prepared for them. If the authors had chosen different settings, the plots would have been different also.

You find the same relationship between setting and action in "Marigolds." At the beginning of the story, Eugenia Collier describes Lizabeth's memories of her hometown. How does the whole story seem to flow from this setting?

> When I think of the home town of my youth, all that I seem to remember is dust—the brown, crumbly dust of late summer—arid, sterile dust that gets into the eyes and makes them water, gets into the throat and between the toes of bare brown feet. I don't know why I should remember only the dust. Surely there must have been lush green lawns and paved streets under leafy shade trees somewhere in town; but memory is an abstract painting— it does not present things as they are, but rather as they *feel*. And so, when I think of that time and that place, I remember only the dry September of the dirt roads and grassless yards of the shanty-town where I lived. And one other thing I remember, another incongruency of memory—a brilliant splash of sunny yellow against the dust—Miss Lottie's marigolds.

Lizabeth remembers a town that was ugly and brown except for the "sunny yellow" of the marigolds. The author uses Lizabeth's memory of the town to prepare you for the action in the story. As a teenager, Lizabeth couldn't understand beauty because she saw her life as ugly. Her anger and lack of understanding made her destroy the only beauty around her—the marigolds.

In one way or another, all the events in the story have their roots in the setting: the children's boredom, Miss Lottie's love for her garden, the father's tears, and Lizabeth's anger and confusion. All those feelings and actions spring naturally out of the setting the author has prepared for us.

1♦Exercise A

Read the following passage and answer the questions about it using what you have learned in this part of the lesson. Use your writing notebook or a separate piece of paper for your answers.

When Miss Lottie's house came into view we stopped, ostensibly to plan our strategy, but actually to reinforce our courage. Miss Lottie's house was the most ramshackle of all our ramshackle homes. The sun and rain had long since faded its rickety frame siding from white to a sullen gray. The boards themselves seemed to remain upright not from being nailed together but rather from leaning together like a house that a child might have constructed from cards. A brisk wind might have blown it down, and the fact that it was still standing implied a kind of enchantment that was stronger than the elements.

1. What does the setting hint about the house's owner? How does it prepare you for Miss Lottie's actions in the future?

2. How does the appearance of the house affect the children? How does it help you predict the children's behavior?

Now check your answers using the suggestions in the Answer Key starting on page 457. Review this part of the lesson if you don't understand why an answer was wrong.

1♦Writing on Your Own

Look at the list you wrote for Develop Your Own Setting on page 155. Now do the following:

1. Choose several items from your list that tell about time.

2. Write a paragraph describing the situation you are in. Include details that show *when* the action is taking place. For example, if you are writing about a cowpuncher riding home after a long day's work, you might say, "She slowed her horse to a walk and drank in the cool evening breeze that flowed up from the river."

3. You may want to change and rewrite your paragraph several times until you get it just the way you like it.

2 ◆ Settings and Feelings

Settings have a powerful effect on feelings. For instance, some people always feel peaceful in a garden. Other people always feel nervous at a party. And most of us get frazzled in a traffic jam.

But our feelings can also affect the way we view a setting. Sometimes your house can make you feel stifled and cooped up. But if you have been away from home for a while, and a bit homesick, that same setting can make you feel safe and secure.

Settings and feelings interact in stories as well. Authors create settings that have a certain effect on characters. And because readers sense the atmosphere, or mood, of the setting, they share the characters' feelings for it.

Think about the relationship between setting and feelings in this passage:

> For the most part, those days are ill-defined in my memory, running together and combining like a fresh water-color painting left out in the rain. I remember squatting in the road drawing a picture in the dust, a picture which Joey gleefully erased with one sweep of his dirty foot. I remember fishing for minnows in a muddy creek and watching sadly as they eluded my cupped hands, while Joey laughed uproariously.

The setting describes a country childhood—playing in the road, fishing for minnows. In some stories, they could be happy memories. But here they are not. The details in the setting hint at Lizabeth's unhappiness. And because she is sad, the reader feels sad too.

2 ◆ Exercise B

Read the following passage and answer the questions about it using what you have learned in this part of the lesson. Use your writing notebook or a separate piece of paper for your answers.

> Miss Lottie's marigolds were perhaps the strangest part of the picture. Certainly they did not fit in with the crumbling decay of the rest of her yard. Beyond the dusty

brown yard, in front of the sorry gray house, rose suddenly and shockingly a dazzling strip of bright blossoms, clumped together in enormous mounds, warm and passionate and sun-golden.

1. How does the setting change in this paragraph? What details tell you about the changing scene?

2. How does that change in setting affect your feelings?

Now check your answers using the suggestions in the Answer Key starting on page 457. Review this part of the lesson if you don't understand why an answer was wrong.

2 ◆ Writing on Your Own

Look at the list you wrote for Develop Your Own Setting on page 155. Then review the paragraph you wrote for 1◆ Writing on Your Own. Now do the following:

1. Choose several items from your list that show what you *see* in this setting.

2. Now rewrite the paragraph you wrote for 1◆ Writing on Your Own, adding details that show your surroundings.
   For example, if you are writing about a cowpuncher, you might want to hint that she's been working hard, maybe even that she's sick: "A tired horse limped up through the canyon. On its back the cowpuncher sagged against the saddle, a lariat dangling loosely from her fingers."

3. You may want to change and rewrite your paragraph several times until you get it just the way you like it.

3 ◆ Setting and the Sense of Really Being There

In theaters, scenery is painted on large canvases called flats. When you stop to think about it, that's a good name for them. They provide only one dimension of the play's setting. But there is more to a theater's setting than just scenery. The actors, their costumes, the sound effects, and the lighting all contribute to the setting. Together, they make the play seem real to the audience.

Authors work to create the same effect in the setting of their stories. They want to give readers more than just flat pictures. They want to put the reader right into the middle of the scene. So authors describe sights, sounds, smells, textures—the little things that make a setting come alive.

Pay attention to how Eugenia Collier involves you in this scene:

> Then I lost my head entirely, mad with the power of inciting such rage, and ran out of the bushes in the storm of pebbles, straight toward Miss Lottie chanting madly, "Old witch, fell in a ditch, picked up a penny and thought she was rich!" The children screamed with delight, dropped their pebbles and joined the crazy dance, swarming around Miss Lottie like bees and chanting, "Old lady witch!" while she screamed curses at us. The madness lasted only a moment, for John Burke, startled at last, lurched out of his chair, and we dashed for the bushes just as Miss Lottie's cane went whizzing at my head.

Notice the different kinds of details you get in this setting. You see the narrator rush out of the bushes "in the storm of pebbles." You hear her begin to chant, and then you hear the other children join in. You watch them dance, "swarming around Miss Lottie like bees." You hear Miss Lottie scream and see her swing her cane. And you watch as John Burke finally gets out of his chair, just before the children scatter into the bushes.

The author combines these details to make you feel as if you are right in the middle of this crazy scene. You can practically feel Miss Lottie's cane whizzing at *your* head. You have the sense of really being there, of really being a part of the story.

3 ✦ Exercise C

Read the following passage and answer the questions about it using what you have learned in this part of the lesson. Use your writing notebook or a separate piece of paper for your answers.

> I leaped furiously into the mounds of marigolds and pulled madly, trampling and pulling and destroying the perfect yellow blooms. The fresh smell of early morning and of dew-soaked marigolds spurred me on as I went tearing and mangling and sobbing while Joey tugged my dress or my waist crying, "Lizabeth, stop, please stop!"
>
> And then I was sitting in the ruined little garden among the uprooted and ruined flowers, crying and crying, and it was too late to undo what I had done.

1. How does the author appeal to your sense of smell in this passage? How does she appeal to your sense of hearing? Give some examples.

2. How does the setting in this passage involve you in Lizabeth's actions? What words help you follow her changing feelings?

Now check your answers using the suggestions in the Answer Key starting on page 457. Review this part of the lesson if you don't understand why an answer was wrong.

3 ✦ Writing on Your Own

Look at the list you wrote for Develop Your Own Setting on page 155. Then review the paragraph you wrote for 2 ◆ Writing on Your Own. Now do the following:

1. Choose some of the smells you notice in your setting.

2. Rewrite your paragraph, adding in some details of smell. For example, if you are writing about a cowpuncher, she might "breathe in the odor of coffee boiling on a smoky campfire."

3. You may want to change and rewrite your paragraph several times until you get it just the way you like it.

4 ◆ Setting and Ideas

It's hard to talk about a story without discussing the ideas it presents. "Marigolds" presents several ideas. One idea is the need for beauty in life. Another idea is the effect that poverty and ignorance can have on people.

Those ideas are part of the story's *themes*. When Eugenia Collier chose her settings, she wanted them to support and express the themes of the story. She wanted the settings to become places for the themes to develop.

Lizabeth makes some discoveries about the importance of beauty. Unfortunately, she learns a lesson at the cost of Miss Lottie's happiness. What does the setting of this passage tell you?

> And there was no rage in the face now, now that the garden was destroyed and there was nothing any longer to be protected.
> . . . The witch was no longer a witch but only a broken old woman who had dared to create beauty in the midst of ugliness and sterility. She had been born in squalor and lived in it all her life. Now at the end of that life she had nothing except a falling-down hut, a wrecked body, and John Burke.

The author uses a picture of Miss Lottie, her home, and her life to show Lizabeth—and us—why that bed of marigolds was so important. We learn that beauty can help people deal with the terrible troubles of life. And when beauty disappears, sometimes hope seems to disappear too.

4 ◆ Exercise D

Read the following passage and answer the questions about it using what you have learned in this part of the lesson. Use your writing notebook or a separate piece of paper for your answers.

> I had never heard a man cry before. I did not know men ever cried. I covered my ears with my hands but could not cut off the sound of my father's harsh, painful, despairing

sobs. My father was a strong man who would whisk a child upon his shoulders and go singing through the house. My father whittled toys for us and laughed so loud that the great oak seemed to laugh with him, and taught us how to fish and hunt rabbits. How could it be that my father was crying?

1. The author uses setting to switch from reality to her memory. What words show the reality that Lizabeth hears? What words show her memories?

2. The setting shows that Lizabeth is learning a painful lesson about life and people. What is she learning?

Now check your answers using the suggestions in the Answer Key starting on page 457. Review this part of the lesson if you don't understand why an answer was wrong.

4♦Writing on Your Own

Look at the list you wrote for Develop Your Own Setting on page 155. Then review the paragraph you wrote for 3♦Writing on Your Own. Now do the following:

1. Choose several items from your list that tell about sounds.

2. Rewrite your paragraph, adding details to the setting that tell what you hear.
    For example, a cowpuncher might hear "the ring of her horse's hooves as they climbed up the stormy riverbed." Or "From a lone tree in the distance, an owl called softly in the twilight."

3. You may want to change and rewrite your paragraph several times until you get it just the way you like it.

Now go on to Reviewing and Interpreting the Story.

Reviewing and Interpreting the Story

Answer these questions without looking back at the story. Choose the best answer to each question and put an *x* in the box beside it, or write your answer on a separate piece of paper.

Remembering Facts

1. In what state does the story take place?

   ☐ a. Maryland

   ☐ b. Kentucky

   ☐ c. California

   ☐ d. Minnesota

2. How many children still live at home with Lizabeth's parents?

   ☐ a. four

   ☐ b. three

   ☐ c. two

   ☐ d. one

Following the Order of Events

3. What happens the first time that Lizabeth goes to Miss Lottie's house?

   ☐ a. She destroys the bed of marigolds.

   ☐ b. The children throw pebbles and dance.

   ☐ c. Joey dares her to sneak up on John Burke.

   ☐ d. Miss Lottie comes outside in a night dress.

4. After Lizabeth's mother mentions Mr. Ellis's coat,

□ a. her father bursts into tears.

□ b. Miss Lottie swings her cane.

□ c. her mother starts an argument.

□ d. Joey ruins his sister's picture.

Understanding
Word Choices
5. Lizabeth is struggling with "the chaotic emotions of adolescence." What does *chaotic* mean?

□ a. happy and peaceful

□ b. curious and intelligent

□ c. short and fat

□ d. wild and confused

6. "I remember fishing for minnows and watching sadly as they eluded my cupped hands. . . ." What does *eluded* mean?

□ a. trapped

□ b. escaped

□ c. worried

□ d. planted

Understanding
Important Ideas
7. Why doesn't Lizabeth's father want Mr. Ellis's coat?

□ a. He already owns a good coat.

□ b. He had just had a fight with Mr. Ellis.

□ c. He hates to take charity.

□ d. He wants his wife to quit her job.

8. Why does Miss Lottie care about the marigolds?

- ☐ a. They are the only beautiful thing in her life.
- ☐ b. She wants to annoy the children.
- ☐ c. She trades them for groceries at the local market.
- ☐ d. They remind her of her childhood.

Understanding Levels of Meaning

9. At the end of the story you learn that Lizabeth no longer lives in the town. Why is that fact important?

- ☐ a. You know that she is now rich.
- ☐ b. You understand why she and Joey were bored during their childhood.
- ☐ c. You learn that it's possible to escape poverty and to learn from past mistakes.
- ☐ d. You predict that Miss Lottie will also move away.

10. Which sentence explains why Lizabeth can't remember any "lush green lawns" or "green leafy shade trees" in her town, even though she admits they must have existed?

- ☐ a. "We children, of course, were only vaguely aware of the extent of our poverty."
- ☐ b. Memory "does not present things as they are, but rather as they *feel*."
- ☐ c. ". . . we were becoming tired of the formlessness of our summer days."
- ☐ d. "But old fears have ways of clinging like cobwebs. . . ."

11. Which adjective best describes John Burke?

  ☐ a. nervous

  ☐ b. mean

  ☐ c. athletic

  ☐ d. slow

12. Which statement best describes Lizabeth's mother?

  ☐ a. Everyone in the family depends on her.

  ☐ b. She had a hard time keeping up with her work.

  ☐ c. Her husband never asks her advice.

  ☐ d. She's thinking of moving to a larger town.

13. Which description tells you most about the children's poverty?

  ☐ a. "The night was silent now except for the sound of crickets and Joey's soft breathing."

  ☐ b. ". . . bored now with the old tires suspended from an oak limb which had kept them entertained for awhile."

  ☐ c. ". . . the girls in faded dresses that were too long or too short, the boys in patchy pants, their sweaty brown chests gleaming in the hot sun."

  ☐ d. "Then the rest of the kids let loose with their pebbles, storming the flowers and laughing wildly and senselessly at Miss Lottie's impotent rage."

14. "The half-dawn light was more eerie than complete darkness, and in it the old house was like the ruin that my world had become—foul and crumbling, a grotesque caricature." The way the setting is described helps you understand Lizabeth's

☐ a. joy.

☐ b. confusion.

☐ c. hunger.

☐ d. curiosity.

Understanding Feelings

15. How does Lizabeth's father feel about his life?

☐ a. bored

☐ b. excited

☐ c. frustrated

☐ d. hopeful

16. As an adult, how does Lizabeth feel about herself as a teenager?

☐ a. She agrees with all her actions.

☐ b. She feels embarrassed about her poverty.

☐ c. She wishes she had planted marigolds with her mother.

☐ d. She is ashamed of the way she acted, but she understands why.

Now check your answers using the Answer Key starting on page 457. Make no mark for right answers. <u>Correct</u> any wrong answers you may have by putting a check mark (✓) in the box next to the right answer. Count the number of questions you answered correctly and plot the total on the Comprehension Scores graph on page 468.

Next, look at the questions you answered incorrectly. What types of questions were they? Count the number you got wrong of each type and enter the numbers in the spaces below.

Remembering Facts	_____
Following the Order of Events	_____
Understanding Word Choices	_____
Understanding Important Ideas	_____
Understanding Levels of Meaning	_____
Understanding Character	_____
Understanding Setting	_____
Understanding Feelings	_____

Now use these numbers to fill in the Comprehension Skills Profile on page 469.

Discussion Guides

The questions below will help you think about the story and the lesson you have just read. If you don't discuss these questions in class, try to think about them or discuss them with your classmates. Perhaps you will want to write a few paragraphs in answer to the questions.

Discussing Setting

1. The events in "Marigolds" take place during late summer. But the author doesn't spend much time telling you about the temperature or the time of year. Instead, she uses details of setting. Review the story and talk about some of the sights, sounds, and smells that the author includes to give you a feeling of summer.

2. In "Marigolds" the author uses setting to make this comparison: "My mother's voice was like a cool, dark room in summer—peaceful, soothing, quiet." Why does the author compare the mother's voice to a room? What do you learn from that description?

3. Miss Lottie's marigolds are an important part of the setting of this story. But imagine if the author had decided to use a different flower. For example, suppose the story were called "Roses." How would the setting change? How would the change in setting affect the story?

Discussing the Story

4. Think about the relationship between Lizabeth and Joey. At one point, Lizabeth says he is inferior because he is younger and a boy. But does Joey always seem inferior? Or does he sometimes seem to take charge of the situation? Find some examples from the story to support your answer.

5. Why does Lizabeth get so upset by her father's tears and her mother's strength? Why do their actions make her wonder how she fits "into this crazy picture"?

6. At the end of the story Lizabeth says, "For one does not have to be ignorant and poor to find that his life is barren as the dusty yards of our town. And I too have planted marigolds." What does she mean by that statement? Do her ideas make you feel depressed or hopeful? Why?

Discussing the Author's Work

7. Like many other authors, Eugenia Collier writes about the place where she grew up—in her case, Maryland. Why do so many writers use details from their own background in their stories?

8. Besides writing short stories, Eugenia Collier also writes poetry. Review "Marigolds" and think about some of the words and phrases that she uses. Does any of her writing remind you of poetry? In what way?

9. Eugenia Collier once wrote about the importance of discovering "the richness, the diversity, the beauty of my black heritage." Do you think that discovery affected the way she felt about Lizabeth when she wrote "Marigolds"? How?

Writing Exercise

Read all the instructions before you begin writing. If you have any questions about how to begin the writing assignment, review Using the Writing Process beginning on page 445, or confer with your writing coach.

1. Think of an important event (real or imagined) that you have been involved in. What strong emotion does the memory of that event create inside of you? Do you feel nervous or afraid? Do you feel angry? Do you feel excited and overjoyed?

2. Write a short story about the event. Use the story's setting to help you describe the event and your feelings about it. Make sure you include the following elements of setting in your story:

   ◆ Time (What's the time of day or time of year? Are you in the past or in the present?)
   ◆ Place (Where is the story taking place?)
   ◆ Sights (What do you see around you?)
   ◆ Smells (What do you smell?)
   ◆ Sounds (What do you hear?)

3. You may want to look back at the writing you did in the four exercises Writing on Your Own. You might find some ideas about ways to use setting in your story.

Unit 5 Use of Language

The Treasure of Lemon Brown

BY WALTER DEAN MYERS

About the Illustration

How would you describe what is happening in this scene from looking at some of the details in the illustration?

Here are some questions to help you think about the story:

◆ Where do you think this scene takes place? What kind of place is the man in? What details about the place lead you to make those conclusions?

◆ What is the man doing?

◆ Do you think the man is frightened? angry? Why?

◆ Describe what you feel when you look at this illustration. Why do you feel that way?

Unit 5

Introduction

About the Story

Greg Ridley isn't doing very well in his math class. In fact, he's just gotten a letter from his principal saying he'll probably fail math unless he starts studying more.

Greg knows what his father will say. He's heard it before. "When I was your age . . . If I'd had the chances that you have . . ." Greg has heard those words so often that he doesn't even listen anymore. All he knows is that his father won't let him play basketball if his grades are poor.

Does Greg's reaction sound familiar to you? Most of us have gone through this kind of struggle with our parents. Greg feels that he can't live up to his father's expectations. What's more, he's not even sure he wants to. His father is always talking about the past, but the past doesn't seem to have any relationship to Greg's life today.

Then Greg meets Lemon Brown, a rag man who lives in an abandoned house in the neighborhood. Lemon shares the secret of his treasure with Greg and tells some stories about his life as a blues musician. Greg learns that a treasure isn't necessarily money or valuables. Sometimes the greatest treasure can be the lessons we learn from the people who love us.

Walter Dean Myers has spent many years writing about important issues in the lives of young people. He was born in 1937 in West Virginia but has spent most of his life in the New York City area. Although he began his career as an editor and a teacher, Myers soon began writing full time. He is best known for his young adult novels, most of which deal with the lives of black teenagers in Harlem. But he also writes ghost stories, fairy tales, and adventure stories. His work has won many awards and honors.

If you are interested in reading other works by Walter Dean Myers, you might look for his award-winning novels *The Young Landlords* and *Motown and Didi: A Love Story* in your library.

About the Lesson

All artists choose a particular tool, one that best expresses their feelings and experiences. Painters use paint. Musicians use instruments. Writers use *words* to share experiences. And like any artist, they must learn how to use that tool skillfully.

The lesson following this story is about the way authors use language. Authors have many reasons for writing. But their biggest concern is to share an experience with another person.

To share that experience, they must solve some problems and ask themselves some questions. For example, how can they reproduce the way people really talk? What words express ideas in a vivid and exciting way? How can they help readers see familiar things through new eyes? How can they draw attention to certain important points in the story?

The following questions will help you focus on the way Walter Dean Myers uses language in "The Treasure of Lemon Brown." Read the story carefully and try to answer these questions as you go along:

◆ What do you learn about the characters—their education, their background—simply from the way they talk?

◆ What descriptions seem particularly vivid or colorful? Why do they stand out in your mind?

◆ What comparisons does Myers draw between objects? How do those comparisons help you see things in a fresh way?

◆ Why does the author use exaggeration? How does it contribute to the story?

Writing Vivid Descriptions

You can understand the importance of language when you write your own descriptions of people, places, or events. Use your writing notebook or a separate piece of paper and try the following suggestions:

1. Describe a person who interests you. The person might be a close friend or someone you've noticed but don't know very well. You might choose a person (or a character) that you've read about in a book or heard of in the news. You could choose someone you admire, or you might decide to write about a person whose ideas you don't agree with.

2. Imagine that person. What do you see? What colors, sounds, shapes, and activities come to mind? What makes that person unique? Make a list of your ideas.

3. Rewrite your list several times until you get it just the way you want it.

The Treasure of Lemon Brown

by Walter Dean Myers

The dark sky, filled with angry, swirling clouds, reflected Greg Ridley's mood as he sat on the stoop of his building. His father's voice came to him again, first reading the letter the principal had sent to the house, then lecturing endlessly about his poor efforts in math.

"I had to leave school when I was thirteen," his father had said, "that's a year younger than you are now. If I'd had half the chances that you have, I'd . . ."

Greg had sat in the small, pale green kitchen listening, knowing the lecture would end with his father saying he couldn't play ball with the Scorpions. He had asked his father the week before, and his father had said it depended on his next report card. It wasn't often the Scorpions took on new players, especially fourteen-year-olds, and this was a chance of a lifetime for Greg. He hadn't been allowed to play high school ball, which he had really wanted to do, but playing for the Community Center team was the next best thing. Report cards were due in a week, and Greg had been hoping for the best. But the principal had ended the suspense early when she sent that letter saying Greg would probably fail math if he didn't spend more time studying.

"And you want to play *basketball?*" His father's brows knitted over deep brown eyes. "That must be some kind of a joke. Now you just get into your room and hit those books."

That had been two nights before. His father's words, like the distant thunder that now echoed through the streets of Harlem, still rumbled softly in his ears.

It was beginning to cool. Gusts of wind made bits of paper dance between the parked cars. There was a flash of nearby lightning, and soon large drops of rain splashed onto his jeans. He stood to go upstairs, thought of the lecture that probably awaited him if he did anything except shut himself in his room with his math book, and started walking down the street instead. Down the block there was an old tenement that had been abandoned for some months. Some of the guys had held an impromptu checker tournament there the week before, and Greg had noticed that the door, once boarded over, had been slightly ajar.

Pulling his collar up as high as he could, he checked for traffic and made a dash across the street. He reached the house just as another flash of lightning changed the night to day for an instant, then returned the graffiti-scarred building to the grim shadows. He vaulted over the outer stairs and pushed tentatively on the door. It was open, and he let himself in.

The inside of the building was dark except for the dim light that filtered through the dirty windows from the streetlamps. There was a room a few feet from the door, and from where he stood at the entrance, Greg could see a squarish patch of light on the floor. He entered the room, frowning at the musty smell. It was a large room that might have been someone's parlor at one time. Squinting, Greg could see an old table on its side against one wall, what looked like a pile of rags or a torn mattress in the corner, and a couch, with one side broken, in front of the window.

He went to the couch. The side that wasn't broken was comfortable enough, though a little creaky. From this spot he could see the blinking neon sign over the bodega on the corner. He sat awhile, watching the sign blink first green then red, allowing his mind to drift to the Scorpions, then to his father. His father had been a postal worker for all Greg's life, and was proud of it, often telling Greg how hard he had worked to pass the test. Greg had heard the story too many times to be interested now.

For a moment Greg thought he heard something that sounded like a scraping against the wall. He listened carefully, but it was gone.

Outside the wind had picked up, sending the rain against the window with a force that shook the glass in its frame. A car passed, its tires hissing over the wet street and its red taillights glowing in the darkness.

Greg thought he heard the noise again. His stomach tightened as he held himself still and listened intently. There weren't any more scraping noises, but he was sure he had heard something in the darkness—something breathing!

He tried to figure out just where the breathing was coming from; he knew it was in the room with him. Slowly he stood, tensing. As he turned, a flash of lightning lit up the room, frightening him with its sudden brilliance. He saw nothing, just the overturned table, the pile of rags and an old newspaper on the floor. Could he have been imagining the sounds? He continued listening, but heard nothing and thought that it might have just been rats. Still, he thought, as soon as the rain let up he would leave. He went to the window and was about to look out when he heard a voice behind him.

"Don't try nothin' 'cause I got a razor here sharp enough to cut a week into nine days!"

Greg, except for an involuntary tremor in his knees, stood stock still. The voice was high and brittle, like dry twigs being broken, surely not one he had ever heard before. There was a shuffling sound as the person who had been speaking moved a step closer. Greg turned, holding his breath, his eyes straining to see in the dark room.

The upper part of the figure before him was still in darkness. The lower half was in the dim rectangle of light that fell unevenly from the window. There were two feet, in cracked, dirty shoes from which rose legs that were wrapped in rags.

"Who are you?" Greg hardly recognized his own voice.

"I'm Lemon Brown," came the answer. "Who're you?"

"Greg Ridley."

"What you doing here?" The figure shuffled forward again, and Greg took a small step backward.

"It's raining," Greg said.

"I can see that," the figure said.

The person who called himself Lemon Brown peered forward, and Greg could see him clearly. He was an old man. His black, heavily wrinkled face was surrounded by a halo of crinkly white hair and whiskers that seemed to separate his head from the layers of dirty coats piled on his smallish frame. His pants were bagged to the knee, where they were met with rags that went down to the old shoes. The rags were held on with strings, and there was a rope around his middle. Greg relaxed. He had seen the man before, picking through the trash on the corner and pulling clothes out of a Salvation Army box. There was no sign of the razor that could "cut a week into nine days."

"What are you doing here?" Greg asked.

"This is where I'm staying," Lemon Brown said. "What you here for?"

"Told you it was raining out," Greg said, leaning against the back of the couch until he felt it give slightly.

"Ain't you got no home?"

"I got a home," Greg answered.

"You ain't one of them bad boys looking for my treasure, is you?" Lemon Brown cocked his head to one side and squinted one eye. "Because I told you I got me a razor."

"I'm not looking for your treasure," Greg answered, smiling. "*If* you have one."

"What you mean, *if* I have one," Lemon Brown said. "Every man got a treasure. You don't know that, you must be a fool!"

"Sure," Greg said as he sat on the sofa and put one leg over the back. "What do you have, gold coins?"

"Don't worry none about what I got," Lemon Brown said. "You know who I am?"

"You told me your name was orange or lemon or something like that."

"Lemon Brown," the old man said, pulling back his shoulders as he did so, "they used to call me Sweet Lemon Brown."

"Sweet Lemon?" Greg asked.

"Yessir. Sweet Lemon Brown. They used to say I sung the blues so sweet that if I sang at a funeral, the dead would commence to rocking with the beat. Used to travel all over Mississippi and as far as Monroe, Louisiana, and east on over to Macon, Georgia. You mean you ain't never heard of Sweet Lemon Brown?"

"Afraid not," Greg said, "What . . . what happened to you?"

"Hard times, boy. Hard times always after a poor man. One day I got tired, sat down to rest a spell and felt a tap on my shoulder. Hard times caught up with me."

"Sorry about that."

"What you doing here? How come you didn't go on home when the rain come? Rain don't bother you young folks none."

"Just didn't." Greg looked away.

"I used to have a knotty-headed boy just like you." Lemon Brown had half walked, half shuffled back to the corner and sat down against the wall. "Had them big eyes like you got. I used to call them moon eyes. Look into them moon eyes and see anything you want."

"How come you gave up singing the blues?" Greg asked.

"Didn't give it up," Lemon Brown said. "You don't give up the blues; they give you up. After a while you do good for yourself, and it ain't nothing but foolishness singing about how hard you got it. Ain't that right?"

"I guess so."

"What's that noise?" Lemon Brown asked, suddenly sitting upright.

Greg listened, and he heard a noise outside. He looked at Lemon Brown and saw the old man was pointing toward the window.

Greg went to the window and saw three men, neighborhood thugs, on the stoop. One was carrying a length of pipe. Greg looked back toward Lemon Brown, who moved quietly across the room to the window. The old man looked out, then beckoned frantically for Greg to follow him. For a moment Greg couldn't move. Then he found himself following Lemon Brown into the hallway and up darkened stairs. Greg followed as closely as he could. They reached the top of the stairs, and Greg felt Lemon Brown's hand first lying on his shoulder, then probing down his arm until he finally took Greg's hand into his own as they crouched in the darkness.

"They's bad men," Lemon Brown whispered. His breath was warm against Greg's skin.

"Hey! Rag man!" A voice called. "We know you in here. What you got up under them rags? You got any money?"

Silence.

"We don't want to have to come in and hurt you, old man, but we don't mind if we have to."

Lemon Brown squeezed Greg's hand in his own hard, gnarled fist.

There was a banging downstairs and a light as the men entered. They banged around noisily, calling for the rag man.

"We heard you talking about your treasure." The voice was slurred. "We just want to see it, that's all."

"You sure he's here?" One voice seemed to come from the room with the sofa.

"Yeah, he stays here every night."

"There's another room over there; I'm going to take a look. You got that flashlight?"

"Yeah, here, take the pipe too."

Greg opened his mouth to quiet the sound of his breath as he sucked it in uneasily. A beam of light hit the wall a few feet opposite him, then went out.

"Ain't nobody in that room," a voice said. "You think he gone or something?"

"I don't know," came the answer. "All I know is that I heard him talking about some kind of treasure. You know they found that shopping bag lady with that money in her bags."

"Yeah. You think he's upstairs?"

"HEY, OLD MAN, ARE YOU UP THERE?"

Silence.

"Watch my back, I'm going up."

There was a footstep on the stairs, and the beam from the flashlight danced crazily along the peeling wallpaper. Greg held his breath. There was another step and a loud crashing noise as the man banged the pipe against the wooden banister. Greg could feel his temples throb as the man slowly neared them. Greg thought about the pipe, wondering what he would do when the man reached them—what he *could* do.

Then Lemon Brown released his hand and moved toward the top of the stairs. Greg looked around and saw stairs going up to the next floor. He tried waving to Lemon Brown, hoping the old man would see him in the dim light and follow him to the next floor. Maybe, Greg thought, the man wouldn't follow them up there. Suddenly, though, Lemon Brown stood at the top of the stairs, both arms raised high above his head.

"There he is!" A voice cried from below.

"Throw down your money, old man, so I won't have to bash your head in!"

Lemon Brown didn't move. Greg felt himself near panic. The steps came closer, and still Lemon Brown didn't move. He was an eerie sight, a bundle of rags standing at the top of the stairs, his shadow on the wall looming over him. Maybe, the thought came to Greg, the scene could be even eerier.

Greg wet his lips, put his hands to his mouth and tried

to make a sound. Nothing came out. He swallowed hard, wet his lips once more and howled as evenly as he could.

"What's that?"

As Greg howled, the light moved away from Lemon Brown, but not before Greg saw him hurl his body down the stairs at the men who had come to take his treasure. There was a crashing noise, and then footsteps. A rush of warm air came in as the downstairs door opened, then there was only an ominous silence.

Greg stood on the landing. He listened, and after a while there was another sound on the staircase.

"Mr. Brown?" he called.

"Yeah, it's me," came the answer. "I got their flashlight."

Greg exhaled in relief as Lemon Brown made his way slowly back up the stairs.

"You OK?"

"Few bumps and bruises," Lemon Brown said.

"I think I'd better be going," Greg said, his breath returning to normal. "You'd better leave, too, before they come back."

"They may hang around outside for a while," Lemon Brown said, "but they ain't getting their nerve up to come in here again. Not with crazy old rag men and howling spooks. Best you stay a while till the coast is clear. I'm heading out west tomorrow, out to east St. Louis."

"They were talking about treasures," Greg said. "You *really* have a treasure?"

"What I tell you? Didn't I tell you every man got a treasure?" Lemon Brown said. "You want to see mine?"

"If you want to show it to me," Greg shrugged.

"Let's look out the window first, see what them scoundrels be doing," Lemon Brown said.

They followed the oval beam of the flashlight into one of the rooms and looked out the window. They saw the men who had tried to take the treasure sitting on the curb near the corner. One of them had his pants leg up, looking at his knee.

"You sure you're not hurt?" Greg asked Lemon Brown.

"Nothing that ain't been hurt before," Lemon Brown said. "When you get as old as me all you say when something hurts is, 'Howdy, Mr. Pain, sees you back again.' Then when Mr. Pain see he can't worry you none, he go on mess with somebody else."

Greg smiled.

"Here, you hold this." Lemon Brown gave Greg the flashlight.

He sat on the floor near Greg and carefully untied the strings that held the rags on his right leg. When he took the rags away, Greg saw a piece of plastic. The old man carefully took off the plastic and unfolded it. He revealed some yellowed newspaper clippings and a battered harmonica.

"There it be," he said, nodding his head. "There it be."

Greg looked at the old man, saw the distant look in his eye, then turned to the clippings. They told of Sweet Lemon Brown, a blues singer and harmonica player who was appearing at different theaters in the South. One of the clippings said he had been the hit of the show, although not the headliner. All of the clippings were reviews of shows Lemon Brown had been in more than 50 years ago. Greg looked at the harmonica. It was dented badly on one side, with the reed holes on one end nearly closed.

"I used to travel around and make money for to feed my wife and Jesse—that's my boy's name. Used to feed them good, too. Then his mama died, and he stayed with his mama's sister. He growed up to be a man, and when the war come he saw fit to go off and fight in it. I didn't have nothing to give him except these things that told him who I was, and what he come from. If you know your pappy did something, you know you can do something too.

"Anyway, he went off to war, and I went off still playing and singing. 'Course by then I wasn't as much as I used to be, not without somebody to make it worth the while. You know what I mean?"

"Yeah," Greg nodded, not quite really knowing.

"I traveled around, and one time I come home, and there was this letter saying Jesse got killed in the war. Broke my heart, it truly did.

"They sent back what he had with him over there, and what it was is this old mouth fiddle and these clippings. Him carrying it around with him like that told me it meant something to him. That was my treasure, and when I give it to him he treated it just like that, a treasure. Ain't that something?"

"Yeah, I guess so," Greg said.

"You *guess* so?" Lemon Brown's voice rose an octave as he started to put his treasure back into the plastic. "Well, you got to guess 'cause you sure don't know nothing. Don't know enough to get home when it's raining."

"I guess . . . I mean, you're right."

"You OK for a youngster," the old man said as he tied the strings around his leg, "better than those scalawags what come here looking for my treasure. That's for sure."

"You really think that treasure of yours was worth fighting for?" Greg asked. "Against a pipe?"

"What else a man got 'cepting what he can pass on to his son, or his daughter, if she be his oldest?" Lemon Brown said. "For a big-headed boy you sure do ask the foolishest questions."

Lemon Brown got up after patting his rags in place and looked out the window again.

"Looks like they're gone. You get on out of here and get yourself home. I'll be watching from the window so you'll be all right."

Lemon Brown went down the stairs behind Greg. When they reached the front door the old man looked out first, saw the street was clear and told Greg to scoot on home.

"You sure you'll be OK?" Greg asked.

"Now didn't I tell you I was going to east St. Louis in the morning?" Lemon Brown asked. "Don't that sound OK to you?"

"Sure it does," Greg said. "Sure it does. And you take care of that treasure of yours."

"That I'll do," Lemon said, the wrinkles about his eyes suggesting a smile. "That I'll do."

The night had warmed and the rain had stopped, leaving puddles at the curbs. Greg didn't even want to think how late it was. He thought ahead of what his father would say and wondered it he should tell him about Lemon Brown. He thought about it until he reached his stoop, and decided against it. Lemon Brown would be OK, Greg thought, with his memories and his treasure.

Greg pushed the button over the bell marked Ridley, thought of the lecture he knew his father would give him, and smiled.

Use of Language

Authors write because they have something to share with their readers. To reach those readers, they have only one tool—words. So authors choose words carefully to create certain effects. Those effects help you see, feel, hear, and even smell the stories you read.

Sometimes authors write for readers who are very familiar with the subject. For example, a writer describing a hospital might have a reader who is a doctor. The language in the story helps the reader relive the feeling of being a doctor in a hospital. The words make the description seem real.

For the most part, however, authors write for strangers. So an author uses language to help us understand new people and places. He or she creates vivid pictures and fresh comparisons. And while showing us a different part of the world, the writer often helps us learn a little more about ourselves.

When he was writing "The Treasure of Lemon Brown," Walter Dean Myers had to create a picture of a teenage boy living in Harlem. He had to describe a rag man, a pair of thugs, and the boy's father. He had to show us the neighborhood. To some readers, these pictures are already familiar. But to many others, they are completely new. Myers had to use language to capture the interest of all his readers.

Figurative language is the use of words and phrases in unusual ways to create strong vivid images, to focus attention on certain ideas, or to compare dissimilar things. In this lesson, we will look at four ways in which Myers uses figurative language:

1 ◆ He uses *dialect*—the pattern of speech used by people of a certain group or of a particular region.

2 ◆ He chooses words carefully to create pictures and explain ideas.

3 ◆ He uses comparisons to create vivid pictures in the reader's mind.

4 ◆ He uses other figures of speech to focus attention on certain ideas.

1 ◆ Using Dialect

Authors develop what you might call an "ear for speech." They pay special attention to conversations that go on around them. They listen to *what* is said, but they also listen to *how* the speaker says it. They notice interesting words and expressions, unusual pronunciations, and slang. All those elements of speech make up dialect.

Dialect is a pattern of speaking that has developed among people of a certain group or a particular region. You've already read some stories that include dialect. In "First Confession," for example, you probably noticed that Frank O'Connor's characters have an unusual way of talking:

> ". . . and she know I don't like her, and she gives pennies to Nora and none to me, and my da sides with her and flakes me, and one night I was so heart-scalded I made up my mind I'd have to kill her."

The author's word choice—*da, flakes, heart-scalded*—is his way of showing dialect. He uses those words to remind you that the character is Irish.

Walter Dean Myers uses dialect in his writing to give you a vivid picture of Lemon Brown. Read the following passage and notice Lemon's grammar:

> "You ain't one of them bad boys looking for my treasure, is you?" Lemon Brown cocked his head to one side and squinted one eye. "Because I told you I got me a razor."

Myers includes slang—*ain't*—and grammatical errors—"them bad boys," "is you," and "got me"—to help you understand more about Lemon Brown's character. You realize that educated speech is not important to him. Maybe he hasn't had much schooling, or maybe he's not interested in "correct" speech. In either case, the dialect forces you to think about his character and pay attention to what you learn about him later in the story.

Read the following passage and answer the questions about it using what you have learned in this part of the lesson. Use your writing notebook or a separate piece of paper for your answers.

> "I used to travel around and make money for to feed my wife and Jesse—that's my boy's name. Used to feed them good, too. Then his mama died, and he stayed with his mama's sister. He growed up to be a man, and when the war come he saw fit to go off and fight in it. I didn't have nothing to give him except these things that told him who I was, and what he come from. If you know your pappy did something, you know you can do something too.
>
> "Anyway, he went off to war, and I went off still playing and singing. 'Course by then I wasn't as much as I used to be, not without somebody to make it worth the while. You know what I mean?"

1. Make a list of words and phrases that show the dialect in this passage.

2. How does Myers make it clear that Lemon is talking to another person? How can you tell that someone is listening to this conversation?

Now check your answers using the suggestions in the Answer Key starting on page 457. Review this part of the lesson if you don't understand why an answer was wrong.

1♦Writing on Your Own

Look at the list you wrote for Writing Vivid Descriptions on page 193. Now do the following:

1. Think about the way the person sounds. What makes that person's speech unique? Does he have a Brooklyn accent? What does a Brooklyn

accent sound like? Maybe she is very well educated. How can you imitate the sound of her speech? Does he have any habits when he talks? Does he clear his throat between words? Does your character say "you know?" after every sentence? What details make that person special?

2. Write a paragraph that shows the person talking on the telephone. As you write, pay special attention to dialect.

3. You may want to change or rewrite your paragraph several times until you get it just the way you like it.

2 ♦ Choosing Words Carefully

Artists choose their tools carefully. Painters, for example, must get familiar with different kinds of brushes, paper, and canvas. They learn how important it is to select just the right colors. They combine lights with darks to achieve contrast. They create highlights with a single dab of paint.

An author paints with words rather than watercolors. Yet words are as varied and expressive as an artist's palette. Just as an artist chooses from twenty different shades of red, a writer chooses from twenty words that have almost the same meaning. But each word, even among synonyms, has its own special shade of color.

Walter Dean Myers chooses a particular word to describe Lemon Brown's way of walking: "The figure *shuffled* forward again." *Shuffled* is a synonym for *walked,* but it adds a shade of meaning that *walked* doesn't have. It tells you that Lemon has trouble picking up his feet when he walks. The word hints that he is old and tired. With just one word, the author paints a picture of an old man.

Imagine if Myers had chosen a different synonym for *walk.* Try substituting some of these words: *staggered, skipped, toddled, lumbered, hiked.* Notice how each synonym changes your picture of Lemon Brown. You can see that Myers chose exactly the right word to create the character.

Colorful language can be more than the choice of a single word. Color also develops from the way an author puts words together. Words in a story combine to create a total effect. As you read, you usually don't stop to admire each individual word any more than you stop to look at the individual brush strokes in a painting. But each word is important because it helps build a well-balanced whole. The story has an overall vividness that holds your interest. Carefully chosen language allows you to understand exactly what is going on and just how the characters feel.

Read the following passage and notice how Walter Dean Myers chooses words that emphasize Greg's fear:

> He tried to figure out just where the breathing was coming from; he knew it was in the room with him. Slowly he stood, tensing. As he turned, a flash of lightning lit up the room, frightening him with its sudden brilliance. He saw nothing, just the overturned table, the pile of rags and

an old newspaper on the floor. Could he have been imagining the sounds? He continued listening, but heard nothing and thought that it might have just been rats. Still, he thought, as soon as the rain let up he would leave. He went to the window and was about to look out when he heard a voice behind him.

The author shows you Greg's growing tension. He contrasts the boy's fear with a picture of the lightning outside. Then he adds a description of the spooky room. Greg imagines that the noise might be rats—which isn't much of a comfort. Then the author suddenly introduces "a voice behind him."

As he builds Greg's fear, the author builds some tension in the reader too. The careful choice of words in this passage keeps our interest and makes the story suspenseful.

2 ◆ Exercise B

Read the following passage and answer the questions about it using what you have learned in this part of the lesson. Use your writing notebook or a separate piece of paper for your answers.

There was a footstep on the stairs, and the beam from the flashlight danced crazily along the peeling wallpaper. Greg held his breath. There was another step and a loud crashing noise as the man banged the pipe against the wooden banister. Greg could feel his temples throb as the man slowly neared them. Greg thought about the pipe, wondering what he would do when the man reached them—what he *could* do.

1. How does the author keep this passage exciting? Make a list of words and phrases that contribute to the suspense.

2. In this passage the author alternates between what is happening in the house and how Greg feels personally. How does that back-and-forth approach add to the total effect of the passage?

Now check your answers using the suggestions in the Answer Key starting on page 457. Review this part of the lesson if you don't understand why an answer was wrong.

2♦Writing on Your Own

Look at the list you wrote for Writing Vivid Descriptions on page 193. Now do the following:

1. Think about the way the person acts in different situations. For example, what verbs describe the way she rides a bike? How does he hold a fork when he eats? How does she behave when she is angry or frightened? How can you tell if he is really interested in a conversation?

2. Write a paragraph or two describing how the person would behave if he or she were lost at the airport or the bus station.
   Choose your words and phrases carefully. Try to create descriptions that show the person's unique behavior in this situation.

3. You may want to change and rewrite your paragraphs several times until they are just the way you want them.

3 ◆ Using Comparisons

Sometimes the best way to describe a thing is to compare it to something else. Take Lemon Brown's voice, for example. Walter Dean Myers describes it this way: "The voice was high and brittle, like dry twigs being broken."

This comparison is called a simile. A *simile* is a direct comparison between unlike things using the word *like, as,* or *resembles* to connect them. Similes help readers look at familiar things in new ways.

Do you think anyone would really mistake the sound of a voice for the sound of dry twigs? Probably not. Then why does the author compare Lemon's voice to twigs?

The author includes this comparison in the story to create a certain effect. He wants you to hear the voice, but he also wants to give you a certain feeling about the character. *A voice like dry twigs* helps you imagine Lemon's age and frailty. But the word *twigs* also gets you thinking about trees. If Lemon's voice is like twigs, how else is he similar to a tree? Trees are old and strong. They protect small plants and animals. How are those qualities like Lemon?

Myers also uses another kind of comparison in this story. Think about this description: "the beam from the flashlight danced crazily along the peeling wallpaper." That sentence contains a *metaphor*—an implied, or suggested, comparison between unlike things. A metaphor hints that one thing *is* another.

In the description of the flashlight, Myers suggests that the beam is a crazy dancer. You know that a beam can't actually dance. But the metaphor helps you picture the beam of light moving up the stairs.

3 ◆ Exercise C

Read the following passages and answer the questions about them using what you have learned in this part of the lesson. Use your writing notebook or a separate piece of paper for your answers.

Passage A
A car passed, its tires hissing over the wet street and its red taillights glowing in the darkness.

Passage B

His father's words, like the distant thunder that now echoed through the streets of Harlem, still rumbled softly in his ears.

1. Both sentences contain comparisons. Write down each comparison and identify it as a simile or a metaphor. Then explain your reasoning.

2. Rewrite each sentence, keeping the author's meaning but leaving out the comparison. Does leaving out the comparison change the feeling you get from the sentence? How?

Now check your answers using the suggestions in the Answer Key starting on page 457. Review this part of the lesson if you don't understand why an answer was wrong.

3♦Writing on Your Own

Look at the list you wrote for Writing Vivid Descriptions on page 193. Now do the following:

1. Write three similes that describe the person. In each simile, show the person in a different situation. Here are some examples:

   □ Grandma perches on her motorcycle like a canary driving a truck.

   □ When she found out she'd won the lottery, Grandma screamed like a baby stuck with a pin.

   □ Wearing her big rain boots, Grandma floats through puddles like a tugboat.

2. Now write three metaphors about the person. Here's an example:

   □ Grandpa is such a moose when he goes for a walk. He tramples down everything that gets in his way.

3. You may want to change and rewrite your comparisons several times until you get them just the way you like them.

4 ◆ Using Other Figures of Speech

Similes and metaphors are figures of speech. There are many kinds of figures of speech, and each has its own name and purpose. Authors use them to create strong vivid images, to focus attention on certain ideas, and to compare dissimilar things.

You have already looked at some of the ways in which Walter Dean Myers uses similes and metaphors in "The Treasure of Lemon Brown." But he uses other figures of speech as well. Like similes and metaphors, these figures of speech tell us more about the characters and the plot.

One example is Myers's use of exaggeration. *Exaggeration* is intentional overstatement to emphasize a point. In the story, Lemon Brown exaggerates his meanness in order to scare Greg:

> "Don't try nothin' 'cause I got a razor here sharp enough
> to cut a week into nine days!"

Lemon knows that Greg doesn't actually believe that a razor can cut up a week. But the old man wants to emphasize how sharp the razor is and let Greg know that he is willing to use it.

Another technique is *personification*—a figure of speech in which an animal, an object, or an idea is described as though it were human. Personification is actually a special kind of metaphor. Think about the way the author describes the sky in this sentence:

> The dark sky, filled with angry, swirling clouds,
> reflected Greg Ridley's mood as he sat on the stoop of his
> building.

A sky can't really be angry. Only humans can show emotions. But the author personifies the sky to show you how the coming thunderstorm reflects Greg's inner feelings.

There are many other kinds of speech. Sometimes they are funny. Sometimes they are dramatic, sad, or thought-provoking. But in the hands of a skilled writer, they call attention to an important image or idea. They help us understand the author's purpose for writing, and they give us a vivid picture of events in the story.

4 ♦ Exercise D

Read the following passage and answer the questions about it using what you have learned in this part of the lesson. Use your writing notebook or a separate piece of paper for your answers.

"Lemon Brown," the old man said, pulling his shoulders as he did so, "they used to call me Sweet Lemon Brown."

"Sweet Lemon?" Greg asked.

"Yessir. Sweet Lemon Brown. They used to say I sung the blues so sweet that if I sang at a funeral, the dead would commence to rocking with the beat. Used to travel all over Mississippi and as far as Monroe, Louisiana, and east on over to Macon, Georgia. You mean you ain't never heard of Sweet Lemon Brown?"

"Afraid not," Greg said. "What . . . what happened to you?"

"Hard times, boy. Hard times always after a poor man. One day I got tired, sat down to rest a spell and felt a tap on my shoulder. Hard times caught up with me."

1. Write down an example of exaggeration in the passage. Why does the author include this example?

2. Write down an example of personification in the passage. Why does the author use this figure of speech?

Now check your answers using the suggestions in the Answer Key starting on page 457. Review this part of the lesson if you don't understand why an answer was wrong.

4 ♦ Writing on Your Own

Look at the list you wrote for Writing Vivid Descriptions on page 193. Then reread the paragraphs you wrote for Writing on Your Own. Now do the following:

1. In the three exercises for Writing on Your Own, you described the

person in different imaginative ways. You thought a lot about the person's special character traits and the behaviors that make him or her unique.

Now imagine that person as the hero of a tall tale. A tall tale is a story with characters who have exaggerated size, talents, strength, and so on. Paul Bunyan appears in many tall tales. So do super-heroes like Batman and Superman.

2. Write a paragraph that exaggerates some of the person's character traits. For example, if your little brother likes to scream, you could turn him into a "ten-foot-tall five year old with a scream loud enough to flatten every tall building in Chicago."

3. You may want to change and rewrite your paragraph several times until you get it just the way you like it.

Now go on to Reviewing and Interpreting the Story.

Reviewing and Interpreting the Story

Answer these questions without looking back at the story. Choose the best answer to each question and put an *x* in the box beside it, or write your answer on a separate piece of paper.

Remembering
Facts

1. Where does Greg live?

   ☐ a. Chicago

   ☐ b. Harlem

   ☐ c. Los Angeles

   ☐ d. St. Louis

2. What course is Greg about to fail?

   ☐ a. English

   ☐ b. math

   ☐ c. science

   ☐ d. music

Following the
Order of Events

3. What happens after Greg sits on the couch in the abandoned house?

   ☐ a. He hears someone breathing in the darkness.

   ☐ b. He tells his father about his problems in school.

   ☐ c. He tries out Lemon Brown's harmonica.

   ☐ d. He threatens the thugs with a razor.

4. Lemon gave the harmonica to his son because

☐ a. Jesse wanted to learn how to play.

☐ b. Lemon had just bought a new one.

☐ c. Jesse's mother had recently died.

☐ d. Jesse had decided to fight in the war.

Understanding
Word Choices
5. "Greg, except for an <u>involuntary</u> tremor in his knees, stood stock still." If the tremor was *involuntary,* then Greg

☐ a. could control it.

☐ b. didn't notice it.

☐ c. could not control it.

☐ d. had never noticed it.

6. "Lemon Brown squeezed Greg's hand in his own hard, <u>gnarled</u> fist." What does *gnarled* mean?

☐ a. smooth and soft

☐ b. bent and twisted

☐ c. bruised and tender

☐ d. weak and fat

Understanding
Important Ideas
7. The harmonica was an important gift because

☐ a. it gave Jesse something he could sell for cash.

☐ b. Lemon knew he would get it back again.

☐ c. Greg learned more about Lemon Brown's career.

☐ d. Jesse could remember his father's accomplishments.

8. At the end of the story Greg discovers that he can
   - ☐ a. learn from his father's past.
   - ☐ b. play basketball for the Scorpions.
   - ☐ c. leave home and travel with Lemon.
   - ☐ d. avoid doing well in school.

Understanding
Levels of
Meaning
9. Why did the author include the thunderstorm in the story?
   - ☐ a. to make the story more realistic
   - ☐ b. to frighten Greg's father
   - ☐ c. to show us that the house leaks
   - ☐ d. to reflect Greg's mood

10. Which of the following ideas is an important point of the story?
   - ☐ a. Young people don't have anything to learn from older people.
   - ☐ b. Playing basketball is more important than doing well in school.
   - ☐ c. People can be smart and kind even if they wear rags and dirty clothes.
   - ☐ d. There is nothing dangerous about living in a big city.

Understanding
Character
11. Which phrase best describes Greg's father?
   - ☐ a. worried about money
   - ☐ b. concerned about his son
   - ☐ c. interested in basketball
   - ☐ d. friendly to Lemon Brown

12. Lemon Brown is

    ☐ a. scared and shy.

    ☐ b. looking for a job.

    ☐ c. able to take care of himself.

    ☐ d. anxious to meet Greg's father.

Understanding
Setting
13. How does the abandoned house contribute to the suspense of the story?

    ☐ a. It shelters Greg during the thunderstorm.

    ☐ b. It's a good place to play checkers.

    ☐ c. It makes Greg feel tense and nervous.

    ☐ d. It protects Greg from his father.

14. Lemon Brown describes the setting of his life as a blues singer. What do you learn from his description?

    ☐ a. A musician must get used to traveling.

    ☐ b. A singer has time for a family.

    ☐ c. The blues are most popular in the North.

    ☐ d. Anyone can sing the blues.

Understanding
Feelings
15. How would you describe Jesse's attitude toward Lemon?

    ☐ a. proud

    ☐ b. embarrassed

    ☐ c. angry

    ☐ d. amused

16. After talking with Lemon Brown, Greg

☐ a. is ready to argue with his father.

☐ b. understands his father better.

☐ c. wants to fight the neighborhood thugs.

☐ d. sets up a meeting with the principal.

Now check your answers using the Answer Key starting on page 457. Make no mark for right answers. <u>Correct</u> any wrong answers you may have by putting a check mark (✓) in the box next to the right answer. Count the number of questions you answered correctly and plot the total on the Comprehension Scores graph on page 468.

Next, look at the questions you answered incorrectly. What types of questions were they? Count the number you got wrong of each type and enter the numbers in the spaces below.

Remembering Facts   _____

Following the Order of Events   _____

Understanding Word Choices   _____

Understanding Important Ideas   _____

Understanding Levels of Meaning   _____

Understanding Character   _____

Understanding Setting   _____

Understanding Feelings   _____

Now use these numbers to fill in the Comprehension Skills Profile on page 469.

Discussion Guides

The questions below will help you think about the story and the lesson you have just read. If you don't discuss these questions in class, try to think about them or discuss them with your classmates. Perhaps you will want to write a few paragraphs in answer to the questions.

Discussing Use of Language

1. Lemon Brown's way of speaking is very different from Greg's. What do you learn about the characters from the way each one talks? How are they similar? How are they different?

2. When Lemon talks about his bumps and bruises, he mentions "Mr. Pain." Why do you think Lemon personifies pain? How does that approach make pain easier to deal with?

3. Think about some of the words that Lemon uses to describe Greg: "knotty-headed boy," "moon eyes." Those are unusual expressions, but they create a vivid picture. What do you learn about Greg's appearance? What do you learn about his personality?

Discussing the Story

4. When Lemon shows Greg his treasure, he brings out a broken harmonica and a pile of old clippings. Are those objects really his treasure? Or is the treasure something more?

5. At the end of the story, Greg wonders if he should tell his father about Lemon Brown. After thinking about it, he decides not to say anything. Why?

6. Do you think the relationship between Greg and his father will change? In what ways? Why?

Discussing the Author's Work

7. Walter Dean Myers grew up in West Virginia but has spent most of his life in the New York City area. Do you think his background helped him develop an ear for dialect? Why?

8. The books that Myers writes are very popular among young adults, but they are also popular with teachers and parents. Think about "The Treasure of Lemon Brown." Why do you think this story appeals to people of so many ages?

9. In addition to writing realistic stories and novels, Myers enjoys inventing fairy tales, ghost stories, and adventure stories. How do you think those imaginative tales help him practice his use of language?

Writing Exercise

Read all the instructions before you begin writing. If you have any questions about how to begin the writing assignment, review Using the Writing Process beginning on page 445, or confer with your writing coach.

1. Imagine that Greg's father learns about Lemon Brown. He is worried that Lemon isn't getting enough to eat and invites him over for dinner.

2. Write a story that describes their meeting. Your story should include the following:

   ◆ Dialect

   ◆ Colorful descriptions

   ◆ A simile or a metaphor

   ◆ An example of exaggeration

   ◆ An example of personification

   Look back at "The Treasure of Lemon Brown" for some examples of Walter Dean Myers's use of language. You may also want to review the four Writing on Your Own exercises you wrote for this lesson.

3. Write, revise, correct, and rewrite your story until you are sure you have got it just the way you want it.

Unit 6   Theme

The Moustache
BY ROBERT CORMIER

About the Illustration

How would you describe the feelings between these two people? Point out some details in the drawing to support your response.

Here are some questions to help you think about the story:

◆ How can you tell that these two people know each other very well? What do you think their relationship might be?

◆ What do you think the old woman's feelings are? What makes you think that?

◆ What do you think the young man's feelings are? What makes you think that?

Unit 6

Introduction

About the Story

The moustache in the title of the story belongs to Mike. Mike is seventeen years old. It's the first moustache he's ever grown, and he is secretly proud of it.

His mother thinks it makes him look too old. His girlfriend isn't crazy about it either. But the moustache has a very different effect on Mike's grandmother. It reminds her of someone else.

Family resemblances are not always obvious. A son is never really the spitting image of his father or a daughter a carbon copy of her mother. In fact, likenesses are apt to skip a generation and pop up in a grandchild. Even then, the resemblance is usually subtle—a certain smile, a way of walking, a crinkling of the eyes. Those traits might not show up in photographs. But an older relative who knows both the older and the younger person may see the similarity right away—

Theme   229

especially when the relative hasn't seen the young person for a while.

In "The Moustache" Mike's grandmother has not seen him since she moved to the nursing home. She suffers from arteriosclerosis, a disease of the arteries that sometimes comes with aging. The disease causes her to become confused. Sometimes she doesn't recognize people she knows. Or she forgets what day or even what year it is. She recalls events of many years ago as if they happened yesterday. But the things that really did happen yesterday, she often can't remember at all.

Lately, Mike's grandmother has been dwelling on events that happened forty years ago. They are not happy memories, but she cannot let go of them. When Mike walks into her room wearing his new moustache and a spiffy raincoat, she is taken aback. It is not her grandson she sees, but someone else. Mike doesn't realize it at first, but he will soon learn that his grandmother has some very tragic memories.

Author Robert Cormier says that he wrote this story and others about young people at a time when he and his wife were bringing up three teenagers. "The house sang in those days," he says, "with the vibrant songs of youth—tender, hectic, tragic, and ecstatic. Hearts were broken on Sunday afternoon and repaired by the following Thursday evening, but how desperate it all was in the interim. The telephone never stopped ringing, the shower seemed to be constantly running, the Beatles became a presence in our lives." Clearly, he loved having a house full of teenagers. And it shows in his stories.

One of his best-known works is a novel for young adults called *The Chocolate War*. It's about a high school freshman who refuses to sell candy for a school fund-raising event. That novel and others by Cormier have been called "brutally real" by some readers. Cormier replies, "As long as what I write is true and believable, why should I have to create happy endings?"

About the Lesson

The lesson that follows this story is about theme. In music, especially in longer pieces of music, a theme is a melody that is repeated in various places throughout the composition. In a song the theme might be the chorus, or refrain, that is repeated after each verse. The idea expressed in the refrain ties together the various verses.

In a story a theme is the underlying message or meaning of a story.

A good story is about a feeling, an experience, or an idea that every reader can identify with. The details that are described in a story may be unique, but the ideas and feelings are familiar to everyone. A story's theme or themes are part of the message an author wants to give the reader.

"The Moustache" contains several themes. One is about aging. Another deals with guilt feelings. You will discover other themes as you read the story.

The questions below will help you focus on the themes in "The Moustache." Read the story carefully and try to answer these questions as you go along:

◆ How has Mike's grandmother changed since she became ill? How does that change make you feel about aging?

◆ What thoughts run through Mike's mind as he gets closer to the nursing home?

◆ What does Mike learn during his visit with his grandmother that changes his image of elderly people?

◆ What feeling prompts Mike to kiss his grandmother?

Develop Your Own Theme

Stories express themes, which are ideas and feelings. Story themes are the ideas and feelings an author expresses, or tells, to readers. Use your writing notebook or a separate piece of paper to write ideas or feelings you might like to express to others in story form. Try the following suggestions to get you started:

1. Think of one or more ideas you would like to express in a story. Write each idea in a sentence. Here are some examples:

   ☐ Many adults don't understand young people.

   ☐ Prejudice is a destructive force in the world.

   ☐ It is difficult to understand the feelings of others.

2. Think of one or more feelings you would like to express in a story. Describe each feeling in a sentence. Here are some examples:

☐ Being loved by someone makes you feel comfortable and safe.

☐ Guilt can make you feel lonely and disappointed with yourself.

☐ Sometimes I feel that when I talk to someone older, I might just as well talk to a blank wall—they can't possibly understand what I feel.

The Moustache

by Robert Cormier

At the last minute Annie couldn't go. She was invaded by one of those twenty-four-hour flu bugs that sent her to bed with a fever, moaning about the fact that she'd also have to break her date with Handsome Harry Arnold that night. We call him Handsome Harry because he's actually handsome, but he's also a nice guy, cool, and he doesn't treat me like Annie's kid brother, which I am, but like a regular person. Anyway, I had to go to Lawnrest alone that afternoon. But first of all I had to stand inspection. My mother lined me up against the wall. She stood there like a one-man firing squad, which is kind of funny because she's not like a man at all, she's very feminine, and we have this great relationship—I mean, I feel as if she really likes me. I realize that sounds strange, but I know guys whose mothers love them and cook special stuff for them and worry about them and all but there's something missing in their relationship.

Anyway. She frowned and started the routine.

"That hair," she said. Then admitted: "Well, at least you combed it."

I sighed. I have discovered that it's better to sigh than argue.

"And that moustache." She shook her head. "I still say a seventeen-year-old has no business wearing a moustache."

"It's an experiment," I said. "I just wanted to see if I could grow one." To tell the truth, I had proved my point about being able to grow a decent moustache, but I also had learned to like it.

"It's costing you money, Mike," she said.

"I know, I know."

The money was a reference to the movies. The Downtown Cinema has a special Friday night offer—half-price admission for high school couples, seventeen or younger. But the woman in the box office took one look at my moustache and charged me full price. Even when I showed her my driver's license. She charged full admission for Cindy's ticket, too, which left me practically broke and unable to take Cindy out for a hamburger with the crowd afterward. That didn't help matters, because Cindy has been getting impatient recently about things like the fact that I don't own my own car and have to concentrate on my studies if I want to win that college scholarship, for instance. Cindy wasn't exactly crazy about the moustache, either.

Now it was my mother's turn to sigh.

"Look," I said, to cheer her up. "I'm thinking about shaving it off." Even though I wasn't. Another discovery: You can build a way of life on postponement.

"Your grandmother probably won't even recognize you," she said. And I saw the shadow fall across her face.

Let me tell you what the visit to Lawnrest was all about. My grandmother is seventy-three years old. She is a resident—which is supposed to be a better word than *patient*—at the Lawnrest Nursing Home. She used to make the greatest turkey dressing in the world and was a nut about baseball and could even quote batting averages, for crying out loud. She always rooted for the losers. She was in love with the Mets until they started to win. Now she has arteriosclerosis, which the dictionary says is "a chronic disease characterized by abnormal thickening and hardening of the arterial walls." Which really means that she can't live at home anymore or even with us, and her memory has betrayed her as well as her body. She used to wander off and sometimes didn't recognize people. My mother visits her all the time, driving the thirty miles to

Lawnrest almost every day. Because Annie was home for a semester break from college, we had decided to make a special Saturday visit. Now Annie was in bed, groaning theatrically—she's a drama major—but I told my mother I'd go, anyway. I hadn't seen my grandmother since she'd been admitted to Lawnrest. Besides, the place is located on the Southwest Turnpike, which meant I could barrel along in my father's new Le Mans. My ambition was to see the speedometer hit seventy-five. Ordinarily, I used the old station wagon, which can barely stagger up to fifty.

Frankly, I wasn't too crazy about visiting a nursing home. They reminded me of hospitals and hospitals turn me off. I mean, the smell of ether makes me nauseous, and I feel faint at the sight of blood. And as I approached Lawnrest—which is a terrible cemetery kind of name, to begin with—I was sorry I hadn't avoided the trip. Then I felt guilty about it. I'm loaded with guilt complexes. Like driving like a madman after promising my father to be careful. Like sitting in the parking lot, looking at the nursing home with dread and thinking how I'd rather be with Cindy. Then I thought of all the Christmas and birthday gifts my grandmother had given me and I got out of the car, guilty, as usual.

Inside, I was surprised by the lack of hospital smell, although there was another odor or maybe the absence of an odor. The air was antiseptic, sterile. As if there was no atmosphere at all or I'd caught a cold suddenly and couldn't taste or smell.

A nurse at the reception desk gave me directions—my grandmother was in East Three. I made my way down the tiled corridor and was glad to see that the walls were painted with cheerful colors like yellow and pink. A wheelchair suddenly shot around the corner, self-propelled by an old man, white-haired and toothless, who cackled merrily as he barely missed me. I jumped aside—here I was, almost getting wiped out by a two-mile-an-hour wheelchair after doing seventy-five on the pike. As I walked through the corridor seeking East Three, I couldn't help glancing into the rooms, and it was like some kind of wax museum—all these figures in various stances and attitudes, sitting in beds or chairs, standing at windows, as if they were frozen forever in these postures. To tell the truth, I began to hurry because I was getting depressed. Finally, I saw a beautiful girl approaching, dressed in white, a nurse or an attendant, and I was so happy to see someone young, someone walking and acting normally, that I gave her a wide smile and a big hello and I must have looked like a kind of nut. Anyway, she looked right through me as if I were a window, which is about par for the course whenever I meet beautiful girls.

I finally found the room and saw my grandmother in bed. My grandmother looks like Ethel Barrymore. I never knew who Ethel Barrymore was until I saw a terrific movie, *None But the Lonely Heart,* on TV, starring Ethel Barrymore and Cary Grant. Both my grandmother and Ethel Barrymore have these great craggy faces like the side of a mountain and wonderful voices like syrup being poured. Slowly. She was propped up in bed, pillows puffed behind her. Her hair had been combed out and fell upon her shoulders. For some reason, this flowing hair gave her an almost girlish appearance, despite its whiteness.

She saw me and smiled. Her eyes lit up and her eyebrows arched and she reached out her hands to me in greeting. "Mike, Mike," she said. And I breathed a sigh of relief. This was one of her good days. My mother had warned me that she might not know who I was at first.

I took her hands in mine. They were fragile. I could actually feel her bones, and it seemed as if they would break if I pressed too hard. Her skin was smooth, almost slippery, as if the years had worn away all the roughness the way the wind wears away the surfaces of stones.

"Mike, Mike, I didn't think you'd come," she said, so happy, and she was still Ethel Barrymore, that voice like a caress. "I've been waiting all this time." Before I could reply, she looked away, out the window. "See the birds? I've been watching them at the feeder. I love to see them come. Even the blue jays. The blue jays are like hawks—they take the food that the small birds should have. But the small birds, the chickadees, watch the blue jays and at least learn where the feeder is."

She lapsed into silence, and I looked out the window. There was no feeder. No birds. There was only the parking lot and the sun glinting on car windshields.

She turned to me again, eyes bright. Radiant, really. Or was it a medicine brightness? "Ah, Mike. You look so grand, so grand. Is that a new coat?"

"Not really," I said. I'd been wearing my Uncle Jerry's old army-fatigue jacket for months, practically living in it, my mother said. But she insisted that I wear my raincoat for the visit. It was about a year old but looked new because I didn't wear it much. Nobody was wearing raincoats lately.

"You always loved clothes, didn't you, Mike?" she said.

I was beginning to feel uneasy because she regarded me with such intensity. Those bright eyes. I wondered—are old people in places like this so lonesome, so abandoned that they go wild when someone visits? Or was she so happy because she was suddenly lucid and everything was sharp and clear? My mother had described those moments when my grandmother suddenly emerged from the fog that so often obscured her mind. I didn't know the answers, but it felt kind of spooky, getting such an emotional welcome from her.

"I remember the time you bought the new coat—the Chesterfield," she said, looking away again, as if watching the birds that weren't there. "That lovely coat with the velvet collar. Black, it was. Stylish. Remember that, Mike? It was hard times, but you could never resist the glitter."

I was about to protest—I had never heard of a Chesterfield, for crying out loud. But I stopped. Be patient with her, my mother had said. Humor her. Be gentle.

We were interrupted by an attendant who pushed a

wheeled cart into the room. "Time for juices, dear," the woman said. She was the standard forty- or fifty-year-old woman: glasses, nothing hair, plump cheeks. Her manner was cheerful but a businesslike kind of cheerfulness. I'd hate to be called "dear" by someone getting paid to do it. "Orange or grape or cranberry, dear? Cranberry is good for the bones, you know."

My grandmother ignored the interruption. She didn't even bother to answer, having turned away at the woman's arrival, as if angry about her appearance.

The woman looked at me and winked. A conspiratorial kind of wink. It was kind of horrible. I didn't think people winked like that anymore. In fact, I hadn't seen a wink in years.

"She doesn't care much for juices," the woman said, talking to me as if my grandmother weren't even there. "But she loves her coffee. With lots of cream and two lumps of sugar. But this is juice time, not coffee time." Addressing my grandmother again, she said, "Orange or grape or cranberry, dear?"

"Tell her I want no juices, Mike," my grandmother commanded regally, her eyes still watching invisible birds.

The woman smiled, patience like a label on her face. "That's all right, dear. I'll just leave some cranberry for you. Drink it at your leisure. It's good for the bones."

She wheeled herself out of the room. My grandmother was still absorbed in the view. Somewhere a toilet flushed. A wheelchair passed the doorway—probably that same old driver fleeing a hit-run accident. A television set exploded with sound somewhere, soap-opera voices filling the air. You can always tell soap-opera voices.

I turned back to find my grandmother staring at me. Her hands cupped her face, her index fingers curled around her cheeks like parenthesis marks.

"But you know, Mike, looking back, I think you were right," she said, continuing our conversation as if there had been no interruption. "You always said, 'It's the things of the spirit that count, Meg.' The spirit! And so you bought the baby-grand piano—a baby grand in the middle of the Depression. A knock came on the door and it was the deliveryman. It took five of them to get it into the house." She leaned back, closing her eyes. "How I loved that piano, Mike. I was never that fine a player, but you loved to sit there in the parlor, on Sunday evenings, Ellie on your lap, listening to me play and sing." She hummed a bit, a fragment of melody I didn't recognize. Then she drifted into silence. Maybe she'd fallen asleep. My mother's name is Ellen, but everyone always calls her Ellie. "Take my hand, Mike," my grandmother said suddenly. Then I remembered—my grandfather's name was Michael. I had been named for him.

"Ah, Mike," she said, pressing my hands with all her feeble strength. "I thought I'd lost you forever. And here you are, back with me again. . . ."

Her expression scared me. I don't mean scared as if I were in danger but scared because of what could happen to her when she realized the mistake she had made. My mother always said I favored her side of the family. Thinking back to the pictures in the old family albums, I recalled my grandfather as tall and thin. Like me. But the resemblance ended there. He was thirty-five when he died, almost forty years ago. And he wore a moustache. I brought my hand to my face. I also wore a moustache now, of course.

"I sit here these days, Mike," she said, her voice a lullaby, her hand still holding mine, "and I drift and dream. The days are fuzzy sometimes, merging together. Sometimes it's like I'm not here at all but somewhere else altogether. And I always think of you. Those years we had. Not enough years, Mike, not enough. . . ."

Her voice was so sad, so mournful that I made sounds of sympathy, not words exactly but the kind of soothings that mothers murmur to their children when they awaken from bad dreams.

"And I think of that terrible night, Mike, that terrible night. Have you ever really forgiven me for that night?"

"Listen . . ." I began. I wanted to say: "Nana, this is Mike your grandson, not Mike your husband."

"Sh . . . sh . . ." she whispered, placing a finger as long and cold as a candle against my lips. "Don't say anything. I've waited so long for this moment. To be here. With you. I wondered what I would say if suddenly you walked in that door like other people have done. I've thought and thought about it. And I finally made up my mind—I'd ask you to forgive me. I was too proud to ask before." Her fingers tried to mask her face. "But I'm not proud anymore, Mike." That great voice quivered and then grew strong again. "I hate you to see me this way—you always said I was beautiful. I didn't believe it. The Charity Ball when we led the grand march and you said I was the most beautiful girl there . . ."

"Nana," I said. I couldn't keep up the pretense any longer, adding one more burden to my load of guilt, leading her on this way, playing a pathetic game of make-believe with an old woman clinging to memories. She didn't seem to hear me.

"But that other night, Mike. The terrible one. The terrible accusations I made. Even Ellie woke up and began to cry. I went to her and rocked her in my arms and you came into the room and said I was wrong. You were whispering, an awful whisper, not wanting to upset little Ellie but wanting to make me see the truth. And I didn't answer you, Mike. I was too proud. I've even forgotten the name of the girl. I sit here, wondering now—was it Laura or Evelyn? I can't remember. Later, I learned that you were telling the truth all the time, Mike. That I'd been wrong . . ." Her eyes were brighter than ever as she looked at me now, but tear-bright, the tears gathering. "It was never the same after that night, was it, Mike? The glitter was gone. From you. From us. And then the accident . . . and I never had the chance to ask you to forgive me . . ."

My grandmother. My poor, poor grandmother. Old people aren't supposed to have those kinds of memories. You see their pictures in the family albums and that's what they are: pictures. They're not supposed to come to life. You drive out in your father's Le Mans doing seventy-five on the pike and all you're doing is visiting an old lady in a nursing home. A duty call. And then you find out that she's a person. She's *somebody*. She's my grandmother, all right, but she's also herself. Like my own mother and father. They exist outside of their relationship to me. I was scared again. I wanted to get out of there.

"Mike, Mike," my grandmother said. "Say it, Mike."

I felt as if my cheeks would crack if I uttered a word.

"Say you forgive me, Mike. I've waited all these years . . ."

I was surprised at how strong her fingers were.

"Say, *'I forgive you, Meg.'*"

I said it. My voice sounded funny, as if I were talking in a huge tunnel. "I forgive you, Meg."

Her eyes studied me. Her hands pressed mine. For the first time in my life, I saw love at work. Not movie love. Not Cindy's sparkling eyes when I tell her that we're going to the beach on a Sunday afternoon. But love like something alive and tender, asking nothing in return. She raised her face, and I knew what she wanted me to do. I bent and brushed my lips against her cheek. Her flesh was like a leaf in autumn, crisp and dry.

She closed her eyes and I stood up. The sun wasn't glinting on the cars any longer. Somebody had turned on another television set, and the voices were the show-off voices of the panel shows. At the same time you could still hear the soap-opera dialogue on the other television set.

I waited awhile. She seemed to be sleeping, her breathing serene and regular. I buttoned my raincoat. Suddenly she opened her eyes again and looked at me. Her eyes were still bright, but they merely stared at me. Without recognition or curiosity. Empty eyes. I smiled at her, but she didn't smile back. She made a kind of moaning sound and turned away on the bed, pulling the blankets around her.

I counted to twenty-five and then to fifty and did it all over again. I cleared my throat and coughed tentatively. She didn't move; she didn't respond. I wanted to say, "Nana, it's me." But I didn't. I thought of saying, "Meg, it's me." But I couldn't.

Finally I left. Just like that. I didn't say goodbye or anything. I stalked through the corridors, looking neither to the right nor the left, nor caring whether that wild old man with the wheelchair ran me down or not.

On the Southwest Turnpike I did seventy-five—no, eighty—most of the way. I turned the radio up as loud as it could go. Rock music—anything to fill the air. When I got home, my mother was vacuuming the living-room rug. She shut off the cleaner, and the silence was deafening. "Well, how was your grandmother?" she asked.

I told her she was fine. I told her a lot of things. How great Nana looked and how she seemed happy and had called me Mike. I wanted to ask her—hey, Mom, you and Dad really love each other, don't you? I mean—there's nothing to forgive between you, is there? But I didn't.

Instead I went upstairs and took out the electric razor Annie had given me for Christmas and shaved off my moustache.

Theme

It's often hard to retell a story to a friend. For example, read the conversation below. A girl is trying to tell a friend about a story she has read.

> "Gee, I just finished this great story. You ought to read it."
>
> "Oh, yeah? What's it about?"
>
> "Well, this guy goes to visit his grandmother in a nursing home. Oh—and he grew this moustache first. Well, *she* thinks *he's* her dead husband, and she starts apologizing for a fight they had forty years ago. . . ."

The story sounds flat. Something has been lost in the retelling. That something is the story's essence, its point—in other words, the story's themes. Themes are the underlying messages or meanings of a story. The details of a story might concern only a particular character in a particular situation. But the themes of a story apply to everyone.

In the example above, the girl has trouble giving an interesting account of the story because she fails to get across the story's themes. Suppose, instead, the girl tells the story this way:

> "Gee, I just finished this great story. You ought to read it."
>
> "Oh, yeah? What's it about?"
>
> "Well, it's about this guy who visits his grandmother in a nursing home. He feels guilty because he hasn't seen her for a while. Then he finds out *she* feels guilty about something too. And he realizes she's not just a grandmother, or just an older person, but a *real* person with an interesting and real past."

The second version is better than the first because the girl hints at some of the story's themes: guilt, aging, and the relationship between a boy and his grandmother. Those themes are good reasons for someone to want to read this story. Everyone has feelings of guilt.

Everyone thinks about growing older and knows people who are older. That's why the story about Mike and his grandmother is worth reading. And that's what the girl is trying to get across to her friend.

Themes may be major or minor. A major theme is an idea that the author returns to time and again. It is one of the most important ideas in the story. Minor themes are ideas that appear in the story less often. Together, the major and minor themes of a story can transform a small tale into a story that touches the lives of all who read it.

Themes in stories are expressed in several ways. In this lesson we'll look at four ways in which author Robert Cormier expresses themes:

1 ◆ The author expresses and emphasizes themes by the way he makes you feel.

2 ◆ He hints at themes by showing the characters' thoughts and conversations.

3 ◆ He suggests themes through character development.

4 ◆ He uses the actions, or events, in the story to suggest themes.

1 ◆ Themes and Feelings

In earlier lessons you learned that authors like to influence your feelings. Writers take great pains to make you feel a certain way. They often use the feelings they create in you to express the themes of the story.

In "The Moustache" author Robert Cormier wants the idea of aging to be a major theme of the story. So he shows you Mike's feelings about his grandmother, who is in failing health. Because Mike is the story's main character, you *identify* with him—you share his feelings. When you share his feelings, you also share the ideas that go through his mind.

In the following passage Mike tells you about his grandmother. How does the author make you feel about Mike's grandmother? How does he want you to feel about aging?

> Let me tell you what the visit to Lawnrest was all about. My grandmother is seventy-three years old. She is a resident—which is supposed to be a better word than *patient*—at the Lawnrest Nursing Home. She used to make the greatest turkey dressing in the world and was a nut about baseball and could even quote batting averages, for crying out loud. She always rooted for the losers. She was in love with the Mets until they started to win. Now she has arteriosclerosis, which the dictionary says is "a chronic disease characterized by abnormal thickening and hardening of the arterial walls." Which really means that she can't live at home anymore or even with us, and her memory has betrayed her as well as her body. She used to wander off and sometimes didn't recognize people.

Mike's grandmother is an elderly woman whose mind is failing. Her memory betrays her. Sometimes she doesn't recognize people. Because of those problems, she can't live at home anymore, or even with her daughter.

It's possible for different people to have different feelings about a situation like this. In real life some people may feel disgusted by a person like Mike's grandmother. Others may react with cruel humor. But *you* probably don't feel amused or disgusted by Mike's grandmother. You probably feel sympathetic, because that's how the author wants you to feel.

Notice how Cormier guides your feelings. He wants you to see Nana as a person, not just as an elderly woman. So he tells you what she was like before she was sick. She made great turkey stuffing. She liked baseball. She always rooted for the losers. She was the kind of person you'd probably like for a friend. And you can't help sharing Mike's grief over his grandmother's present condition.

That theme is one of the important ideas that Robert Cormier wants you to think about. Elderly people in failing health were once active, interesting people. Like Mike's grandmother, they have been "betrayed" by old age. If you now feel sympathetic toward the problems of older people, then you have grasped one of the themes of "The Moustache."

The author also guides your feelings when he wants to make a point about nursing homes. Read the passage in Exercise A and try to decide what idea the author wants you to think about.

1 ◆ Exercise A

Read the following passage and answer the questions about it using what you have learned in this part of the lesson. Use your writing notebook or a separate piece of paper for your answers.

> Inside [the nursing home], I was surprised by the lack of hospital smell, although there was another odor or maybe the absence of an odor. The air was antiseptic, sterile. As if there was no atmosphere at all or I'd caught a cold suddenly and couldn't taste or smell.
>
> . . . As I walked through the corridor seeking East Three, I couldn't help glancing into the rooms, and it was like some kind of wax museum—all these figures in various stances and attitudes, sitting in beds or chairs, standing at windows, as if they were frozen forever in these postures.

1. In the second part of the passage Mike compares the nursing home to something else. That comparison is one way the author shapes your feelings about nursing homes. What does the author compare the nursing home to?

2. Many magazine and newspaper articles give readers the idea that some nursing homes are like "warehouses" for elderly people who

are sick and disabled. How does Robert Cormier express that theme in the passage? Do you agree with him?

Now check your answers using the suggestions in the Answer Key starting on page 457. Review this part of the lesson if you don't understand why an answer is wrong.

1♦Writing on Your Own

Look at the sentences about ideas and feelings that you have written for Develop Your Own Theme on page 231. Now do one or both of the following:

1. Write a paragraph that expresses your feelings about an idea you have described in one of your sentences. Try to use a comparison to explain your feelings about the idea, just as Robert Cormier does in the story.

2. Choose a feeling that you have described in one of your sentences. Write a paragraph that explains *how* that feeling is like what you have described in your sentence. For example, how does being loved by someone make you feel comfortable and safe? (When I am loved it makes me feel taken care of and protected.) How can guilt make you feel lonely and disappointed with yourself? (When you feel guilty, you often feel isolated because you can't discuss it with anyone. You may feel disappointed with yourself for what you have done.) Why might you feel talking to someone older is like talking to a blank wall? (You might feel they have never experienced the feelings that you have, and like a blank wall, they can't understand anything you say.)

3. You may want to change and rewrite your paragraphs several times to get them just right.

2 ◆ Themes, Thoughts, and Conversations

There is no such thing as idle talk in a story. Authors carefully choose everything their characters say. The thoughts and conversations of the characters help to develop a story's themes.

Imagine, for example, that someone you love is very ill. You try to go about your daily routine. But you can't help thinking about that person's illness. The topics of illness and death crop up in your conversations. From the things you say, friends might conclude that death and dying are very much on your mind. If you were a character in a story, then death and dying would be themes of the story.

In "The Moustache" you learn what is on Mike's mind in two ways: from his thoughts and from his conversations. You know what Mike is thinking because he tells you. When he is not talking to another character, he talks directly to the reader.

His thoughts and conversations provide clues to an important theme. The following thoughts run through Mike's mind as he gets closer to the nursing home. See if you can find the important idea his thoughts contain.

> And as I approached Lawnrest—which is a terrible cemetery kind of name, to begin with—I was sorry I hadn't avoided the trip. Then I felt guilty about it. I'm loaded with guilt complexes. Like driving like a madman after promising my father to be careful. Like sitting in the parking lot, looking at the nursing home with dread and thinking how I'd rather be with Cindy. Then I thought of all the Christmas and birthday gifts my grandmother had given me and I got out of the car, guilty, as usual.

One idea in this passage stands out—the idea of guilt. Mike feels guilty about many things. Why doesn't he visit his grandmother more often? Why does he drive too fast? Why does he wish he were with his girlfriend instead of visiting his grandmother? "I'm loaded with guilt complexes," he says.

In other parts of the story you hear more about Mike's guilt. For example, you learn that Mike feels guilty for letting his grandmother go on thinking that he is her husband.

Clearly, guilt is a major theme of "The Moustache." It is mentioned several times because it is an important part of Mike's life. And, like aging, it is a part of readers' lives too. We can all identify with Mike's feelings of guilt, because all of us have things that we feel guilty about. The idea of guilt, like the idea of aging, is a theme that every reader can relate to.

In Exercise B you learn that something has been bothering Mike's grandmother for almost forty years. She reveals her thoughts in her conversation with Mike, who she thinks is her husband. Look for the theme hidden behind her words.

2 ◆ Exercise B

Read the following passage and answer the questions about it using what you have learned in this part of the lesson. Use your writing notebook or a separate piece of paper for your answers.

> "But that other night, Mike. The terrible one. The terrible accusations I made. Even Ellie woke up and began to cry. I went to her and rocked her in my arms and you came into the room and said I was wrong. You were whispering, an awful whisper, not wanting to upset little Ellie but wanting to make me see the truth. And I didn't answer you, Mike. I was too proud. . . . Later, I learned that you were telling the truth all the time, Mike. That I'd been wrong . . ." Her eyes were brighter than ever as she looked at me now, but tear-bright, the tears gathering. "It was never the same after that night, was it, Mike? The glitter was gone. From you. From us. And then the accident . . . and I never had the chance to ask you to forgive me . . ."

1. Mike's grandmother reveals that she has been carrying a feeling of guilt for many years. The reason for her guilt was that she never answered her husband when he told her that she was wrong to think he was involved with another woman. What was it that had kept her from answering her husband?

2. The author develops an important theme about young people versus older people in the grandmother's conversation with Mike. What is it? Do you agree?

Now check your answers using the suggestions in the Answer Key starting on page 457. Review this part of the lesson if you don't understand why an answer was wrong.

2 ✦ Writing on Your Own

Read the sentences about ideas and feelings that you have written for Develop Your Own Theme on page 231. Now do the following:

1. Write a paragraph as though you were talking to someone. In this conversation you want to show the other person how you feel about an idea or a feeling you have. Here's an example:

   > Just yesterday, my mother said, "No swimming (basketball, baseball, gymnastics, etc.) practice until your homework is done!" This is typical. She doesn't realize that if I don't get in my practice time I'll bomb in the meet (game, trials) on Saturday. People are depending on me. Probably when she was a kid all she ever did was homework!

2. You may want to change and rewrite your paragraph several times until you get it just the way you like it.

3 ♦ Theme and Character Development

The characters in a story can also express the themes. When a character develops, he or she seems to grow up or change. Character development always affects the main character, who usually illustrates the most important theme of the story. A good way to find that important theme is to ask yourself the question, What does the main character learn in the course of the story? If you can answer that question, then you have probably found the most important theme.

Ask yourself what Mike has learned in the course of this story. Then read the following passage from "The Moustache." What has Mike just learned? What theme does the passage suggest?

> My grandmother. My poor, poor grandmother. Old people aren't supposed to have those kinds of memories. You see their pictures in the family albums and that's what they are: pictures. They're not supposed to come to life. You drive out in your father's Le Mans doing seventy-five on the pike and all you're doing is visiting an old lady in a nursing home. A duty call. And then you find out that she's a person. She's *somebody*. She's my grandmother, all right, but she's also herself.

Mike has just learned to see beyond his stereotype of a grandmother. He thought grandmothers were just little old ladies who made great turkey stuffing and gave lavish presents to their grandchildren. Now he sees that grandmothers are real people. They carry the same emotional load that he does—the terrible mistakes, the pangs of remorse, the bitter memories as well as the sweet.

Mike has made a big discovery. He simply hadn't thought about his grandmother in those terms. He has learned an important lesson. He has learned that other people—even elderly people—have complicated feelings, just as he does.

When you answered the question, What has Mike learned? you uncovered an important theme. We must all realize that other people are just as complicated as we are. Everyone must be given credit for having deep and sometimes troubled feelings.

Minor characters as well as main characters may also be used to develop a theme. Think about the attendant who brings fruit juices to Mike's grandmother. She isn't part of the story line. In fact, she interrupts it. The part she plays doesn't reveal anything about Mike that we don't already know. But she *does* help develop one of the themes of the story. Go on to Exercise C and try to decide what ideas the attendant develops.

3 ♦ Exercise C

Read the following passage and answer the questions about it using what you have learned in this part of the lesson. Use your writing notebook or a separate piece of paper for your answers.

> We were interrupted by an attendant who pushed a wheeled cart into the room. "Time for juices, dear," the woman said. She was the standard forty- or fifty-year-old woman: glasses, nothing hair, plump cheeks. Her manner was cheerful but a businesslike kind of cheerfulness. I'd hate to be called "dear" by someone getting paid to do it. "Orange or grape or cranberry, dear? Cranberry is good for the bones, you know." . . .
>
> The woman looked at me and winked. A conspiratorial kind of wink. It was kind of horrible. I didn't think people winked like that anymore. In fact, I hadn't seen a wink in years.
>
> "She doesn't care much for juices," the woman said, talking to me as if my grandmother weren't even there. . . . Addressing my grandmother again, she said, "Orange or grape or cranberry, dear?"
>
> "Tell her I want no juices, Mike," my grandmother commanded regally, her eyes still watching invisible birds.
>
> The woman smiled, patience like a label on her face. "That's all right, dear. I'll just leave some cranberry for you. Drink it at your leisure. It's good for the bones."

1. Make a list of at least three things Mike doesn't like about the attendant.

2. The attendant seems to think about the grandmother in the same way that Mike used to think about her. How was Mike's attitude similar to the attendant's attitude?

Now check your answers using the suggestions in the Answer Key starting on page 457. Review this part of the lesson if you don't understand why an answer was wrong.

3♦Writing on Your Own

Look at the sentences about ideas and feelings that you have written for Develop Your Own Theme on page 231. Now do the following:

1. Think of a character that might go with one of the ideas and feelings you have already described. For example, that character could be an adult who you think doesn't understand young people; a prejudiced person who you know is hurtful to others; a person who loves you; or someone who constantly feels guilty.

2. Write a paragraph that describes that person. Include in the description how the person doesn't understand, is prejudiced and hurtful, how you are loved, or one of the other emotions you have listed.

3. You may want to change and rewrite your paragraph several times until you get it just the way you like it.

4 ◆ Theme and Action

People naturally express ideas and feelings through their actions. For instance, a person who is speechless with anger might kick something. That action expresses fury and rage. When someone is overjoyed, she might toss her hat into the air—an action that shows high spirits. On Memorial Day a person might lay a wreath on a grave. The action expresses respect for the person buried there. You can see that actions are not just empty gestures. They are full of meaning.

Authors give a lot of thought to the actions they include in their stories. They think about what an action will "say" in the story. In other words, they decide how the action will express an idea or theme.

There are many actions in "The Moustache" that express the themes of the story. One such action comes toward the end of Mike's visit. Think about the action in the following passage:

> "Say you forgive me, Mike. I've waited all these years . . ."
> I was surprised at how strong her fingers were.
> "Say, *'I forgive you, Meg.'* "
> I said it. . . . "I forgive you, Meg."
> Her eyes studied me. Her hands pressed mine. For the first time in my life, I saw love at work. Not movie love. Not Cindy's sparkling eyes when I tell her that we're going to the beach on a Sunday afternoon. But love like something alive and tender, asking nothing in return. She raised her face, and I knew what she wanted me to do. I bent and brushed my lips against her cheek.

The meaningful action in this passage is the kiss. It completes the act of forgiveness that Mike's grandmother asks for from her husband. (Remember, she thinks Mike is her husband.)

The kiss helps express an important theme in the story. That theme is love. Mike has just learned something new about love. Before, he thought of love only as it was presented in the movies—as romantic or passionate. But now he sees that real love goes deeper. The kind of love he sees in his grandmother's eyes is unselfish—"love like something alive and tender, asking nothing in return." So Mike responds with an equally unselfish act of love, and he kisses his grandmother.

Another action that expresses a theme comes at the very end of the story. Review the ending by reading the passage in Exercise D. Try to decide how the final action helps to explain an important theme.

4 ◆ Exercise D

Read the following passage and answer the questions about it using what you have learned in this part of the lesson. Use your writing notebook or a separate piece of paper for your answers.

> When I got home, my mother was vacuuming the living-room rug. She shut off the cleaner, and the silence was deafening. "Well, how was your grandmother?" she asked.
>
> I told her she was fine. I told her a lot of things. How great Nana looked and how she seemed happy and had called me Mike. I wanted to ask her—hey, Mom, you and Dad really love each other, don't you? I mean—there's nothing to forgive between you, is there? But I didn't.
>
> Instead I went upstairs and took out the electric razor Annie had given me for Christmas and shaved off my moustache.

1. As a result of visiting the nursing home, Mike has something on his mind about his parents. He wants to ask his mother about what he is thinking, but he doesn't. What does he want to ask?

2. The author doesn't say why Mike shaved off his moustache. But that action is related to an idea in the story. What is that idea or theme?

Now check your answers using the suggestions in the Answer Key starting on page 457. Review this part of the lesson if you don't understand why an answer was wrong.

4 ◆ Writing on Your Own

Look at the sentences about ideas and feelings that you have written for Develop Your Own Theme on page 231. Also look at the paragraph you wrote about a character in 3◆Writing on Your Own, page 253. Now do the following:

1. Write a paragraph that describes an action by the character you wrote about in 3♦Writing on Your Own. Try to have the action express an idea or theme. If you have already begun to write about an action in your paragraph, add to the action now.

2. You may want to change and rewrite your paragraph several times until you get it just the way you like it.

Now go on to Reviewing and Interpreting the Story.

Reviewing and Interpreting the Story

Answer these questions without looking back at the story. Choose the best answer to each question and put an *x* in the box beside it, or write your answer on a separate piece of paper.

Remembering
Facts

1. Who is Meg?

   ☐ a. Mike's older sister

   ☐ b. the young nurse

   ☐ c. Mike's mother

   ☐ d. Mike's grandmother

2. Whom does Mike resemble?

   ☐ a. his father

   ☐ b. his sister

   ☐ c. his grandmother

   ☐ d. his mother's father

Following the
Order of Events

3. Mike's grandmother has been confused about events in the world around her

   ☐ a. just for the past year or two.

   ☐ b. ever since Mike's mother was born.

   ☐ c. for as long as Mike has known her.

   ☐ d. ever since her husband died.

4. At what point in the story does Mike realize his grandmother thinks he is someone else?

□ a. as soon as she greets him

□ b. when she admires his coat

□ c. when she recalls playing the piano for him and Ellie

□ d. not until after he has left

Understanding Word Choices

5. Mike glances into some of the rooms in the nursing home. He sees "all these figures in various <u>stances</u> and <u>attitudes</u> . . . as if they were frozen forever in these <u>postures</u>." The words *stances, attitudes,* and *postures* all seem to

□ a. relate to poses or positions.

□ b. be difficult and unrelated.

□ c. mean freezing in cold rooms.

□ d. suggest peace and happiness.

6. Mike says, "My mother had described those moments when my grandmother suddenly emerged from the fog that so often <u>obscured</u> her mind." Instead of *obscured,* the author could have used the word

□ a. destroyed.

□ b. eased.

□ c. clouded.

□ d. penetrated.

7. What kind of feeling does Mike often have that his grandmother seems to have also?

☐ a. confusion

☐ b. guilt

☐ c. loneliness

☐ d. boredom

8. What does Mike's grandmother wish she had done before her husband died?

☐ a. demanded an apology from him

☐ b. learned to play the piano better

☐ c. asked him to forgive her

☐ d. been a better mother to Ellie

9. A person whose behavior is condescending tends to look down on other people. Who in the story has a condescending air?

☐ a. Cindy

☐ b. the juice lady

☐ c. Mike

☐ d. Nana

10. What happened between Mike's grandmother and grandfather when they were young?

☐ a. They couldn't agree on how to raise Ellie.

☐ b. He thought she was seeing another man.

☐ c. She thought he was seeing another woman.

☐ d. They had a big argument over money.

11. Mike feels that his mother

☐ a. doesn't like him.

☐ b. likes him.

☐ c. gets along better with Annie.

☐ d. is nervous about sending him to the nursing home.

12. The things Mike's grandmother thought she saw were

☐ a. scenes around the nursing home.

☐ b. dreams brought on by her medicine.

☐ c. ideas suggested by Mike.

☐ d. drawn from her memories.

13. The setting is partly in Mike's home and partly in the nursing home. In other words, the setting of the story goes from

☐ a. bad to worse.

☐ b. a world of worry to a world of peace.

☐ c. the real world to an unreal world.

☐ d. worse to better.

14. Mike says the air in the nursing home is "antiseptic, sterile." He says there is no atmosphere at all. The author wants to suggest that

☐ a. it is like being nowhere that is real.

☐ b. the home is kept very clean.

☐ c. this smell is better than a hospital smell.

☐ d. no smell at all is better than an offensive smell.

15. **The scenes at the nursing home make Mike feel**

    ☐ a. relieved.

    ☐ b. suspicious.

    ☐ c. depressed.

    ☐ d. angry.

16. **When Mike realizes that his grandmother has mistaken him for her dead husband, he feels**

    ☐ a. proud to look so grown up.

    ☐ b. vaguely nervous and frightened.

    ☐ c. as if he might cry.

    ☐ d. disgusted with an older person's foolishness.

Now check your answers using the Answer Key starting on page 457. Make no mark for right answers. <u>Correct</u> any wrong answers you may have by putting a check mark (✓) in the box next to the right answer. Count the number of questions you answered correctly and plot the total on the Comprehension Scores graph on page 468.

Next, look at the questions you answered incorrectly. What types of questions were they? Count the number you got wrong of each type and enter the numbers in the spaces below.

Remembering Facts   _____

Following the Order of Events   _____

Understanding Word Choices   _____

Understanding Important Ideas   _____

Understanding Levels of Meaning   _____

Understanding Character   _____

Understanding Setting   _____

Understanding Feelings   _____

Now use these numbers to fill in the Comprehension Skills Profile on page 469.

Discussion Guides

The questions below help you think about the story and the lesson you have just read. If you don't discuss these questions in class, try to think about them or discuss them with your classmates. Perhaps you will want to write a few paragraphs in answer to the questions.

Discussing Theme

1. Relationships between family members is a theme of *8 Plus 1,* a collection of short stories from which this story was taken. What kind of relationship does Mike seem to have with his family? Is he close to his mother? His sister? How can you tell? What is the author trying to tell you about families?

2. Minor characters are sometimes used to comment on a theme (see part 3 of the lesson). Think about the old man in the wheelchair who almost runs Mike down in the corridor. What does he add to the theme of aging?

3. Guilt is a theme in the story. How do the characters Mike and Nana both illustrate that theme? Do you think guilt is a theme that every reader can understand? Why do you think the author wants Mike and you to think about guilt?

Discussing the Story

4. Do you think that Mike should have made his grandmother understand that he wasn't her husband? Why or why not?

5. Mike drives home from the nursing home at eighty miles an hour with the radio blaring. Why do you think he behaves this way?

6. Think about the events that lead up to Mike's actions at the end of the story. Do you think he makes the right decision when he shaves off his moustache? Why or why not?

Discussing the Author's Work

7. How can you tell that Robert Cormier knows a lot about teenagers? What are some of the little touches, or details, that the author uses to make Mike seem like a real teenager?

8. Sometimes Mike's grandmother seems to be living in the distant past, sometimes in the real present, and sometimes in a confused

present in which she doesn't see things as they really are. Find places in the story where each of these happens. What does her changing view of reality add to the story?

9. Robert Cormier says, "As long as what I write is true and believable, why should I have to create happy endings?" Do you think "The Moustache" has a happy ending? What makes the ending happy? What makes it unhappy?

Writing Exercise

Read all the instructions before you begin writing. If you have any questions about how to begin the writing assignment, review Using the Writing Process on page 445, or confer with your writing coach.

1. At the beginning of the unit you were asked to think of some ideas and feelings that you would like to express as themes in the story. If you haven't done that yet, read the instructions for Develop Your Own Theme on page 231, and write these themes as sentences now.

    Develop your themes by following the instructions in the four Writing on Your Own exercises.

2. Write a short story that expresses some of the themes you thought about. Your story should express your themes using one or more of the techniques you learned about in this unit:

    ◆ **Expressing themes through feelings:** Tell how a character in the story feels under certain circumstances.

    ◆ **Expressing themes through thoughts and conversations:** Let your ideas come through in what your character thinks and says.

    ◆ **Expressing themes through character development:** Show what your characters have learned in the course of the story.

    ◆ **Expressing themes through actions:** Relate things the characters do to the ideas and feelings you are expressing in your story.

3. Write, revise, correct, and rewrite your story until you are sure you have got it just the way you want it.

Unit 7   Tone and Mood

Sucker

BY CARSON McCULLERS

About the Illustration

How would you describe the feelings of the boy who is sitting up in the bed? What do you think might have made him feel that way? Point out some details in the drawing to support your response.

Here are some questions to help you think about the story:

◆ How would you describe the expression on the young boy's face?

◆ Who do you think the older boy in the drawing might be? How do you think he feels? What details about him make you think that?

◆ What do you think might be happening in this scene?

Unit 7

Introduction

About the Story

In households where there are many people but not many rooms, the children are usually expected to share a bedroom. This often means two to a bed. Such is the case with Pete and Richard, two boys growing up in the depression years of the 1930s. At the time of the story, Pete is sixteen and Richard is twelve.

If you have ever had to share a room with someone, you probably know that roommates often bicker with each other. But this is not the case with Pete and Richard. As Pete tells it:

> It was always like I had a room to myself. Sucker [Richard] slept in my bed with me but that didn't interfere with anything. The room was mine and I used it as I wanted to.

It almost seems that Richard doesn't exist for Pete, except for those times when Pete feels like playing tricks on him. And when Pete *does* notice him, he calls him by the very uncomplimentary name of "Sucker." But Sucker worships Pete. He would do anything to have Pete pay attention to him and like him.

Pete is having a similar problem with Maybelle Watts. He has a crush on Maybelle, but she ignores him. It's as if Pete doesn't exist as far as she is concerned—except for the times when she chooses to embarrass him in public.

Here we have two boys who live about as close together as people can and yet who are miles apart. Each boy is looking for attention and love. Each is made miserable by the person whose affection he craves. Where this all leads is what the story is about.

Author Carson McCullers is best remembered for her novel *The Heart Is a Lonely Hunter*. This book was made into a movie in 1968, and it is still shown on TV from time to time. McCullers also wrote *Member of the Wedding,* which was a popular movie in 1952 and remained popular for many years after. If you enjoy "Sucker," you will probably enjoy reading both of these fine books.

Carson McCullers (1917–1967) is one of the great examples of what a person can accomplish despite having a severe physical disability. A series of strokes left her paralyzed on the left side of her body for most of her adult life. She finished one of her novels by typing steadily, at the rate of one page a day, with only one hand. She is recognized as one of the outstanding writers of stories set in the southern United States, where she was born and grew up.

About the Lesson

The lesson that follows the story is about tone and mood. Every piece of writing has a tone, just as your voice has a tone when you speak. And the tone of a story changes constantly, just as your manner of speaking changes according to how you feel. The way you feel is called your mood.

How the author feels is the author's mood. And the author develops the moods of the characters. You can tell from the tone of the story how the author feels about the characters, the actions, and the ideas that are being presented. Tone, therefore, is sometimes called the author's *attitude*. And tone and mood, as you will see in the lesson, work very closely together.

The questions below will help you focus on tone and mood as they develop in the story "Sucker." Read the story carefully and try to answer these questions as you go along:

◆ How does the tone change with each new turn in the story? What are some of the different feelings (moods) that the characters experience?

◆ How does the author let you know how she feels, and how she wants *you* to feel, about Maybelle Watts by the way she describes Maybelle?

◆ What does Maybelle contribute to the tone and mood of the scenes in which she appears? What feeling do you get from the scenes set in the boys' bedroom?

◆ The only dialogue—conversation—in the story is between Pete and Sucker. How do their conversations make you feel?

Using Tone to Describe Moods

People's moods change from day to day, even from hour to hour, according to how they feel. You can often tell a person's mood by how he or she acts, what that person says, and how the person says it. This is the *tone* the person conveys as a result of the mood he or she is in.

Use your writing notebook or a separate piece of paper and try the following suggestions:

1. Write two sentences that show how a mood can change rather quickly. Write one sentence that tells how good you feel getting up on a bright, sunny morning. Write a second sentence that tells how you feel fifteen minutes later when you remember you have a math test that you haven't studied for.

2. Write two sentences that show how you can change your tone with the words you use. Write one sentence that tells how happy you are when you are with a special person. Write a second sentence that tells how you feel when you can't be with that person. Underline the words that clearly show what your mood is each time.

3. Write two sentences that describe two different characters. One character is a pleasant person whom you like. The other person is someone you don't like. The tone you use in your writing is bound to be different in each case.

    After each sentence write in parentheses what you think the tone of the sentence is (happy, loving, airy, sunny, etc.; depressed, angry, annoyed, frightened, etc.).

4. Write two short conversations between two people. In the first conversation the two people seem to like each other. In the second conversation the two people seem to dislike each other. After you have written the conversations, give your paper to a friend and ask how he or she can tell the difference in the tone and feeling (mood) in each conversation.

Sucker

by Carson McCullers

It was always like I had a room to myself. Sucker slept in my bed with me but that didn't interfere with anything. The room was mine and I used it as I wanted to. Once I remember sawing a trap door in the floor. Last year when I was a sophomore in high school I tacked on my wall some pictures of girls from magazines and one of them was just in her underwear. My mother never bothered me because she had the younger kids to look after. And Sucker thought anything I did was always swell.

Whenever I would bring any of my friends back to my room all I had to do was just glance once at Sucker and he would get up from whatever he was busy with and maybe half smile at me, and leave without saying a word. He never brought kids back there. He's twelve, four years younger than I am, and he always knew without me even telling him that I didn't want kids that age meddling with my things.

Half the time I used to forget that Sucker isn't my brother. He's my first cousin but practically ever since I remember he's been in our family. You see his folks were killed in a wreck when he was a baby. To me and my kid sisters he was like our brother.

Sucker used to always remember and believe every word I said. That's how he got his nick-name. Once a couple of years ago I told him that if he'd jump off our garage with an umbrella it would act as a parachute and he wouldn't fall hard. He did it and busted his knee. That's just one instance. And the funny thing was that no matter how many times he got fooled he would still believe me. Not that he was dumb in other ways—it was just the way he acted with me. He would look at everything I did and quietly take it in.

There is one thing I have learned, but it makes me feel guilty and is hard to figure out. If a person admires you a lot you despise him and don't care—and it is the person who doesn't notice you that you are apt to admire. This is not easy to realize. Maybelle Watts, this senior at school, acted like she was the Queen of Sheba and even humiliated me. Yet at this same time I would have done anything in the world to get her attentions. All I could think about day and night was Maybelle until I was nearly crazy. When Sucker was a little kid and on up until the time he was twelve I guess I treated him as bad as Maybelle did me.

Now that Sucker has changed so much it is a little hard to remember him as he used to be. I never imagined anything would suddenly happen that would make us both very different. I never knew that in order to get what has happened straight in my mind I would want to think back on him as he used to be and compare and try to get things settled. If I could have seen ahead maybe I would have acted different.

I never noticed him much or thought about him and when you consider how long we have had the same room together it is funny the few things I remember. He used to talk to himself a lot when he'd think he was alone—all about him fighting gangsters and being on ranches and that sort of kids' stuff. He'd get in the bathroom and stay as long as an hour and sometimes his voice would go up high and excited and you could hear him all over the house. Usually, though, he was very quiet. He didn't have many boys in the neighborhood to buddy with and his face had the look of a kid who is watching a game and waiting to be asked to play. He didn't mind wearing the sweaters and coats that I outgrew, even if the sleeves did flop down too big and make his wrists look as thin and white as a little girl's. That is how I remember him—getting a little bigger every year but still being the same. That was Sucker up until a few months ago when all this trouble began.

Maybelle was somehow mixed up in what happened so I guess I ought to start with her. Until I knew her I hadn't given much time to girls. Last fall she sat next to me in General Science class and that was when I first began to notice her. Her hair is the brightest yellow I ever saw and occasionally she will wear it set into curls with some sort of gluey stuff. Her fingernails are pointed and manicured and painted a shiny red. All during class I used to watch Maybelle, nearly all the time except when I thought she was going to look my way or when the teacher called on me. I couldn't keep my eyes off her hands, for one thing. They are very little and white except for that red stuff, and when she would turn the pages of her book she always licked her thumb and held out her little finger and turned very slowly. It is impossible to describe Maybelle. All the boys are crazy about her but she didn't even notice me. All I could do was sit and look at her in class—and sometimes it was like the whole room could hear my heart beating and I wanted to holler or light out and run for Hell.

At night, in bed, I would imagine about Maybelle. Often this would keep me from sleeping until as late as one or two o'clock. Sometimes Sucker would wake up and ask me why I couldn't get settled and I'd tell him to hush his mouth. I suppose I was mean to him lots of times. I guess I wanted to ignore somebody like Maybelle did me. You could always tell by Sucker's face when his feelings were hurt. I don't remember all the ugly remarks I must have made because even when I was saying them my mind was on Maybelle.

That went on for nearly three months and then somehow she began to change. In the halls she would speak to me and every morning she copied my homework. At lunchtime once I danced with her in the gym. One afternoon I got up nerve and went around to her house with a carton of cigarettes. I knew she smoked in the girls' basement and sometimes outside of school—and I didn't want to take her candy because I think that's been run into the ground. She was very nice and it seemed to me everything was going to change.

It was that night when this trouble really started. I had come into my room late and Sucker was already asleep. I felt too happy and keyed up to get in a comfortable position and I was awake thinking about Maybelle a long time. Then I dreamed about her and it seemed I kissed her. It was a surprise to wake up and see the dark. I lay still and a little while passed before I could come to and understand where I was. The house was quiet and it was a very dark night.

Sucker's voice was a shock to me. "Pete? . . ."

I didn't answer anything or even move.

"You do like me as much as if I was your own brother, don't you, Pete?"

I couldn't get over the surprise of everything and it was like this was the real dream instead of the other.

"You have liked me all the time like I was your own brother, haven't you?"

"Sure," I said.

Then I got up for a few minutes. It was cold and I was glad to come back to bed. Sucker hung on to my back. He felt little and warm and I could feel his warm breathing on my shoulder.

"No matter what you did I always knew you liked me."

I was wide awake and my mind seemed mixed up in a strange way. There was this happiness about Maybelle and all that—but at the same time something about Sucker and his voice when he said these things made me take notice. Anyway I guess you understand people better when you are happy than when something is worrying you. It was like I had never really thought about Sucker until then. I felt I had always been mean to him. One night a few weeks before I had heard him crying in the dark. He said he had lost a boy's beebee gun and was scared to let anybody know. He wanted me to tell him what to do. I was sleepy and tried to make him hush and when he wouldn't I kicked at him. That was just one of the things I remembered. It seemed to me he had always been a lonesome kid. I felt bad.

There is something about a dark cold night that makes you feel close to someone you're sleeping with. When you talk together it is like you are the only people awake in the town.

"You're a swell kid, Sucker," I said.

It seemed to me suddenly that I did like him more than anybody else I knew—more than any other boy, more than my sisters, more in a certain way even than Maybelle. I felt good all over and it was like when they play sad music in the movies. I wanted to show Sucker how much I really thought of him and make up for the way I had always treated him.

We talked for a good while that night. His voice was fast and it was like he had been saving up these things to tell me for a long time. He mentioned that he was going to try to build a canoe and that the kids down the block wouldn't let him in on their football team and I don't know what all. I talked some too and it was a good feeling to think of him taking in everything I said so seriously. I even spoke of Maybelle a little, only I made out like it was her who had been running after me all this time. He asked questions about high school and so forth. His voice was excited and he kept on talking fast like he could never get the words out in time. When I went to sleep he was still talking and I could feel his breathing on my shoulder, warm and close.

During the next couple of weeks I saw a lot of Maybelle. She acted as though she really cared for me a little. Half the time I felt so good I hardly knew what to do with myself.

But I didn't forget about Sucker. There were a lot of old things in my bureau drawer I'd been saving—boxing gloves and Tom Swift books and second-rate fishing tackle. All this I turned over to him. We had some more talks together and it was really like I was knowing him for the first time. When there was a long cut on his cheek I knew he had been monkeying around with this new first razor set of mine, but I didn't say anything. His face seemed different now. He used to look timid and sort of like he was afraid of a whack over the head. That expression was gone. His face, with those wide-open eyes and his ears sticking out and his mouth never quite shut, had the look of a person who is surprised and expecting something swell.

Once I started to point him out to Maybelle and tell her he was my kid brother. It was an afternoon when a murder mystery was on at the movie. I had earned a dollar working for my Dad and I gave Sucker a quarter to go and get candy and so forth. With the rest I took Maybelle. We were sitting near the back and I saw Sucker come in. He began to stare at the screen the minute he stepped past the ticket man and he stumbled down the aisle without noticing where he was going. I started to punch Maybelle but couldn't quite make up my mind. Sucker looked a little silly—walking like a drunk with his eyes glued to the movie. He was wiping his reading glasses on his shirttail and his knickers flopped down. He went on until he got to the first few rows where the kids usually sit. I never did punch Maybelle. But I got to thinking it was good to have both of them at the movie with the money I earned.

I guess things went on like this for about a month or six weeks. I felt so good I couldn't settle down to study or put my mind on anything. I wanted to be friendly with everybody. There were times when I just had to talk to some person. And usually that would be Sucker. He felt as good as I did. Once he said: "Pete, I am gladder that you are like my brother than anything else in the world."

Then something happened between Maybelle and me. I never have figured out just what it was. Girls like her are hard to understand. She began to act different toward me. At first I wouldn't let myself believe this and tried to think it was just my imagination. She didn't act glad to see me anymore. Often she went out riding with this fellow on the football team who owns this yellow roadster. The car was the color of her hair and after school she would ride off with him, laughing and looking into his face. I couldn't think of anything to do about it and she was on my mind all day and night. When I did get a chance to go out with her she was snippy and didn't seem to notice me. This made me feel like something was the matter—I would worry about my shoes clopping too loud on the floor, or the fly of my pants, or the bumps on my chin. Sometimes when Maybelle was around, a devil would get into me and I'd hold my face stiff and call grown men by their last names without the Mister and say rough things. In the night I would wonder what made me do all this until I was too tired for sleep.

At first I was so worried I just forgot about Sucker. Then later he began to get on my nerves. He was always hanging around until I would get back from high school, always looking like he had something to say to me or wanted me to tell him. He made me a magazine rack in his Manual Training class and one week he saved his lunch money and bought me three packs of cigarettes. He couldn't seem to take it in that I had things on my mind and didn't want to fool with him. Every afternoon it would be the same—him in my room with this waiting expression on his face. Then I wouldn't say anything or I'd maybe answer him rough-like and he would finally go on out.

I can't divide that time up and say this happened one day and that the next. For one thing I was so mixed up the weeks just slid along into each other and I felt like Hell and didn't care. Nothing definite was said or done. Maybelle still rode around with this fellow in his yellow roadster and sometimes she would smile at me and sometimes not. Every afternoon I went from one place to another where I thought she would be. Either she would act almost nice and I would begin thinking how things would finally

clear up and she would care for me—or else she'd behave
so that if she hadn't been a girl I'd have wanted to grab
her by that white little neck and choke her. The more
ashamed I felt for making a fool of myself the more I ran
after her.

Sucker kept getting on my nerves more and more. He
would look at me as though he sort of blamed me for
something, but at the same time knew that it wouldn't last
long. He was growing fast and for some reason began to
stutter when he talked. Sometimes he had nightmares or
would throw up his breakfast. Mom got him a bottle of cod
liver oil.

Then the finish came between Maybelle and me. I met
her going to the drugstore and asked for a date. When she
said no I remarked something sarcastic. She told me she
was sick and tired of my being around and that she had
never cared a rap about me. She said all that. I just stood
there and didn't answer anything. I walked home very
slowly.

For several afternoons I stayed in my room by myself.
I didn't want to go anywhere or talk to anyone. When
Sucker would come in and look at me sort of funny I'd yell
at him to get out. I didn't want to think of Maybelle and
I sat at my desk reading *Popular Mechanics* or whittling
at a toothbrush rack I was making. It seemed to me I was
putting that girl out of my mind pretty well.

But you can't help what happens to you at night. That
is what made things how they are now.

You see a few nights after Maybelle said those words to
me I dreamed about her again. It was like that first time
and I was squeezing Sucker's arm so tight I woke him up.
He reached for my hand.

"Pete, what's the matter with you?"

All of a sudden I felt so mad my throat choked—at myself and the dream and Maybelle and Sucker and every
single person I knew. I remembered all the times Maybelle
had humiliated me and everything bad that had ever

happened. It seemed to me for a second that nobody would ever like me but a sap like Sucker.

"Why is it we aren't buddies like we were before? Why—?"

"Shut your damn trap!" I threw off the cover and got up and turned on the light. He sat in the middle of the bed, his eyes blinking and scared.

There was something in me and I couldn't help myself. I don't think anybody ever gets that mad but once. Words came without me knowing what they would be. It was only afterward that I could remember each thing I said and see it all in a clear way.

"Why aren't we buddies? Because you're the dumbest slob I ever saw! Nobody cares anything about you! And just because I felt sorry for you sometimes and tried to act decent don't think I give a damn about a dumb-bunny like you!"

If I'd talked loud or hit him it wouldn't have been so bad. But my voice was slow and like I was very calm. Sucker's mouth was partway open and he looked as though he'd knocked his funny bone. His face was white and sweat came out on his forehead. He wiped it away with the back of his hand and for a minute his arm stayed raised that way as though he was holding something away from him.

"Don't you know a single thing? Haven't you ever been around at all? Why don't you get a girl friend instead of me? What kind of a sissy do you want to grow up to be anyway?"

I didn't know what was coming next. I couldn't help myself or think.

Sucker didn't move. He had on one of my pajama jackets and his neck stuck out skinny and small. His hair was damp on his forehead.

"Why do you always hang around me? Don't you know when you're not wanted?"

Afterward I could remember the change in Sucker's face. Slowly that blank look went away and he closed his mouth. His eyes got narrow and his fists shut. There had never been such a look on him before. It was like every second he was getting older. There was a hard look to his eyes you don't see usually in a kid. A drop of sweat rolled down his chin and he didn't notice. He just sat there with those eyes on me and he didn't speak and his face was hard and didn't move.

"No, you don't know when you're not wanted. You're too dumb. Just like your name—a dumb Sucker."

It was like something had busted inside me. I turned off the light and sat down in the chair by the window. My legs were shaking and I was so tired I could have bawled. The room was cold and dark. I sat there for a long time and smoked a squashed cigarette I had saved. Outside the yard was black and quiet. After a while I heard Sucker lie down.

I wasn't mad any more, only tired. It seemed awful to me that I had talked like that to a kid only twelve. I couldn't take it all in. I told myself I would go over to him and try to make it up. But I just sat there in the cold until a long time had passed. I planned how I could straighten it out in the morning. Then, trying not to squeak the springs, I got back in bed.

Sucker was gone when I woke up the next day. And later when I wanted to apologize as I had planned he looked at me in this new hard way so that I couldn't say a word.

All of that was two or three months ago. Since then Sucker has grown faster than any boy I ever saw. He's almost as tall as I am and his bones have gotten heavier and bigger. He won't wear any of my old clothes anymore and has bought his first pair of long pants—with some leather suspenders to hold them up. Those are just the changes that are easy to see and put into words.

Our room isn't mine at all anymore. He's gotten up this gang of kids and they have a club. When they aren't digging trenches in some vacant lot and fighting they are always in my room. On the door there is some foolishness written in Mercurochrome saying "Woe to the Outsider who Enters" and signed with crossed bones and their secret initials. They have rigged up a radio and every afternoon it blares out music. Once as I was coming in I heard a boy telling something in a low voice about what he saw in the back of his big brother's automobile. I could guess what I didn't hear. *That's what her and my brother do. It's the truth—parked in the car.* For a minute Sucker looked surprised and his face was almost like it used to be. Then he got hard and tough again. "Sure, dumbell. We know all that." They didn't notice me. Sucker began telling them how in two years he was planning to be a trapper in Alaska.

But most of the time Sucker stays by himself. It is worse when we are alone together in the room. He sprawls across the bed in those long corduroy pants with the suspenders and just stares at me with that hard, half-sneering look. I fiddle around my desk and can't get settled because of those eyes of his. And the thing is I just have to study because I've gotten three bad cards this term already. If I flunk English I can't graduate next year. I don't want to be a bum and I just have to get my mind on it. I don't care a flip for Maybelle or any particular girl anymore and it's only this thing between Sucker and me that is the trouble now. We never speak except when we have to before the family. I don't even want to call him Sucker anymore and unless I forget I call him by his real name, Richard. At night I can't study with him in the room and I have to hang around the drugstore, smoking and doing nothing, with the fellows who loaf there.

More than anything I want to be easy in my mind again. And I miss the way Sucker and I were for a while in a funny, sad way that before this I never would have believed. But everything is so different that there seems to be nothing I can do to get it right. I've sometimes thought if we could have it out in a big fight that would help. But I can't fight him because he's four years younger. And another thing—sometimes this look in his eyes makes me almost believe that if Sucker could he would kill me.

Tone and Mood

When you stop to think about it, it's amazing how much you can do with the tone of your voice. For example, read these two words aloud: *Oh, Dad.* Now see how many different ways you can say these words—just these two words—to give them a different feeling and a different meaning each time.

Raise your voice a little at the end and it means that you are about to ask a question. Say it sharply and it sounds as though you are peeved about something. Say it slowly, with a sob in your voice, and you express sympathy or sorrow. You can express fear, anger, joy, disgust—all with the way you adjust your tone of voice. The way you say the words—your tone—often provides more meaning for a listener than the words themselves.

Other things besides your voice can have tone as well. Music has tone. Places have tone. Think of the atmospheres or tones that you connect with a church, a school, a ballpark, and your home. People also have tone. A person in authority often projects an assertive, capable tone, while a clown projects a humorous tone.

Stories, or any writing for that matter, must have tone too. If an author fails to provide a variety of tones in a story, you soon become extremely bored with it. What is worse, you will have a very difficult time trying to figure out what the author wants you to know, feel, or understand about the story.

Tone carries with it a *mood*. Mood is a feeling or an emotion. A person may have a blue mood or a happy mood, a carefree mood or a troubled mood. He or she may be suspicious, angry, satisfied, eager, or disappointed. There is virtually no limit to the kinds of moods or feelings that a person may experience.

The tone of a march may put you in a patriotic mood. A love song may make you feel a bit dreamy. The tone of a church may inspire feelings of awe or reverence. The tone of a ballpark may make you feel carefree and excited.

Tone and mood are very similar because they both involve feelings. They are so similar, in fact, that many people say there is no difference at all between them. For our purposes, however, we will say that the difference is this: *Tone* is a manner, atmosphere, or attitude that carries, or conveys, a feeling. *Mood* is the feeling itself.

Here is how tone and mood work together in a story: As an author writes, he or she is in a particular mood, just as you are when you speak. The author feels a certain way about an idea or a character and expresses this mood or feeling through the tone of the story. You sense the tone as you read, you notice that the story has a certain mood. And if the author has successfully fashioned the tone and mood of the story, you begin to feel just the way he or she wants you to feel.

When you speak, there are several things that contribute to the tone you use to express your feelings. Your choice of words, the level of your voice, the expression on your face, and your movements all help to provide the tone that conveys your mood. An author, however, as we say many times in the lessons in this book, has only words to work with. As you have surely seen in the story you have just read, a good author provides exactly the tone needed to control the mood of the story and your mood as a reader as well.

In this lesson we will look at four things that help develop true-to-life tones and moods in Carson McCullers' story.

1 ◆ The author changes tones and moods to reflect the kinds of changes in tone and mood that occur in real life.

2 ◆ The author chooses words carefully to create the tones and moods she wants.

3 ◆ Characters and settings are used to create tone and mood.

4 ◆ Dialogue—conversation between characters—is used to create tone and mood.

1 ♦ Changing Tones and Moods

People's moods are like the weather—always changing. You may feel happy upon awakening, bored in a dull class, excited at a pep rally, nervous taking a test, thoughtful on your way home from school, and warm in the company of a favorite friend.

Tones change too—tones of place, people, and voices. Classrooms, gyms, auditoriums—all have their own sights, sounds, and smells that provide each with a special and different tone. The people whom you meet in your life all bring their own special tones with them. There is a difference between a severe principal and your favorite teacher. You sense a different tone in each, and each puts you in a different mood.

People and places are *dynamic*. This means they are always changing. And as they change, tones and moods change with them. For a story to be convincing, its tone and mood must change continually, just as happens in real life. These changes are what keep your interest alive. The changing tones and moods are used to pass along information that the author wants you to have about the characters and ideas in the story.

In the story "Sucker," Carson McCullers begins with a rather light tone. As a reader, you respond with a light mood. You are even somewhat amused at the way Pete keeps his room. But five paragraphs later, the tone has made a definite change. You begin to feel that something has gone wrong between Pete and Sucker. You feel a bit uneasy, just as Pete is worried and uneasy. Watch for the change in tone and mood between these two passages:

> It was always like I had a room to myself. Sucker slept in my bed with me but that didn't interfere with anything. The room was mine and I used it as I wanted to. Once I remember sawing a trap door in the floor. Last year . . . I tacked on my wall some pictures of girls from magazines and one of them was just in her underwear. My mother never bothered me because she had the younger kids to look after. And Sucker thought anything I did was always swell.

The passage above has a light, amusing tone. Both boys seem comfortable and satisfied with the way things are at this point. The mood is comfortable. But notice how different the tone and its corresponding mood are in this passage:

> Now that Sucker has changed so much it is a little hard to remember him as he used to be. I never imagined anything would suddenly happen that would make us both very different. I never knew that in order to get what has happened straight in my mind I would want to think back on him as he used to be and compare and try to get things settled. If I could have seen ahead maybe I would have acted different.

Pete has become thoughtful and a bit sad. The author used the change of tone between the two passages to do two things. She communicates Pete's new feeling to you to let you know that things are not as they should be between the two boys, and she makes you worry about this a bit, just as Pete is worried. What this does, of course, is draw you into the story as you become anxious to know what has caused the tone of the story, and Pete's mood, to go from light to heavy or threatening.

1 ⬥ Exercise A

Read the following passages and answer the questions about them using what you have learned in this part of the lesson. Use your writing notebook or a separate piece of paper for your answers.

Passage A

> We talked for a good while that night. His voice was fast and it was like he had been saving up these things to tell me for a long time. . . . I talked some too and it was a good feeling to think of him taking in everything I said so seriously. . . . His voice was excited and he kept on talking fast like he could never get the words out in time. When I went to sleep he was still talking and I could still feel his breathing on my shoulder, warm and close.

Passage B

> At first I was so worried I just forgot about Sucker. Then later he began to get on my nerves. . . . He couldn't seem

to take it in that I had things on my mind and didn't want to fool with him. Every afternoon it would be the same— him in my room with this waiting expression on his face. Then I wouldn't say anything or I'd maybe answer him rough-like and he would finally go on out.

1. Find words or phrases that show a change of feeling from one passage to the next. (Example: warm and close—rough-like)

2. What is the difference between the two passages as far as the mood or feeling expressed by the author is concerned?

Now check your answers using the suggestions in the Answer Key starting on page 457. Review this part of the lesson if you don't understand why an answer was wrong.

1♦Writing on Your Own

Look at the sentences you have written for Using Tone to Describe Moods on page 271. Now do the following:

1. In one set of the sentences you showed how a mood can change rather quickly. Using each sentence, write two short paragraphs that show how a person's mood can change from cheerful to depressed.

2. You may want to change and rewrite your paragraphs several times until you get them just the way you want them.

2 ♦ Tone, Mood, and Word Choice

If you were to receive a gift of striped socks for your birthday, you might say, "Gee, thanks. That was very thoughtful of you. I do like striped socks."

But if you were given a new pet, a puppy that you'd wanted for years, you would probably explode with, "A dog! Just what I've always wanted! Oh, thank you!"

In both cases, you would have expressed your appreciation for a gift. But it wouldn't have been hard to tell from your tone of voice how you felt about a new puppy as compared to a pair of socks. Your choice of words and the way you said the words would have created a tone that gave away your feelings—your mood.

In much the same way, an author might describe a sunrise in a story in a number of different ways:

A sudden burst of gold announced a glorious new day.

The merciless ball of fire crept over the barren hills.

Dawn broke on another day.

All of these sentences express the same idea—morning has come. But, in each case, the choice of words creates a tone that would clearly show how the author and the characters in a story felt about the arrival of a new day.

When Maybelle is described in "Sucker," you can tell at once, from the tone of the description, how the author feels about Maybelle and how she wants *you* to feel about her. And, of course, you can tell how poor Pete feels. All of this information is conveyed by just the right choice of words.

> Maybelle was somehow mixed up in what happened so I guess I ought to start with her. Until I knew her I hadn't given much time to girls. Last fall she sat next to me in General Science class and that was when I first began to notice her. Her hair is the brightest yellow I ever saw and occasionally she will wear it set into curls with some sort of gluey stuff. Her fingernails are pointed and manicured and painted a shiny red. All during class I used to watch Maybelle, nearly all the time except when I thought she

was going to look my way or when the teacher called on me. I couldn't keep my eyes off her hands, for one thing. They are very little and white except for that red stuff, and when she would turn the pages of her book she always . . . held out her little finger and turned very slowly.

Poor Pete seems to be struck dumb by Maybelle's "great beauty." But, from the tone the author creates with a few choice words in just the right place, readers know just how to feel about Maybelle. Maybelle's hair is bright yellow and "set into curls *with some sort of gluey stuff.*" Her hands, which Pete loves to watch, are very small and white *"except for that red stuff."* Through her choice of words, Carson McCullers creates a tone that says, in effect, "I think Maybelle is a pretty little snob. And I'm sure, dear reader, that you will feel the same way when I get through with her."

2 ◆ Exercise B

Read the following passage and answer the questions about it using what you have learned in this part of the lesson. Use your writing notebook or a separate piece of paper for your answers.

Afterward I could remember the change in Sucker's face. Slowly that blank look went away and he closed his mouth. His eyes got narrow and his fists shut. There had never been such a look on him before. It was like every second he was getting older. There was a hard look to his eyes you don't see usually in a kid. A drop of sweat rolled down his chin and he didn't notice. He just sat there with those eyes on me and he didn't speak and his face was hard and didn't move.

1. The author describes Sucker's body language to set the tone of the passage and to show Sucker's feelings. Make a list of those signs. (There are at least six.)

2. How did Sucker's feelings toward Pete change? If you were Pete, how would you feel with Sucker staring at you, knowing you had hurt him?

Now check your answers using the suggestions in the Answer Key starting on page 457. Review this part of the lesson if you don't understand why an answer was wrong.

2◆Writing on Your Own

Look at the sentences you have written for Using Tone to Describe Moods on page 271. Now do the following:

1. Plan to write two short paragraphs: one that tells how happy you are to be with a special person, and another that tells how you feel when you can't be with that person. Plan your paragraphs by making lists of words or phrases that describe your feelings. Make a separate list for each paragraph.

2. Write the paragraphs.

3. You may want to change and rewrite your paragraphs several times until you get them just the way you want them.

3 ♦ Tone and Mood—Characters and Setting

In earlier lessons you learned how authors use setting and characters to provide just the right atmosphere for the action in their stories. The same sort of thing is done all the time in TV commercials. If a sponsor wants to create a macho image for a product, the scene might be set in a hot, dry valley. The action might include cowboys doing chores that require strength and endurance. On the other hand, in a commercial for a luxury item, the scene may be the front of a fine theater or mansion, and the actors might be dressed in expensive formal attire. Characters and setting are used to create any tone the sponsor wants to project. It is hoped, of course, that the tone will influence your mood and make you want to buy the products that you see advertised.

There are three characters in "Sucker." Each creates a special feeling. There are two settings. Most of the story is set in the bedroom that the boys share. But there is one scene in which the three characters appear together in a movie theater. Let's look at that scene first. Then in Exercise C you can examine one of the scenes in the boys' room. Each setting and the characters involved create a different tone and mood.

> Once I started to point him out to Maybelle and tell her he was my kid brother. It was an afternoon when a murder mystery was on at the movie. . . . We were sitting near the back and I saw Sucker come in. He began to stare at the screen the minute he stepped past the ticket man and he stumbled down the aisle without noticing where he was going. I started to punch Maybelle but couldn't quite make up my mind. Sucker looked a little silly—walking like a drunk with his eyes glued to the movie. He was wiping his reading glasses on his shirttail and his knickers flopped down. He went on until he got to the first few rows where the kids usually sit. I never did punch Maybelle. But I got to thinking it was good to have both of them at the movie with the money I earned.

Notice that whenever Sucker appears you tend to feel sympathetic toward him. Pete is always a bit edgy. In this scene he feels warm and good about having done something nice for Sucker, but he also feels embarrassed by Sucker in Maybelle's presence. Maybelle has a chilling effect on this scene, as she does on other parts of the story.

The movie theater is used in much the same way the boys' room is used. It brings the characters together in a close, quiet atmosphere.

3 ◆ Exercise C

Read the following passages and answer the questions about them using what you have learned in this part of the lesson. Use your writing notebook or a separate piece of paper for your answers.

> It was that night when this trouble really started. I had come into my room late and Sucker was already asleep. I felt too happy and keyed up to get in a comfortable position and I was awake thinking about Maybelle a long time. Then I dreamed about her and it seemed I kissed her. It was a surprise to wake up and see the dark. I lay still and a little while passed before I could come to and understand where I was. The house was quiet and it was a very dark night. . . .

> [Sucker talks with Pete]

> Then I got up for a few minutes. It was cold and I was glad to come back to bed. Sucker hung on to my back. He felt little and warm and I could feel his warm breathing on my shoulder. . . .
> There is something about a dark cold night that makes you feel close to someone you're sleeping with. When you talk together it is like you are the only people awake in the town.

1. How are the house and the night described so that they set the tone for this scene?

2. In contrast to the feeling created by the night, Pete's feeling toward Sucker is described as warm and close. This is an example of how an author can emphasize a character's mood by creating an *opposite* kind of tone in the setting. When it is storming and threatening outside, why do you often feel safe, warm, and secure in your home?

Now check your answers using the suggestions in the Answer Key starting on page 457. Review this part of the lesson if you don't understand why an answer was wrong.

3 ♦ Writing on Your Own

Look at the sentences you have written for Using Tone to Describe Moods on page 271. Now do the following:

1. You have written two sentences that describe two different characters—one whom you like and one whom you don't like. Plan to write two or three paragraphs about one of these people.

2. In your planning, think of a scene where you will appear with this person.

3. Write your paragraphs describing what goes on between you and the other person. In your paragraphs describe the setting and how you feel.

4. You may want to change and rewrite your paragraphs several times until you get them just the way you want them.

4 ◆ Tone, Mood, and Dialogue

Authors often set the tones and express the moods of stories in much the same way you set the tone and mood of situations when you speak. They use dialogue—conversation between characters. There are only two examples of dialogue in "Sucker," but between them, they sum up the two major moods of the story. We will look at the first example below, and you can study the second yourself in Exercise D.

> The house was quiet and it was a very dark night.
> Sucker's voice was a shock to me. "Pete? . . ."
> I didn't answer anything or even move.
> "You do like me as much as if I was your own brother, don't you Pete?"
> I couldn't get over the surprise of everything and it was like this was the real dream instead of the other.
> "You have liked me all the time like I was your own brother, haven't you?"
> "Sure," I said. . . .
> "No matter what you did I always knew you liked me."
> I was wide awake and my mind seemed mixed up in a strange way. There was this happiness about Maybelle and all that—but at the same time something about Sucker and his voice when he said these things made me take notice.

Pete is in a happy mood because Maybelle has finally noticed him. It is at this point that Sucker makes his very moving appeal for love. Sucker is an orphan, remember, and has probably always felt like an outsider in this family. Pete's habit of ignoring Sucker certainly hasn't helped matters.

To set the tone for this moment, Carson McCullers did two things. First, she established a feeling of closeness between the boys on a cold, dark night. (You saw this in the passage used in Exercise C.) Then she made the dialogue very simple. That is how conversation usually is when people are expressing very deep feelings.

"You do like me . . . You have liked me . . ." is Sucker's simple appeal. "Sure," Pete says. And that's all Sucker wants to hear. That simple dialogue sets the tone and mood of the scene.

4 ♦ Exercise D

Read the following passage and answer the questions about it using what you have learned in this part of the lesson. Use your writing notebook or a separate piece of paper for your answers.

> "Pete, what's the matter with you?"
>
> All of a sudden I felt so mad my throat choked—at myself and the dream and Maybelle and Sucker and every single person I knew. I remembered all the times Maybelle had humiliated me and everything bad that had ever happened. It seemed to me for a second that nobody would ever like me but a sap like Sucker.
>
> "Why is it we aren't buddies like we were before? Why—?"
>
> "Shut your damn trap!" I threw off the cover and got up and turned on the light. He sat in the middle of the bed, his eyes blinking and scared.
>
> There was something in me and I couldn't help myself. I don't think anybody ever gets that mad but once. Words came without me knowing what they would be. . . .
>
> "Why aren't we buddies? Because you're the dumbest slob I ever saw! Nobody cares anything about you! And just because I felt sorry for you sometimes and tried to act decent don't think I give a damn about a dumb-bunny like you!"
>
> If I'd talked loud or hit him it wouldn't have been so bad. But my voice was slow and like I was very calm.

1. Both the tone of the passage and the mood of the character, Pete, express uncontrolled and unreasonable anger. Why do you think Pete's anger was uncontrolled and unreasonable?

2. The author describes Pete's tone of voice as slow and calm. Why do you think this tone hurt Sucker more than a loud angry tone might have?

Now check your answers using the suggestions in the Answer Key starting on page 457. Review this part of the lesson if you don't understand why an answer was wrong.

4♦Writing on Your Own

Look at the sentences you have written for Using Tone to Describe Moods on page 271. Now do the following:

1. You have written two conversations between two people. In one conversation they express a liking for each other. In the other conversation they dislike each other.

2. Choose one of the conversations. Rewrite it and expand the conversation to at least two notebook pages.

3. As the conversation goes along, show how the mood can change. For example, one person may start angry and end the conversation in a more quiet tone. The other person may begin with a happy tone and end up crying.

4. You may want to change and rewrite your conversation several times until you get it just the way you want it.

Now go on to Reviewing and Interpreting the Story section.

Reviewing and Interpreting the Story

Answer these questions without looking back at the story. Choose the best answer to each question and put an *x* in the box beside it, or write your answer on a separate piece of paper.

Remembering
Facts

1. Pete and Sucker are

   ☐ a. brothers.

   ☐ b. cousins.

   ☐ c. friends.

   ☐ d. unrelated.

2. When Pete went to the movies with Maybelle

   ☐ a. he paid for both Sucker and Maybelle.

   ☐ b. Sucker had to pay his own way.

   ☐ c. they each paid their own way.

   ☐ d. his parents paid for everyone.

Following the
Order of Events

3. When did Pete first begin to act kindly toward Sucker?

   ☐ a. after the date at the movies

   ☐ b. when Maybelle became tired of Pete

   ☐ c. when Sucker broke his knee

   ☐ d. when Maybelle began to pay attention to Pete

4. Which of the following events happened first?

    ☐ a. Pete told Sucker he was a slob.

    ☐ b. Pete saw Sucker at the movies.

    ☐ c. Pete told Sucker that he liked him.

    ☐ d. Pete visited Maybelle at her home.

Understanding
Word Choices
5. "Maybelle Watts . . . acted like she was the Queen of Sheba and even <u>humiliated</u> me." The word *humiliated* means

    ☐ a. uplifted.

    ☐ b. amazed.

    ☐ c. embarrassed.

    ☐ d. horrified.

6. "He used to look <u>timid</u> and sort of like he was afraid of a whack over the head." The word *timid* means

    ☐ a. shy or afraid.

    ☐ b. ignorant or stupid.

    ☐ c. funny or laughable.

    ☐ d. confused or muddled.

Understanding
Important Ideas
7. Which one of the following quotations from the story best sums up a very important thought Pete had?

    ☐ a. "Whenever I would bring any of my friends back to my room all I had to do was just glance once at Sucker and he would get up . . . and leave. . . ."

    ☐ b. "Maybelle was somehow mixed up in what happened so I guess I ought to start with her."

    ☐ c. "If a person admires you a lot you despise him and don't care—and it is the person who doesn't notice you that you are apt to admire."

    ☐ d. "Once I started to point him out to Maybelle and tell her he was my kid brother."

8. Which one of the following quotations from the beginning of the story best sums up what the story is about?

    ☐ a. "Yet at this same time I would have done anything in the world to get her attentions."

    ☐ b. "I never imagined anything would suddenly happen that would make us both very different."

    ☐ c. "I never noticed him much or thought about him. . . ."

    ☐ d. "Maybelle was somehow mixed up in what happened so I guess I ought to start with her."

Understanding
Levels of
Meaning

9. Which one of these ideas is suggested in the story?

    ☐ a. Maybelle and Pete were plotting against Sucker.

    ☐ b. It was Sucker's fault that Pete and Maybelle broke up.

    ☐ c. It is better if young people don't have strong feelings about other people.

    ☐ d. Maybelle treated Pete much the same as Pete treated Sucker.

10. At the movies, Pete started to point out Sucker to Maybelle, but he decided not to. Why do you think Pete didn't tell Maybelle about Sucker?

☐ a. Pete was embarrassed by Sucker's appearance.

☐ b. Pete was too much in love with Maybelle to think of Sucker.

☐ c. Maybelle didn't give Pete a chance to talk.

☐ d. Sucker was too timid to meet Maybelle.

11. Which one of the following quotations from the story marks the big change in Sucker's character?

☐ a. "It was that night when this trouble really started. I had come into my room late and Sucker was already asleep."

☐ b. "Slowly that blank look went away and he closed his mouth. His eyes got narrow and his fists shut."

☐ c. "During the next couple of weeks I saw a lot of Maybelle. She acted as though she really cared for me a little."

☐ d. "Then something happened between Maybelle and me. I never have figured out just what it was."

12. At the beginning of the story Pete says: "The room was mine. . . ." Near the end of the story he says: "Our room isn't mine any more." This change suggests that Sucker

☐ a. is probably pleased that he and Pete are no longer friends.

☐ b. and Pete have finally learned to share.

- [ ] c. has changed because he has gone from knickers to long pants.
- [ ] d. is not timid any more where Pete is concerned.

13. Much of the action takes place in the room that Pete and Sucker share. Why is this a good setting for examining the interaction between them?

- [ ] a. Boys fight more over their rooms than anything else.
- [ ] b. The two characters can be observed at close quarters.
- [ ] c. It makes the story a matter of turf warfare.
- [ ] d. It shows how poor the family is.

14. The setting in the movie theater is used to show one of Pete's feelings at that time. Which one of the following quotations from the story best describes Pete's feelings in the movie theater?

- [ ] a. "His face seemed different now."
- [ ] b. "Then something happened between Maybelle and me."
- [ ] c. ". . . it was good to have both of them . . ."
- [ ] d. ". . . he stumbled down the aisle without noticing where he was going."

15. Which one of the following statements best describes Sucker's feelings early in the story?

- [ ] a. He is jealous of Maybelle.
- [ ] b. He is lonesome.
- [ ] c. He misses his mother.
- [ ] d. He is afraid of Pete.

16. Which one of the following statements expresses how Pete felt after breaking up with Maybelle?

☐ a. He feels it is part of growing up.

☐ b. He was pleased that she still noticed him sometimes.

☐ c. He is lonesome.

☐ d. He was worried because now Sucker was always on his mind.

Now check your answers using the Answer Key starting on page 457. Make no mark for right answers. Correct any wrong answers you may have by putting a check mark (✓) in the box next to the right answer. Count the number of questions you answered correctly and plot the total on the Comprehension Scores graph on page 468.

Next, look at the questions you answered incorrectly. What types of questions were they? Count the number you got wrong of each type and enter the numbers in the spaces below.

Remembering Facts _____

Following the Order of Events _____

Understanding Word Choices _____

Understanding Important Ideas _____

Understanding Levels of Meaning _____

Understanding Character _____

Understanding Setting _____

Understanding Feelings _____

Now use these numbers to fill in the Comprehension Skills Profile on page 469.

Discussion Guides

The questions below will help you think about the story and the lesson you have just read. If you don't discuss these questions in class, try to think about them or discuss them with your classmates. Perhaps you will want to write a few paragraphs in answer to the questions.

Discussing Tone and Mood

1. One explanation of tone is that it is the author's attitude toward a character, a situation, or an idea in a story. It is a reflection of the author's mood—how she feels. It is clear that the author is sympathetic toward Sucker and that she doesn't like Maybelle. How does the author feel about Pete? And how is her attitude reflected in the tone of the story?

2. Early in the story, Pete feels close to Sucker in their cold, dark, quiet room. Later, after Pete's cruel outburst at Sucker, he says, "My legs were shaking and I was so tired I could have bawled. The room was cold and dark. . . . Outside the yard was black and quiet." What makes the tone of these two scenes, which take place in the very same setting, so entirely different?

3. In the last part of the story, the author emphasizes the look in Sucker's eyes. How do Sucker's eyes affect tone and mood in the story? Drawing on your own experience, describe how people's eyes can affect tones and moods in real life.

Discussing the Story

4. Sucker wanted Pete to like him. Pete wanted Maybelle to like him. Maybelle wanted many boys to like her. And it seemed that no one was happy. Why do you think this is so?

5. Pete presents a puzzle at the beginning of the story. He says, "There is one thing . . . makes me feel guilty and hard to figure out. If a person admires you a lot you despise him and don't care—and it is the person who doesn't notice you that you are apt to admire." This is true in many relationships. Describe a situation like this from your own experience.

6. People change in this story. Pete tells you at the beginning of the story that people have changed. He says, "Sucker has changed so much. . . . I never imagined anything would suddenly happen that

would make us both very different." Make a list of the ways in which Sucker was different at the end of the story. How was Pete different?

Discussing the Author's Work

7. It has been said that in nearly all her stories Carson McCullers wrote about loneliness. Is this story about loneliness? Explain your answer.

8. It has also been said that once you know that Carson McCullers suffered from a severe physical disability, you can find many characters in her stories who also suffer disabilities. What handicaps do you think the characters in this story have?

9. Carson McCullers' best-known book is titled *The Heart Is a Lonely Hunter*. Why might this also be a good title for the story you have just read? (The title comes from a poem by William Sharp that begins, "My heart is a lonely hunter that hunts on a lonely hill.")

Writing Exercise

Read all the instructions before you begin writing. If you have any questions about how to begin the writing assignment, review Using the Writing Process beginning on page 445, or confer with your writing coach.

1. At the beginning of the unit you were asked to write sentences that express tones and moods in different ways. If you haven't done this yet, read the instructions for Using Tone to Describe Moods on page 271, and write these sentences now.

2. Write a short story about someone with whom you were once friendly, but now have fallen out. In the story tell about how it was when you were friends, how it was when you fell out with the person, and how you feel about it now.

3. Try to use words, characters, settings, and conversations to set the tones of your story and express the moods.

4. Write, revise, correct, and rewrite your story until you are sure you have got it just the way you want it.

Unit 8   Folk Story

Naftali the Storyteller and His Horse, Sus
BY ISAAC BASHEVIS SINGER

About the Illustration

How would you describe this scene? Point out some details in the drawing to support your response.

Here are some questions to help you think about the story:

◆ What do the children's style of dress and the man's tell you about them and about where they live?

◆ How can you tell that the story is set in another place and time?

◆ What do you think the man and the children are doing?

◆ Why do you think the horse is there?

Unit 8

Introduction

About the Story

"Naftali the Storyteller and His Horse, Sus" is set in Poland, about a hundred years ago. At that time Poland had a large Jewish population. Many of the Jews lived in small rural villages called *shtetls* (SHTE-tels). They had their own language (Yiddish), customs, and traditions. Learning played an important part in their lives, especially as it applied to their religion and to their role in life as Jews.

Naftali grew up in a Polish shtetl. His father was a coachman and it was expected that, like other boys, Naftali would follow his father's trade. But Naftali had other ideas. He had become interested in stories and storytelling. He could not live without stories, he said. So, to be close to what he loved best, he decided to become a traveling bookseller. He bought some books and built a wagon, which he trained his horse to pull. The horse was his beloved Sus.

You will find this story to be a very easy one. It has no conflict and therefore very little plot. It simply tells about Naftali and how he spent his life as a bookseller. What makes the story interesting is the ideas it contains and the pictures it creates in your mind. It gives you a view of a kind of life you probably aren't familiar with. And it stirs your imagination. If you could do anything you wanted to do for a living, what would it be? Would you bring good to the world? Or would you be interested only in money?

"Naftali the Storyteller and His Horse, Sus" is written as a folk story. Among other things, this means it is designed to teach a lesson. What it teaches is the value of reading. In a very simple way, it discusses many of the ideas you have been dealing with throughout this book. But don't be fooled by the simplicity of the story. The ideas run deep and the lessons are very important, as you will see.

Isaac Bashevis Singer was born in Poland in 1904. He was the son and grandson of rabbis and knew the shtetl life very well. He came to the United States in 1935 and has lived in New York City most of his life. Though he speaks and writes English perfectly well, he prefers to write his stories in Yiddish. They are then translated into English and many other languages. "I had to stay with my language," he said, "and with the people whom I know best. If you write about the things and the people you know best, you discover your roots."

In more than fifty years as a writer, Isaac Singer has written a huge number of stories that have been published throughout the world in newspapers, magazines, and books. He has won many awards for his work. In 1978 he won his highest award, the Nobel Prize in literature. Some people collect Isaac Singer stories, trying to see if they can find all of them. You may want to do the same. Start with his short stories. *Gimpel the Fool and Other Stories* is one of his most famous collections. Some of his novels are *The Family Moskat, The Magician of Lublin, The Manor,* and *The Slave.*

Because this story takes place in another country, among a group of people who have a language and customs that are probably foreign to you, it contains some words and expressions that you may not be familiar with. Some of these words and expressions are listed here, in the order in which they appear in the story. The definitions and explanations will help you to understand their importance to the characters in the story.

Yiddish. A language that evolved from German during

the Middle Ages. Jews carried the language with them when they went to Poland and Russia.

Reb. A title of respect, as in Reb Zebulun and Reb Falik—two characters in the story. It is usually reserved for learned, prominent, or wealthy people.

groshen. a coin worth very little

Pentateuch. Consists of the first five books of the Bible, the books given by Moses. It is the most important part of the Bible for Jews—often called the Law.

Yeshiva. A school that teaches general subjects but emphasizes religious studies.

Cossack. Russian cavalryman in the czarist army. They were famous for their horsemanship and for their brutality, especially toward the Jews of Russia and Poland.

cabalists. A special sect of Jews who lead simple, religious lives and believe that they have certain knowledge—some of it mystical and magical—that brings them closer to God.

Succoth. Jewish harvest festival of thanksgiving occurring in the fall

Western Wall. or Wailing Wall, is the last remains of the Temple at Jerusalem, destroyed by the Romans. A very holy place for Jews

Cave of Machpelah. The place where Abraham was buried. He is considered the founder of Judaism.

Rachel's Tomb. Rachel was the wife of Jacob, an important figure in the Old Testament of the Bible. She is considered an ancestor of some of the tribes of Israel.

Hasidim. members of a very religious Jewish sect

Passover. a major Jewish holiday celebrating the Jews' exodus from slavery in Egypt

Scriptures. the books of the Bible

About the Lesson

The lesson that follows the story is about folk stories. Stories are as old as the human race. In fact, the ability to imagine stories and tell them is one of the things that separates people from the beasts. Isaac Singer tells us about the importance of storytelling and imagining stories in "Naftali the Storyteller and His Horse, Sus."

Simple stories that have been told and retold for so long that their authors have been lost or forgotten are called folk stories. Long before they were written down and put into books, they were passed on by word of mouth. Such stories have special characteristics that mark them as folktales, or folk stories. You will learn about these characteristics in the lesson.

Some authors, such as Isaac Singer, like to write stories in a *folk style*. Stories in this style are not real folktales, because they were not passed down through generations by word of mouth, but they do contain the characteristics of a folktale. "Naftali the Storyteller" illustrates many of the elements of a true folktale.

The questions below will help you focus on the special features of a folk story as you read. Read the story carefully and try to answer these questions as you go along:

◆ How would you describe the style of the story? Is it difficult or easy? Is the language elaborate or plain and simple?

◆ Magic and fantasy occur in two places in the story. Can you find these two places? Make a note of them when you find them.

◆ What do you learn about the times and the Jewish people in Poland from reading the story?

◆ What lessons do you learn from the story about living a good and useful life?

Create Your Own Folk Story

The first step you take when you create your own story is to choose an idea. What will my story be about? Discuss ideas with your classmates, or try the following suggestions. Use your writing notebook or a separate piece of paper to list your ideas.

1. Here are some ideas to help you get started with your story.

   □ Every culture has its own folk stories and fables that teach a lesson. Investigate your own heritage for ideas. Ask your parents and grandparents about the stories they heard as children. Find out more about the folklore, legends, myths, superstitions, and customs of your family's culture.

   □ Aesop's fables are famous throughout the world. In those stories animals talk. You may want a talking animal as a character in your story or as the main character.

   □ Where will your story take place? A different country? A city? A forest?

2. Make a list of the ideas, people, places, and events that will be in your story. Your list should include

   □ who is in the story (character)
   □ where the story will take place (setting)
   □ what the story will be about (theme or moral)

3. Rewrite your list putting the events in the order in which they will occur in the story. Rewrite your list until you get the order just the way you want it.

Naftali the Storyteller and His Horse, Sus

by Isaac Bashevis Singer

I

The father, Zelig, and the mother, Bryna, both complained that their son, Naftali, loved stories too much. He could never go to sleep unless his mother first told him a story. At times she had to tell him two or three stories before he would close his eyes. He always demanded: "Mama, more, more! . . ."

Fortunately, Bryna had heard many stories from her mother and grandmother. Zelig himself, a coachman, had many things to tell—about spirits who posed as passengers and imps who stole into stables at night and wove braids into the horses' tails and elflocks into their manes. The nicest story was about when Zelig had still been a young coachman.

One summer night Zelig was coming home from Lublin with an empty wagon. It just so happened that he hadn't picked up any passengers from Lublin to his hometown, Janów. He drove along a road that ran through a forest. There was a full moon. It cast silvery nets over the pine branches and strings of pearls over the bark of the tree trunks. Night birds cried. From time to time a wolf's howl was heard. In those days the Polish woods still swarmed with bears, wolves, foxes, martens, and many other wild beasts. That night Zelig was despondent. When his wagon was empty of passengers, his wallet was empty of money, and there wouldn't be enough for Bryna to prepare for the Sabbath.

Suddenly Zelig saw lying in the road a sack that appeared to be full of flour or ground sugar. Zelig stopped his horse and got down to take a look. A sack of flour or sugar would come in handy in a household.

Zelig untied the sack, opened it, took a lick, and decided that it was ground sugar. He lifted the sack, which was unusually heavy. Zelig was accustomed to carrying his passengers' baggage and he wondered why a sack of sugar should feel so heavy.

"It seems I didn't have enough to eat at the inn," Zelig thought. "And when you don't eat enough, you lose your strength."

He loaded the sack into the wagon. It was so heavy that he nearly strained himself.

He sat down on the driver's box and pulled on the reins, but the horse didn't move.

Zelig tugged harder and cried out, *"Wyszta!"* which in Polish means "Giddap!"

But even though the horse pulled with all his might, the wagon still wouldn't move forward.

"What's going on here?" Zelig wondered. "Can the sack be so heavy that the horse cannot pull it?"

This made no sense, for the horse had often drawn a wagonful of passengers along with their baggage.

"There is something here that's not as it should be," Zelig said to himself. He got down again, untied the sack, and took another lick. God in heaven, the sack was full of salt, not sugar!

Zelig stood there dumfounded. How could he have made such a mistake? He licked again, and again, and it was salt.

"Well, it's one of those nights!" Zelig mumbled to himself.

He decided to heave the sack off the wagon, since it was clear that evil spirits were toying with him. But by now the sack had become as heavy as if it were filled with lead.

The horse turned his head backward and stared, as if curious to what was going on.

Suddenly Zelig heard laughter coming from inside the sack. Soon afterward the sack crumbled and out popped a creature with the eyes of a calf, the horns of a goat, and the wings of a bat. The creature said in a human voice, "You didn't lick sugar or salt but an imp's tail."

And with these words the imp burst into wild laughter and flew away.

Dozens of times Zelig the coachman told this same story to Naftali but Naftali never grew tired of hearing it. He could picture it all—the forest, the night, the silver moon, the curious eye of the horse, the imp. Naftali asked all kinds of questions: Did the imp have a beard? Did it have feet? How did its tail look? Where did it fly off to?

Zelig couldn't answer all the questions. He had been too frightened at the time to notice the details. But to the last question Zelig replied, "He probably flew to beyond the Dark Regions, where people don't go and cattle don't stray, where the sky is copper, the earth iron, and where the evil forces live under roofs of petrified toadstools and in tunnels abandoned by moles."

II

Like all the children in town, Naftali rose early to go to cheder. He studied more diligently than the other children. Why? Because Naftali was eager to learn to read. He had seen older boys reading storybooks and he had been envious of them. How happy was one who could read a story from a book!

At six, Naftali was already able to read a book in Yiddish, and from then on he read every storybook he could get his hands on. Twice a year a bookseller named Reb Zebulun visited Janów, and among the other books in the sack he carried over his shoulder were some storybooks. They cost two groshen a copy, and although Naftali got only two groshen a week allowance from his father, he saved up enough to buy a number of storybooks each season. He also read the stories in his mother's Yiddish Pentateuch and in her books of morals.

When Naftali grew older, his father began to teach him how to handle horses. It was the custom in those days for a son to take over his father's livelihood. Naftali loved horses very much but he wasn't anxious to become a coachman driving passengers from Janów to Lublin and from Lublin to Janów. He wanted to become a bookseller with a sackful of storybooks.

His mother said to him, "What's so good about being a bookseller? From toting the sack day in day out, your back becomes bent, and from all the walking, your legs swell."

Naftali knew that his mother was right and he thought a lot about what he would do when he grew up. Suddenly he came up with a plan that seemed to him both wise and simple. He would get himself a horse and wagon, and instead of carrying the books on his back, he would carry them in the wagon.

His father, Zelig, said, "A bookseller doesn't make enough to support himself, his family, and a horse besides."

"For me it will be enough."

One time when Reb Zebulun the bookseller came to town, Naftali had a talk with him. He asked him where he got the storybooks and who wrote them. The bookseller told him that in Lublin there was a printer who printed these books, and in Warsaw and Vilna there were writers who wrote them. Reb Zebulun said that he could sell many more storybooks, but he lacked the strength to walk to all the towns and villages, and it didn't pay him to do so.

Reb Zebulun said, "I'm liable to come to a town where there are only two or three children who want to read storybooks. It doesn't pay me to walk there for the few groshen I might earn nor does it pay me to keep a horse or hire a wagon."

"What do these children do without storybooks?" Naftali asked. And Reb Zebulun replied, "They have to make do. Storybooks aren't bread. You can live without them."

"I couldn't live without them," Naftali said.

During this conversation Naftali also asked where the writers got all these stories and Reb Zebulun said, "First of all, many unusual things happen in the world. A day doesn't go by without some rare event happening. Besides, there are writers who make up such stories."

"They make them up?" Naftali asked in amazement. "If that is so, then they are liars."

"They are not liars," Reb Zebulun replied. "The human brain really can't make up a thing. At times I read a story that seems to me completely unbelievable, but I come to some place and I hear that such a thing actually happened. The brain is created by God, and human thoughts and fantasies are also God's works. Even dreams come from God. If a thing doesn't happen today, it might easily happen tomorrow. If not in one country, then in another. There are endless worlds and what doesn't happen on earth can happen in another world. Whoever has eyes that see and ears that hear absorbs enough stories to last a lifetime and to tell to his children and grandchildren."

That's what old Reb Zebulun said, and Naftali listened to his words agape.

Finally, Naftali said, "When I grow up, I'll travel to all the cities, towns, and villages, and I'll sell storybooks everywhere, whether it pays me or not."

Naftali had decided on something else too—to become a writer of storybooks. He knew full well that for this you had to study, and with all his heart he determined to learn. He also began to listen more closely to what people said, to what stories they told, and to how they told them. Each person had his or her own manner of speaking. Reb Zebulun told Naftali, "When a day passes, it is no longer there. What remains of it? Nothing more than a story. If stories weren't told or books weren't written, man would live like the beasts, only for the day."

Reb Zebulun said, "Today we live, but by tomorrow today will be a story. The whole world, all human life, is one long story."

III

Ten years went by. Naftali was now a young man. He grew up tall, slim, fair-skinned, with black hair and blue eyes. He had learned a lot at the studyhouse and in the yeshiva and he was also an expert horseman. Zelig's mare had borne a colt and Naftali pastured and raised it. He called him Sus. Sus was a playful colt. In the summer he liked to roll in the grass. He whinnied like the tinkling sound of a bell. Sometimes, when Naftali washed and curried him and tickled his neck, Sus burst out in a sound that resembled laughter. Naftali rode him bareback like a Cossack. When Naftali passed the marketplace astride Sus, the town girls ran to the windows to look out.

After a while Naftali built himself a wagon. He ordered the wheels from Leib the blacksmith. Naftali loaded the wagon with all the storybooks he had collected during the years and he rode with his horse and his goods to the nearby towns. Naftali bought a whip, but he swore solemnly to himself that he would never use it. Sus didn't need to be whipped or even to have the whip waved at him. He pulled the light wagonful of books eagerly and easily. Naftali seldom sat on the box but walked alongside his horse and told him stories. Sus cocked his ears when Naftali spoke to him and Naftali was sure that Sus understood him. At times, when Naftali asked Sus whether he had liked a story, Sus whinnied, stomped his foot on the ground, or licked Naftali's ear with his tongue as if he meant to say, "Yes, I understand . . ."

Reb Zebulun had told him that animals live only for the day, but Naftali was convinced that animals have a memory too. Sus often remembered the road better than he, Naftali, did. Naftali had heard the story of a dog whose masters had lost him on a distant journey and months after they had come home without their beloved pet, he showed up. The dog crossed half of Poland to come back to his owners. Naftali had heard a similar story about a cat. The fact that pigeons fly back to their coops from very far away was known throughout the world. In those days, they were often used to deliver letters. Some people said this was memory, others called it instinct. But what did it matter what it was called? Animals didn't live for the day only.

Naftali rode from town to town; he often stopped in villages and sold his storybooks. The children everywhere loved Naftali and his horse, Sus. They brought all kinds of good things from home for Sus—potato peels, turnips, and pieces of sugar—and each time Sus got something to eat he waved his tail and shook his head, which meant "Thank you."

Not all the children were able to study and learn to read, and Naftali would gather a number of young children, seat them in the wagon, and tell them a story, sometimes a real one and sometimes a made-up one.

Wherever he went, Naftali heard all kinds of tales—of demons, hobgoblins, windmills, giants, dwarfs, kings, princes, and princesses. He would tell a story nicely, with all the details, and the children never grew tired of listening to him. Even grownups came to listen. Often the grownups invited Naftali home for a meal or a place to sleep. They also liked to feed Sus.

When a person does his work not only for money but out of love, he brings out the love in others. When a child couldn't afford a book, Naftali gave it to him free. Soon Naftali became well known throughout the region. Eventually, he came to Lublin.

In Lublin, Naftali heard many astonishing stories. He met a giant seven feet tall who traveled with a circus and a troupe of midgets. At the circus Naftali saw horses who danced to music, as well as dancing bears. One trickster swallowed a knife and spat it out again, another did a somersault on a high wire, a third flew in the air from one trapeze to another. A girl stood on a horse's back while it raced round and round the circus ring. Naftali struck up an easy friendship with the circus people and he listened to their many interesting stories. They told of fakirs in India who could walk barefoot over burning coals. Others let themselves be buried alive, and after they were dug out several days later, they were healthy and well. Naftali heard astounding stories about sorcerers and miracle workers who could read minds and predict the future. He met an old man who had walked from Lublin to the Land of Israel, then back again. The old man told Naftali about cabalists who lived in caves behind Jerusalem, fasted from one Sabbath to the next, and learned the secrets of God, the angels, the seraphim, the cherubim, and the holy beasts.

The world was full of wonders and Naftali had the urge to write them down and spread them far and wide over all the cities, towns, and villages.

In Lublin, Naftali went to the bookstores and bought storybooks, but he soon saw that there weren't enough storybooks to be had. The storekeepers said that it didn't pay the printers to print them since they brought in so little money. But could everything be measured by money? There were children and even grownups everywhere who yearned to hear stories and Naftali decided to tell all that he had heard. He himself hungered for stories and could never get enough of them.

IV

More years passed, Naftali's parents were no longer living. Many girls had fallen in love with Naftali and wanted to marry him, but he knew that from telling stories and selling storybooks he could not support a family. Besides, he had become used to wandering. How many stories could he hear or tell living in one town? He therefore decided to stay on the road. Horses normally live some twenty-odd years, but Sus was one of those rare horses who live a long time. However, no one lives forever. At forty Sus began to show signs of old age. He seldom galloped now, nor were his eyes as good as they once were. Naftali was already gray himself and the children called him Grandpa.

One time Naftali was told that on the road between Lublin and Warsaw lay an estate where all booksellers came, since the owner was very fond of reading and hearing stories. Naftali asked the way and he was given directions to get there. One spring day he came to the estate. Everything that had been said turned out to be true. The owner of the estate, Reb Falik, gave him a warm welcome and bought many books from him. The children in the nearby town had already heard about Naftali the storyteller and they snatched up all the storybooks he had brought with him. Reb Falik had many horses grazing and when they saw Sus they accepted him as one of their own. Sus promptly began to chew the grass where many yellow flowers grew and Naftali told Reb Falik one story after another. The weather was warm, birds sang, twittered, and trilled, each in its own voice.

The estate contained a tract of forest where old oaks grew. Some of the oaks were so thick they had to be hundreds of years old. Naftali was particularly taken by one oak standing in the center of a meadow. It was the thickest oak Naftali had ever seen in his life. Its roots were spread over a wide area and you could tell that they ran deep. The crown of the oak spread far and wide, and it cast a huge shadow. When Naftali saw this giant oak, which had to be older than all the oaks in the region, it occurred to him: "What a shame an oak hasn't a mouth to tell stories with!"

This oak had lived through many generations. It may have gone back to the times when idol worshippers still lived in Poland. It surely knew the time when the Jews had come to Poland from the German states where they had been persecuted and the Polish king, Kazimierz I, had opened the gates of the land to them. Naftali suddenly realized that he was tired of wandering. He now envied the oak for standing so long in one place, deeply rooted in God's earth. For the first time in his life Naftali got the urge to settle down in one place. He also thought of his horse. Sus was undoubtedly tired of trekking over the roads. It would do him good to get some rest in the few years left him.

Just as Naftali stood there thinking these thoughts, the owner of the estate, Reb Falik, came along in a buggy. He stopped the buggy near Naftali and said, "I see you're completely lost in thought. Tell me what you're thinking."

At first Naftali wanted to tell Reb Falik that many kinds of foolish notions ran through the human mind and that not all of them could be described. But after a while he thought, "Why not tell him the truth?"

Reb Falik seemed a goodhearted man. He had a silver-white beard and eyes that expressed the wisdom and goodness that sometimes come with age. Naftali said, "If you have the patience, I'll tell you."

"Yes, I have the patience. Take a seat in the buggy. I'm going for a drive and I want to hear what a man who is famous for his storytelling thinks about."

Naftali sat down in the buggy. The horses hitched to the buggy walked slowly and Naftali told Reb Falik the story of his life, as well as what his thoughts were when he saw the giant oak. He told him everything, kept nothing back.

When Naftali finished, Reb Falik said, "My dear Naftali, I can easily fulfill all your wishes and fantasies. I am, as you know, an old man. My wife died some time ago. My children live in the big cities. I love to hear stories and I also have lots of stories to tell. If you like, I'll let you build a house in the shade of the oak and you can stay there as long as I live and as long as you live. I'll have a stable built for your horse near the house and you'll both live out your lives in peace. Yes, you are right. You cannot wander forever. There comes a time when every person wants to settle in one place and drink in all the charms that the place has to offer."

When Naftali heard these words, a great joy came over him. He thanked Reb Falik again and again, but Reb Falik said, "You need not thank me so much. I have many peasants and servants here, but I don't have a single person I can talk to. We'll be friends and we'll tell each other lots of stories. What's life, after all? The future isn't here yet and you cannot foresee what it will bring. The present is only a moment and the past is one long story. Those who don't tell stories and don't hear stories live only for that moment, and that isn't enough."

V

Reb Falik's promise wasn't merely words. The very next day he ordered his people to build a house for Naftali the storyteller. There was no shortage of lumber or of crafts-men on the estate. When Naftali saw the plans for the house, he grew disturbed. He needed only a small house for himself and a stable for Sus. But the plans called for a big house with many rooms. Naftali asked Reb Falik why such a big house was being built for him, and Reb Falik replied, "You will need it."

"What for?" Naftali asked.

Gradually, the secret came out. During his lifetime Reb Falik had accumulated many books, so many that he couldn't find room for them in his own big house and many books had to be stored in the cellar and in the attic. Besides, in his talks with Reb Falik, Naftali had said that he had many of his own stories and stories told him by others written down on paper and that he had collected a chestful of manuscripts, but he hadn't been able to have these stories printed, for the printers in Lublin and in the other big cities demanded a lot of money to print them and the number of buyers of storybooks in Poland wasn't large enough to cover such expenses.

Alongside Naftali's house, Reb Falik had a print shop built. He ordered crates of type from Lublin (in those days there was no such thing as a typesetting machine) as well as a hand press. From now on Naftali would have the opportunity to set and print his own storybooks. When he learned what Reb Falik was doing for him, Naftali couldn't believe his ears. He said, "Of all the stories I have ever heard or told, for me this will be by far the nicest."

That very summer everything was ready—the house, the library, the print shop. Winter came early. Right after Succoth the rains began, followed by snow. In winter there is little to do on an estate. The peasants sat in their huts and warmed themselves by their stoves or they went to the tavern. Reb Falik and Naftali spent lots of time together. Reb Falik himself was a treasure trove of stories. He had met many famous squires. In his time he had visited the fairs in Danzig, Leipzig, and Amsterdam. He had even made a trip to the Holy Land and had seen the Western Wall, the Cave of Machpelah, and Rachel's Tomb. Reb Falik told many tales and Naftali wrote them down.

Sus's stable was too big for one horse. Reb Falik had a number of old horses on his estate that could no longer work so Sus wasn't alone. At times, when Naftali came into the stable to visit his beloved Sus, he saw him bowing his head against the horse on his left or his right, and it seemed to Naftali that Sus was listening to stories told him by the other horses or silently telling his own horsy story. It's true that horses cannot speak, but God's creatures can make themselves understood without words.

That winter Naftali wrote many stories—his own and those he heard from Reb Falik. He set them in type and printed them on his hand press. At times, when the sun shone over the silvery snow, Naftali hitched Sus and another horse to a sleigh and made a trip through the nearby towns to sell his storybooks or give them away to those who couldn't afford to buy them. Sometimes Reb Falik went along with him. They slept at inns and spent time with merchants, landowners, and Hasidim on their way to visit their rabbis' courts. Each one had a story to tell and Naftali either wrote them down or fixed them in his memory.

The winter passed and Naftali couldn't remember how. On Passover, Reb Falik's sons, daughters, and grandchildren came to celebrate the holiday at the estate, and again Naftali heard wondrous tales of Warsaw, Cracow, and even of Berlin, Paris, and London. The kings waged wars, but scientists made all kinds of discoveries and inventions. Astronomers discovered stars, planets, comets. Archaeologists dug out ruins of ancient cities. Chemists found new elements. In all the countries, tracks were being laid for railroad trains. Museums, libraries, and theaters were being built. Historians uncovered writings from generations past. The writers in every land described the life and the people among whom they dwelled. Mankind could not and would not forget its past. The history of the world grew ever richer in detail.

That spring something happened that Naftali had been expecting and, therefore, dreading. Sus became sick and stopped grazing. The sun shone outside, and Naftali led Sus out to pasture where the fresh green grass and many flowers sprouted. Sus sat down in the sunshine, looked at the grass and the flowers, but no longer grazed. A stillness shone out from his eyes, the tranquillity of a creature that has lived out its years and is ready to end its story on earth.

One afternoon, when Naftali went out to check on his beloved Sus, he saw that Sus was dead. Naftali couldn't hold back his tears. Sus had been a part of his life.

Naftali dug a grave for Sus not far from the old oak where Sus had died, and he buried him there. As a marker over the grave, he thrust into the ground the whip that he had never used. Its handle was made of oak.

Oddly enough, several weeks later Naftali noticed that the whip had turned into a sapling. The handle had put down roots into the earth where Sus lay and it began to sprout leaves. A tree grew over Sus, a new oak which drew sustenance from Sus's body. In time young branches grew out of the tree and birds sang upon them and built their nests there. Naftali could hardly bring himself to believe that this old dried-out stick had possessed enough life within it to grow and blossom. Naftali considered it a miracle. When the tree grew thicker, Naftali carved Sus's name into the bark along with the dates of his birth and death.

Yes, individual creatures die, but this doesn't end the story of the world. The whole earth, all the stars, all the planets, all the comets represent within them one divine history, one source of life, one endless and wondrous story that only God knows in its entirety.

A few years afterward, Reb Falik died, and years later, Naftali the storyteller died. By then he was famous for his storybooks not only throughout Poland but in other countries as well. Before his death Naftali asked that he be buried beneath the young oak that had grown over Sus's grave and whose branches touched the old oak. On Naftali's tombstone were carved these words from the Scriptures:

LOVELY AND PLEASANT IN THEIR LIVES,
AND IN THEIR DEATH
THEY WERE NOT DIVIDED

The Folk Story

The best place to start talking about folk stories is with the word *folk* itself. *Folk* is a very old word in the English language. It comes from the German *volk*, which means "people." So a folk story is a people's story. But since we are all people, how are folk stories different from any other stories that people might read or tell?

You will recall that in another lesson we said that words that have similar meanings—synonyms—usually have different shades of meaning. For example, *skinny* means almost the same thing as *slim*—but not quite. A *leap* is somewhat greater than a *jump,* and a *risk* seems more uncertain than a *chance.*

Although *folk* is a synonym for *people,* it more accurately suggests plain, or simple, people. Most, but not all, people are folk. Rulers are not thought of as folk. Rich people are not folk. Folks are you and me and our families. We have the folks over for dinner.

Volkswagen means "folk car." When those cars were first introduced into the United States, they were intended for the people. It was not a car usually driven by the president of a bank; it was driven by the everyday working person who didn't have a lot of money. *Folklore* is learning or knowledge that comes from among the people. It is not knowledge that is acquired by scientists. Folklore, or folk learning, deals with natural medicines, ways to make clothes, and many other useful arts.

The first stories you were told as a small child were probably folk stories, or folktales as they are also called. "Jack and the Beanstalk" is a folktale. So are "Goldilocks and the Three Bears" and "Little Red Riding Hood." The stories of Paul Bunyan and Pecos Bill are folk stories that were passed among the people of the American frontier during the nineteenth century.

The identities of the authors of folk stories have usually been lost in time. But this is not always the case. Some modern authors have chosen to write in the *style* of the folk story, as Isaac Singer has done. Many of Washington Irving's stories, such as "The Legend of Sleepy Hollow," are very much like folk stories. The Uncle Remus tales by Joel Chandler Harris are considered American folk stories. Perhaps you can add some of your own favorites to the list.

Folk stories have certain identifying features. These are the four features that we will discuss in the lesson:

1 ◆ **Simplicity.** Folk stories are simple tales about simple people.

2 ◆ **Fantasy, magic, and the supernatural.** Folk stories usually have one or more of these elements.

3 ◆ **Customs, traditions, and beliefs.** Folk stories are important for reminding people who they are and where they come from.

4 ◆ **A lesson.** Folk stories always contain a lesson, or moral.

1 ◆ Simplicity

Everything about a folk story is simple. The language is easy to understand. The ideas are clear and straightforward. The characters are either good or bad, strong or weak, rich or poor, wise or foolish. There are no in-betweens. Consider this passage in which Naftali learns how stories are written.

> During this conversation Naftali also asked where the writers got all these stories and Reb Zebulun said, "First of all, many unusual things happen in the world. A day doesn't go by without some rare event happening. Besides, there are writers who make up such stories."
>
> "They make them up?" Naftali asked in amazement. "If that is so, then they are liars."
>
> "They are not liars," Reb Zebulun replied. "The human brain really can't make up a thing. . . . The brain is created by God, and human thoughts and fantasies are also God's works. Even dreams come from God. If a thing doesn't happen today, it might easily happen tomorrow. If not in one country, then in another. There are endless worlds and what doesn't happen on earth can happen in another world. Whoever has eyes that see and ears that hear absorbs enough stories to last a lifetime and to tell to his children and grandchildren."

The language is so simple here that a five-year-old child could understand what is going on. And yet you don't get the feeling that the author is talking down to you.

Notice how simply Isaac Singer has explained some very complicated ideas. He has explained where a writer's ideas come from. He has said in a few words that all things are possible—somewhere, somehow. Scholars have filled whole libraries writing about these two ideas. By expressing them in about a dozen lines in this story, Singer has said just enough, simply enough, so that anyone—the folk—can understand.

Naftali, his parents, and Zebulun the bookseller are poor, simple people. Reb Falik, who enters the story later, is a very rich man. This is the way it is in folk stories. There are no in-betweens. Each character stands out simply and clearly, with no uncertainties, no questions about what kind of a person he or she is.

1 ♦ Exercise A

Read the following passage and answer the questions about it using what you have learned in this part of the lesson. Use your writing notebook or a separate piece of paper for your answers.

> Naftali had decided on something else too—to become a writer of storybooks. He knew full well that for this you had to study, and with all his heart he determined to learn. He also began to listen more closely to what people said, to what stories they told, and to how they told them. Each person had his or her own manner of speaking. Reb Zebulun told Naftali, "When a day passes, it is no longer there. What remains of it? Nothing more than a story. If stories weren't told or books weren't written, man would live like the beasts, only for the day."
>
> Reb Zebulun said, "Today we live, but by tomorrow today will be a story. The whole world, all human life, is one long story."

1. Even though the story is simple, it contains a very deep thought: What makes us human is that we have a past, a history. The study of history, therefore, is the study of humanity. Do you agree? Support your answer with evidence from the passage.

2. The story tells in very simple terms how to become a writer. What did Naftali do to become a better writer and storyteller? Do you think Singer gives us good advice?

Now check your answers using the suggestions in the Answer Key starting on page 457. Review this part of the lesson if you don't understand why an answer was wrong.

1 ♦ Writing on Your Own

Look at the list you have written for Create Your Own Folk Story on page 314 that tells you about your own story idea. Now do the following:

1. Select items from your list that tell who your character is and where the story takes place.

2. Write a few paragraphs that begin your story.

☐ Remember that folk stories have simple characters who are either good or bad, honest or dishonest. Using simple language, describe your character. For example, your character may be a farmer who is honest and hardworking. He or she wears simple clothes and doesn't have many belongings.

☐ Describe the setting and hint at the problem your character has. Perhaps the farmer needs money for his or her children.

☐ Now think about what your character needs? Knowledge? Money? Medicine? Why?

3. You may want to change and rewrite your paragraphs several times until you have the order and descriptions just right.

2 ◆ Fantasy, Magic, and the Supernatural

In almost every folk story, something very unusual happens. Trees and animals speak. Gods descend from heaven and change things around in magical ways. There are wizards, witches, fairies, imps, and goblins. All have their mischief to make or their wonders to perform.

Fantasy, magic, and the supernatural make a good story. People love a good scare. And they like to dream that someone or something magical will come along to solve all their problems and, maybe, make them rich. In other words, people like to *fantasize*. Most stories, especially folk stories, allow us to fantasize.

But fantasy serves another purpose in folk stories. We said in part one of the lesson that folk stories present ideas in simple ways. Well, very often magic and fantasy are used to explain those ideas. It's not easy, for example, to explain how the world began or how the first person came to be, so every culture has folk stories that explain these things as magic or as wonderful deeds of the gods. Parents have always had to teach their children to be cautious in the world, to watch out for evil things, and it's not easy to teach about evil. So stories were made up about imps and demons who are always waiting to trip you up. "Naftali the Storyteller and His Horse, Sus" begins with a story about an imp. It is a story within a story. Zelig tells the story often, and young Naftali never tires of hearing it.

> Dozens of times Zelig the coachman told this same story to Naftali but Naftali never grew tired of hearing it. He could picture it all—the forest, the night, the silver moon, the curious eye of the horse, the imp. Naftali asked all kinds of questions: Did the imp have a beard? Did it have feet? How did its tail look? Where did it fly off to?
>
> Zelig couldn't answer all the questions. He had been too frightened at the time to notice the details. But to the last question Zelig replied, "He probably flew to beyond the Dark Regions, where people don't go and cattle don't stray, where the sky is copper, the earth iron, and where the evil forces live under roofs of petrified toadstools and in tunnels abandoned by moles."

Surely this must have been an exciting story to listen to. The forest, the night, the moon, and the imp must have sent chills up and down young Naftali's spine. The story also undoubtedly excited Naftali's imagination. This is the beginning of his desire to be a writer and storyteller himself. Naftali's interest in stories really becomes a part of his education.

The story also teaches a lesson, as all folk stories do. In answer to Naftali's question about where the imp flew off to, Zelig said that there is a Dark Region where evil forces live. He described it as a horrible place where people and even animals are afraid to go. The lesson is that the evil in life should be avoided.

2 ◆ Exercise B

Read the following passage and answer the questions about it using what you have learned in this part of the lesson. Use your writing notebook or a separate piece of paper for your answers.

> Naftali dug a grave for Sus not far from the old oak where Sus had died, and he buried him there. As a marker over the grave, he thrust into the ground the whip that he had never used. Its handle was made of oak.
>
> Oddly enough, several weeks later Naftali noticed that the whip had turned into a sapling. The handle had put down roots into the earth where Sus lay and it began to sprout leaves. A tree grew over Sus, a new oak which drew sustenance from Sus's body. . . . When the tree grew thicker, Naftali carved Sus's name into the bark along with the dates of his birth and death.
>
> Yes, individual creatures die, but this doesn't end the story of the world. The whole earth, all the stars, all the planets, all the comets represent within them one divine history, one source of life, one endless and wondrous story that only God knows in its entirety.

1. Reread the last sentence of the passage. What do you think that sentence means? Do you agree with Singer?

2. What is the lesson that can be learned from the magical sprouting of the whip?

Now check your answers using the suggestions in the Answer Key starting on page 457. Review this part of the lesson if you don't understand why an answer was wrong.

2 ◆ Writing on Your Own

Look at the list you have written for Create Your Own Folk Story on page 314 that tells you about your own story idea. Now do the following:

1. Select an item from your list that tells about the event that will occur in your story. What will happen in the story? For example, the farmer needs money to travel to a large town to buy medicine for a sick child. The farmer must walk many miles and cross a huge river. Remember that your character is honest and good and won't give up.

2. Write a paragraph that introduces an element of fantasy or the supernatural into your story. For example, your farmer needs to cross the river but a troll or imp refuses to let anyone pass. How will the troll be defeated? Will the farmer outsmart him or use magic?

3. You may want to change and rewrite your paragraph several times before you get the order and events just right.

3 ◆ Customs, Traditions, and Beliefs

Customs, traditions, and beliefs are part of our history. And, as Singer points out, history is important to people. He tells us that without a past, without history, we would be like the beasts.

Our customs and traditions give us roots. They make us feel that we are a part, a continuation, of all that has come before us. They are our link with history. We learn from the past, and we pass our knowledge on to future generations. Animals live simply for each day as it comes, but we live by building on the past and planning for the future.

Many countries, for example, have an Independence Day. In the United States it is July 4, in Mexico it is September 16. In Canada they celebrate Canada Day on July 1, and France celebrates Bastille Day on July 14. Each of these holidays celebrates a time when the common people broke away from the tyranny of the powerful ruling class. Knowing that our ancestors could accomplish such a thing makes us feel that we are part of these great events. So they have become part of our traditions. Stories, customs, and traditions have grown up around them.

For many people religious traditions and beliefs give them a sense of moral values. Religions help teach the difference between good and bad, right and wrong. And they help people to deal with forces in the world that are beyond their understanding. Customs that people follow in the practice of their religions help them maintain their beliefs.

Because customs, traditions, and beliefs are part of our folklore, they are frequently included in folk stories. Notice how Isaac Singer works traditional Jewish experiences into his story.

> Naftali heard astounding stories about sorcerers and miracle workers who could read minds and predict the future. He met an old man who had walked from Lublin to the Land of Israel, then back again. The old man told Naftali about cabalists who lived in caves behind Jerusalem, fasted from one Sabbath to the next, and learned the secrets of God, the angels, the seraphim, the cherubim, and the holy beasts.

> [Later in the story]

> This oak had lived through many generations. It may have

gone back to the times when idol worshippers still lived in Poland. It surely knew the time when the Jews had come to Poland from the German states where they had been persecuted and the Polish king, Kazimierz I, had opened the gates of the land to them.

The first of those passages tells of a man who had made a pilgrimage to the Holy Land on foot and who had seen and had learned wonderful things. This passage is an example of people's devotion to religion. It also mentions the cabalists. They are a very religious Jewish sect who feel they have special knowledge that brings them very close to God and to the other inhabitants of heaven.

In the second passage, Singer has included a bit of Jewish history. The Jews were driven from Germany in the Middle Ages and were welcomed into Poland by Kazimierz, or Casimir, I. Not long before that, he tells us, the Poles were idol worshippers.

3 ✦ Exercise C

Read the following passage and answer the questions about it using what you have learned in this part of the lesson. Use your writing notebook or a separate piece of paper for your answers.

> Like all the children in town, Naftali rose early to go to cheder [KHAY-der]. He studied more diligently than the other children. Why? Because Naftali was eager to learn to read. He had seen older boys reading storybooks and he had been envious of them. How happy was one who could read a story from a book!
>
> At six, Naftali was already able to read a book in Yiddish, and from then on he read every storybook he could get his hands on. . . . He also read the stories in his mother's Yiddish Pentateuch [Bible] and in her books of morals.

1. The passage, in fact, the whole story, stresses the importance of two particular skills. These skills have traditionally been important to Jewish people, as well as many other cultures. What skills are emphasized in the story? How does knowing a little more about the Jewish culture help you understand more about the story?

2. Naftali loved to read. How do you think his love of stories and reading grew?

Now check your answers using the suggestions in the Answer Key starting on page 457. Review this part of the lesson if you don't understand why an answer was wrong.

3♦Writing on Your Own

Look at the list you have written for Create Your Own Folk Story on page 314 that tells you about your own story idea. Now do the following:

1. Select an item from the list that tells about the event or what will happen in your story. Try to add a custom or tradition from your heritage into the story. For example, the farmer may come from Poland, Ireland, Africa, Canada, Portugal, Japan, Cuba, etc. Add some of the history and traditions of that country to your story.

2. Write a short paragraph telling what happened and adding some information about the farmer's beliefs and culture.

3. You may want to change and rewrite your paragraph several times until you get it just the way you like it.

4 ◆ Teaching a Moral, or Lesson

When you were a small child, someone probably told you at least one of Aesop's fables. They are very famous short stories, and they have been told for many generations. Aesop's fables always involve animals, and they always teach a moral. They are simple folk stories.

Aesop himself is a folk legend. No one is sure if he was a real person or not. Some say that he was a slave who lived about 600 B.C. on the Greek island of Samos. Others say that he was a crippled storyteller who told stories to ancient Greek kings. Whoever he was, his simple fables have survived for more than 2,000 years. It is the morals, or lessons, which they teach that make them so lasting. Parents often use them to teach their children the lessons of life. Consider the moral in the "Fox and the Grapes," from which we get the expression "sour grapes."

> A hungry fox saw some luscious clusters of grapes hanging high on a vine. He tried all the tricks he knew to get at them, but try as he would he could not reach them. At last he gave up. To mask his disappointment he announced, "The grapes are very likely sour and not worth my attention."
> The moral: We often pretend to despise what we cannot have.

Notice that the moral is stated at the end of the fable. Aesop always ended his tales that way to be sure that the reader wouldn't miss the lesson. Not all folk stories are as blunt about pointing out the moral as Aesop's fables are. But all folk stories do contain lessons that are rather obvious.

Earlier in the lesson you saw how Naftali's father used the story of the imp to teach his son about the forces of evil in the world. Later, Singer told of the sprouting whip to teach that life continues after death: through death comes new life, in a continuous cycle. There are also many lessons about the value of reading. What lesson is the author trying to teach in this passage?

> Wherever he went, Naftali heard all kinds of tales—of demons, hobgoblins, windmills, giants, dwarfs, kings, princes and princesses. He would tell a story nicely, with all the details, and the children never grew tired of

listening to him. Even grownups came to listen. Often the grownups invited Naftali home for a meal or a place to sleep. They also liked to feed Sus.

When a person does his work not only for money but out of love, he brings out the love in others. When a child couldn't afford a book, Naftali gave it to him free. Soon Naftali became well known throughout the region.

The lesson in this passage is stated for you, almost as Aesop would have done, except the statement is buried in the middle of the passage instead of being placed at the end. The moral is this, When a person does his work not only for money but out of love, he brings out the love in others.

It is quite true that people are happiest when they are working at something that they like to do. If you work only for money, chances are that you will be quite miserable at your job. The happiest people are those who work for others. If you can perform a service for others and make a good living too, you have the best of both worlds.

Sometimes in folk stories the moral is discovered during the main character's *quest*. A quest is an adventure in which the hero is searching for something. A quest could be a search for riches that are to be used for some good purpose, or it could be a search for the answer to an important question. (Notice that the word *quest* forms the beginning of the word *question*. Both words come from the Latin word *quaerere* meaning "to ask" or "to seek.") Try to find Naftali's moral quest in Exercise D.

4 ✦ Exercise D

Read the following passage and answer the questions about it using what you have learned in this part of the lesson. Use your writing notebook or a separate piece of paper for your answers.

The world was full of wonders and Naftali had the urge to write them down and spread them far and wide over all the cities, towns, and villages.

In Lublin, Naftali went to the bookstores and bought storybooks, but he soon saw that there weren't enough storybooks to be had. The storekeepers said that it didn't pay the printers to print them since they brought in so little money. But could everything be measured by money? There were children and even grownups everywhere who yearned to hear stories and Naftali decided to tell all that he had heard.

1. You have probably heard it said that you can't buy everything in life. That is an important lesson. Why does Naftali feel that there are some things in life that are more important than money? Do you agree?

2. How would you describe Naftali's moral quest?

Now check your answers using the suggestions in the Answer Key staring on page 457. Review this part of the lesson if you don't understand why an answer was wrong.

4♦Writing on Your Own

Look at the list you have written for Create Your Own Folk Story on page 314 that tells you about your own story idea. Now do the following:

1. Select an item from the list that will be a good ending for your story. Remember that a folk story ends with a moral, or lesson. For example, the farmer has traveled for miles and must outwit a troll to cross the river. What does he teach us? Perhaps he shows us something about determination and perseverance.

2. Write a paragraph that tells what happens at the end of the story. Be sure to include the moral.

3. You may want to change and rewrite your paragraph several times before you get the ending just right.

No go on to Reviewing and Interpreting the Story.

Reviewing and Interpreting the Story

Answer these questions without looking back at the story. Choose the best answer to each question and put an *x* in the box beside it, or write your answer on a separate piece of paper.

Remembering Facts

1. Reb Zebulun was a
   - ☐ a. land owner.
   - ☐ b. coachman.
   - ☐ c. printer.
   - ☐ d. bookseller.

2. What did Naftali have that he never used?
   - ☐ a. a wagon
   - ☐ b. a whip
   - ☐ c. money
   - ☐ d. his horse

Following the Order of Events

3. As he viewed the old oak on the large estate, Naftali decided that he wanted to
   - ☐ a. write his first story.
   - ☐ b. bury Sus there.
   - ☐ c. settle down.
   - ☐ d. become a printer.

4. When did Naftali meet Reb Falik?

   ☐ a. when Naftali started selling books

   ☐ b. on Naftali's return from Israel

   ☐ c. when Naftali was a child

   ☐ d. when Naftali was an old man

Understanding
Word Choices
5. An oak tree drew <u>sustenance</u> from Sus's body.
   Sustenance is

   ☐ a. knowledge to go on living.

   ☐ b. faith that lasts after death.

   ☐ c. food to maintain life.

   ☐ d. love that binds friends together.

6. Naftali studied more <u>diligently</u> than other
   children. *Diligently* means that he

   ☐ a. studied harder.

   ☐ b. was smarter.

   ☐ c. studied faster.

   ☐ d. found studying easier.

Understanding
Important Ideas
7. Which of the following is an important idea that
   is often repeated in the story?

   ☐ a. Life itself is a long story.

   ☐ b. Life is good to those who like stories.

   ☐ c. Beware of imps and evil spirits.

   ☐ d. Be kind to animals.

8. According to the story, what happens when people do their work out of love?

   ☐ a. They remain poor.

   ☐ b. They become very religious.

   ☐ c. They are made fun of by others.

   ☐ d. They bring out love in others.

Understanding
Levels of
Meaning

9. Naftali's ambition was to be a traveling bookseller because he

   ☐ a. wanted to earn enough money to support a family.

   ☐ b. wanted to do what he enjoyed the most.

   ☐ c. was a very good reader.

   ☐ d. liked horses as his father did.

10. "When a day passes it is no longer there." That sentence shows us that storytelling

   ☐ a. preserves the events of the day forever.

   ☐ b. helps the days pass by more quickly.

   ☐ c. makes the days seem longer.

   ☐ d. keeps us from dwelling on the past.

Understanding
Character

11. Which phrase best describes Naftali's attitude toward life?

   ☐ a. disliked traveling

   ☐ b. often unhappy with his life

   ☐ c. eager to learn and to teach

   ☐ d. filled with regret

12. In the story Reb Zebulun teaches Naftali what he knows. Reb shares his knowledge with Naftali because Reb

☐ a. thought they could share Sus.

☐ b. wanted to retire.

☐ c. wanted him to join his business.

☐ d. also loved stories, imagination, and reading.

Understanding
Setting

13. In this story, Singer does not describe Naftali's surroundings in any detail. Why did the author say so little about the setting?

☐ a. He felt the setting wasn't vivid enough.

☐ b. The setting is really ideas, values, and lessons.

☐ c. The setting created too many problems for the author.

☐ d. He felt readers would become bored with the descriptions.

14. When Naftali looked at the oaks on the estate, he was attracted by one that had roots spreading over a wide area. How were Naftali and the oak similar?

☐ a. Both had lived a long time and had spread their "roots" far and wide.

☐ b. They were old and tired.

☐ c. Both were no longer interested in passing their knowledge on to another generation.

☐ d. Both were strong and proud.

Understanding
Feelings

15. Sus is one of the characters in the story. Which description best explains how Naftali felt about Sus?

☐ a. angry and impatient

☐ b. cautious and fearful

☐ c. unfeeling and uninterested

☐ d. loving and respectful

16. Children and adults would gather to listen to Naftali's stories. People invited him into their homes to eat and sleep. People appreciated him because

☐ a. they didn't have very many visitors.

☐ b. he took care of their children.

☐ c. he taught them something about life and themselves.

☐ d. they were allowed to use his horse.

Now check your answers using the Answer Key starting on page 457. Make no mark for right answers. <u>Correct</u> any wrong answers you may have by putting a check mark (✓) in the box next to the right answer. Count the number of questions you answered correctly and plot the total on the Comprehension Scores graph on page 468.

Next, look at the questions you answered incorrectly. What types of questions were they? Count the number you got wrong of each type and enter the numbers in the spaces below.

Remembering Facts _____

Following the Order of Events _____

Understanding Word Choices _____

Understanding Important Ideas _____

Understanding Levels of Meaning _____

Understanding Character _____

Understanding Setting _____

Understanding Feelings _____

Now use these numbers to fill in the Comprehension Skills Profile on page 469.

Discussion Guides

The questions below will help you think about the story and the lesson you have just read. If you don't discuss these questions in class, try to think about them or discuss them with your classmates. Perhaps you will want to write a few paragraphs in answer to the questions.

Discussing Folk Stories

1. A feature of many folk stories that is not discussed in the lesson is *wish fulfillment*. This means that someone who wants something very much wishes for it and gets it. There may be a genie, fairy, imp, god, or magician to make the wish come true. What is Naftali's wish, and how does it come true?

2. In part 4 of the lesson you learned that many folk stories tell about a quest. A quest usually involves travel. Describe Naftali's quest in detail. Was he successful in his quest? Explain your opinion.

3. Most folk stories are set in the country among plain country people. How does "Naftali the Storyteller" fit this pattern? Can you think of a folk story that takes place in a city?

Discussing the Story

4. In the story, Reb Falik says: "What's life, after all? The future isn't here yet and you cannot foresee what it will bring. The present is only a moment and the past is one long story. Those who don't tell stories and don't hear stories live only for that moment, and that isn't enough." Explain what you think Reb Falik means. Do you agree?

5. The story ends with a quotation from the Scriptures (the Bible). What does the quotation mean and how does it apply to the story? (The quotation is from the Second Book of Samuel, Chapter 1, verse 23. David is mourning the death of King Saul and his son Jonathan, who were slain in battle.)

6. Are there people like Naftali in the world? If you don't think there are, explain why not. If you think there are, tell who they are and in what way they are like Naftali. (You can think of groups of people or of organizations rather than just one person.)

Discussing the Author's Work

7. The way Isaac Singer tells this story seems almost childish at times. Still, people of all ages enjoy the story. What is your opinion of the simple way in which the story is told? How would the story change if the language and the situations were more "grown up"?

8. Isaac Singer writes in Yiddish. His work is then translated into English and other languages. A great many of his stories are set among Jewish people in Poland in the last century or before. How different would the story be, do you think, if the people were Polish and Catholic? English and Protestant? Japanese and Buddhist?

9. When Isaac Singer was given the Nobel Prize in literature in 1978, he was praised for "bringing universal conditions to life." What "universal conditions" does he bring to life in "Naftali the Storyteller and His Horse, Sus"?

Writing Exercise

Read all the instructions before you begin writing. If you have any questions about how to begin the writing assignment, review Using the Writing Process beginning on page 445, or confer with your writing coach.

1. At the beginning of the unit you were asked to make a list of characters, settings, and themes or morals. If you haven't done that yet, read the instructions for Create Your Own Folk Story on page 314, and make your list now.

2. Write a rough draft of a folk story based on your idea and the list you made. Try to include all the elements you've learned about in this lesson:

   ◆ **Simplicity:** Use simple and straightforward language in your story and to describe your characters.

   ◆ **Fantasy:** Most folk stories have an element of fantasy, magic, or the supernatural.

   ◆ **Customs:** Customs, traditions, and beliefs remind us of where we come from and who we are.

   ◆ **Moral:** Folk stories always teach us a lesson about life.

3. If you have written the paragraphs in the four Writing on Your Own exercises, you may use them to help you write your story. Use your four paragraphs and

   a. Make an outline of which parts of the story come first, second, third, and fourth.

   b. Rewrite your story. If you are having trouble, you might want to look at other collections of folk stories or fables.

   c. Reread your story once again. Make changes and corrections. You may want a friend, teacher, or your writing coach to make suggestions at this point.

   d. Write your story in its final form. Some authors write a final draft two or three times until they get the story just the way they want it.

Unit 9   Science Fiction

A Sound of Thunder

BY RAY BRADBURY

About the Illustration

What is fantastic about the scene depicted in this drawing? What details lead you to suspect that this is a story that could only happen in someone's imagination?

Here are some questions to help you think about the story:

◆ What kind of animal is in this picture? When would you guess the story takes place?

◆ What things in the picture are out of place with the setting? Where would you guess they came from?

◆ What do you think the men in the picture are doing? Support your response.

Unit 9

Introduction

About the Story

"A Sound of Thunder" is about time travel. As the story opens, a man named Eckels hands over a check for ten thousand dollars, the price of a ride in a time machine. What great moment in history does he wish to visit? you wonder. Maybe he will choose an important battle. Or perhaps he will want to meet a famous leader or visit some distant ancestor.

While these are all good guesses, Eckels has something else in mind. Ten thousand dollars buys him a place in a safari, a safari back in time to hunt the biggest game of all: *Tyrannosaurus rex,* the "thunder lizard"! (Even great writers sometimes make mistakes. If you haven't already spotted the mistake that Ray Bradbury made in this story, get a good dictionary and look up "thunder lizard" or "brontosaurus.") Tyrannosaurus rex is why Eckels has come to the small office of Time Safari, Inc. "Safaris to any year in the past," it advertises. "You name the animal. We take you there. You shoot it."

The year is 2055, and the place is the United States. It is the day after a presidential election that marked the end of a bitterly fought campaign. Eckels and the others are relieved that Keith won, and not Deutscher. "If Deutscher had gotten in," says the man behind the desk, "we'd have the worst kind of dictatorship. . . . Anyway, Keith's President now. All you got to worry about is—"

"Shooting my dinosaur," Eckels finishes for him.

Actually, there are a few other concerns—staying alive, for one. Hunting dinosaurs is dangerous business. Equally risky is the danger of tampering with the past. A wrong step in the past could easily change the course of history, forever.

The leaders of Time Safari, Inc. take every precaution not to disturb the past. They hunt only those creatures that would have died a natural death a minute or two later. And they erect an "anti-gravity path" that floats just above the ground so that no one will disturb prehistoric plants or insects. "Stay on the Path," demands Travis, the safari leader.

So Eckels sets out on his time safari like a small boy setting out on an innocent adventure. But the world he leaves is not the world he returns to, because along the way, disaster occurs. The past is violated. And the consequences of that one false step echo through eons of time.

The author, Ray Bradbury, has been called "the world's greatest living science-fiction writer." Some admirers, however, insist that he writes not as much about science as about people and their behavior. Probably the truth lies somewhere in between. Bradbury's special brand of science fiction explores the impact of scientific development on human life. Bradbury feels that scientific knowledge, if improperly used, can do humanity more harm than good. His stories, he has said, "are intended as much to instruct how to prevent dooms, as to predict them."

About his writing he says, "I write for fun. . . . I have fun with ideas. I play with them. I approach my craft with enthusiasm and respect. If my work sparks serious thought, fine. But I don't write with that in mind."

If you enjoy "A Sound of Thunder," you'll probably want to read some other Bradbury favorites, such as *Farenheit 451* and *Something Wicked This Way Comes* (both novels), and *The Martian Chronicles, The Illustrated Man, The Small Assassin, The Golden Apples of the Sun,* and *Dandelion Wine,* which are short-story collections.

About the Lesson

The lesson that follows "A Sound of Thunder" is about science fiction. Good science fiction is both good science and good fiction. You learn something about scientific theories from reading it, and you also learn something about people—maybe even about yourself. You get a glimpse of the future—at least one person's vision of the future. And some of the visions of science-fiction writers have been uncannily accurate!

Writers of science fiction don't predict the future. Instead, they try to present a variety of possible tomorrows for us to think about today. Some of these looks into the future are positively chilling, while others create a captivating new world. What really happens in the future depends on the choices we make today. Science fiction asks us to think about those choices before we make them.

The questions below will help you focus on some of the characteristics of science fiction you will find in "A Sound of Thunder." Read the story and try to answer these questions as you go along:

◆ Through this story, you will enter a world of the future, where some things are familiar and other things are strange and hard to believe. What is strange and unbelievable about this new world? What seems familiar to you?

◆ You will learn something about evolution—how things evolve, or develop, over long periods of time. How does this scientific theory help make the rest of the story more believable?

◆ You will see how one man acts under great stress. Why is this scene a good picture of human nature?

◆ How does the story draw you into its fantasy world?

Create Your Own Science-Fiction Story

It can be fun to let your imagination run wild. As a science-fiction writer, you are able to combine elements of science with weird or unbelievable worlds, creatures, and inventions. In science fiction, the impossible does not exist.

You can understand better how a science-fiction writer creates a startling new world by thinking about ideas for your own science-fiction story. Use your writing notebook or a separate piece of paper and think of a topic of your own or consider the following suggestions:

1. Choose one of the following ideas for a story, or think of an idea of your own.

   ☐ Genetic engineering is a process in which new organisms are designed. Imagine designing a new bacteria that protects people from all illnesses—a world where no one is ever sick and no one ever dies.

   ☐ Scientists predict that people will one day live in outer space. Create your own space colony. What problems will your colony encounter? How will society be different from what we know now?

   ☐ Imagine a world in which fantasy becomes reality. Through a technological advance known as virtual reality, people are able to become part of a world that does not really exist.

2. Make a list of characters, settings, and events that will be in your story. For example, if you choose virtual reality, what world will your character enter? How will a person enter this fantasy world? Will the person live permanently in this fantasy world, or will he or she be able to return to the world of reality?

3. Rewrite your list putting the events in the order in which they will occur. Rewrite your list until you get the order just the way you want it.

A Sound of Thunder

by Ray Bradbury

*T*he sign on the wall seemed to quaver under a film of sliding warm water. Eckels felt his eyelids blink over his stare, and the sign burned in the momentary darkness:

TIME SAFARI, INC.
SAFARIS TO ANY YEAR IN THE PAST.
YOU NAME THE ANIMAL.
WE TAKE YOU THERE.
YOU SHOOT IT.

A warm phlegm gathered in Eckels' throat; he swallowed and pushed it down. The muscles around his mouth formed a smile as he put his hand slowly out upon the air, and in that hand waved a check for ten thousand dollars to the man behind the desk.

"Does this safari guarantee I come back alive?"

"We guarantee nothing," said the official, "except the dinosaurs." He turned. "This is Mr. Travis, your Safari Guide in the Past. He'll tell you what and where to shoot. If he says no shooting, no shooting. If you disobey instructions, there's a stiff penalty of another ten thousand dollars, plus possible government action, on your return."

Eckels glanced across the vast office at a mass and tangle, a snaking and humming of wires and steel boxes, at an aurora that flickered now orange, now silver, now blue. There was a sound like a gigantic bonfire burning all of Time, all the years and all the parchment calendars, all the hours piled high and set aflame.

A touch of the hand and this burning would, on the instant, beautifully reverse itself. Eckels remembered the wording in the advertisements to the letter. Out of chars and ashes, out of dust and coals, like golden salamanders, the old years, the green years, might leap; roses sweeten the air, white hair turn Irish-black, wrinkles vanish; all, everything fly back to seed, flee death, rush down to their beginnings, suns rise in western skies and set in glorious easts, moons eat themselves opposite to the custom, all and everything cupping one in another like Chinese boxes, rabbits into hats, all and everything returning to the fresh death, the seed death, the green death, to the time before the beginning. A touch of a hand might do it, the merest touch of a hand.

"Hell and damn," Eckels breathed, the light of the Machine on his thin face. "A real Time Machine." He shook his head. "Makes you think. If the election had gone badly yesterday, I might be here now running away from the results. Thank God Keith won. He'll make a fine President of the United States."

"Yes," said the man behind the desk. "We're lucky. If Deutscher had gotten in, we'd have the worst kind of dictatorship. There's an anti-everything man for you, a militarist, anti-Christ, anti-human, anti-intellectual. People called us up, you know, joking but not joking. Said if Deutscher became President they wanted to go live in 1492. Of course it's not our business to conduct Escapes, but to form Safaris. Anyway, Keith's President now. All you got to worry about is—"

"Shooting my dinosaur," Eckels finished it for him.

"A *Tyrannosaurus rex*. The Thunder Lizard, the damnedest monster in history. Sign this release. Anything happens to you, we're not responsible. Those dinosaurs are hungry."

Eckels flushed angrily. "Trying to scare me!"

"Frankly, yes. We don't want anyone going who'll panic at the first shot. Six Safari leaders were killed last year, and a dozen hunters. We're here to give you the damnedest thrill a *real* hunter ever asked for. Traveling you back sixty million years to bag the biggest damned game in all Time. Your personal check's still there. Tear it up."

Mr. Eckels looked at the check for a long time. His fingers twitched.

"Good luck," said the man behind the desk. "Mr. Travis, he's all yours."

They moved silently across the room, taking their guns with them, toward the Machine, toward the silver metal and the roaring light.

First a day and then a night and then a day and then a night, then it was day-night-day-night-day. A week, a month, a year, a decade! A.D. 2055. A.D. 2019. 1999! 1957! Gone! The Machine roared.

They put on their oxygen helmets and tested the intercoms.

Eckels swayed on the padded seat, his face pale, his jaw stiff. He felt the trembling in his arms and he looked down and found his hands tight on the new rifle. There were four other men in the Machine. Travis, the Safari Leader, his assistant, Lesperance, and two other hunters, Billings and Kramer. They sat looking at each other, and the years blazed around them.

"Can these guns get a dinosaur cold?" Eckels felt his mouth saying.

"If you hit them right," said Travis on the helmet radio. "Some dinosaurs have two brains, one in the head, another far down the spinal column. We stay away from those. That's stretching luck. Put your first two shots into the eyes, if you can, blind them, and go back into the brain."

The Machine howled. Time was a film run backward. Suns fled and ten million moons fled after them. "Good God," said Eckels. "Every hunter that ever lived would envy us today. This makes Africa seem like Illinois."

The Machine slowed; its scream fell to a murmur. The Machine stopped.

The sun stopped in the sky.

The fog that had enveloped the Machine blew away and they were in an old time, a very old time indeed, three hunters and two Safari Heads with their blue metal guns across their knees.

"Christ isn't born yet," said Travis. "Moses has not gone to the mountain to talk with God. The Pyramids are still in the earth, waiting to be cut out and put up. *Remember* that. Alexander, Caesar, Napoleon, Hitler—none of them exists."

The men nodded.

"That"—Mr. Travis pointed—"is the jungle of sixty million two thousand and fifty-five years before President Keith."

He indicated a metal path that struck off into green wilderness, over steaming swamp, among giant ferns and palms.

"And that," he said, "is the Path, laid by Time Safari for your use. It floats six inches above the earth. Doesn't touch so much as one grass blade, flower, or tree. It's an anti-gravity metal. It's purpose is to keep you from touching this world of the past in any way. Stay on the Path. Don't go off it. I repeat. *Don't go off.* For *any* reason! If you fall off, there's a penalty. And don't shoot any animal we don't okay."

"Why?" asked Eckels.

They sat in the ancient wilderness. Far birds' cries blew on a wind, and the smell of tar and an old salt sea, moist grasses, and flowers the color of blood.

"We don't want to change the Future. We don't belong here in the Past. The government doesn't *like* us here. We have to pay big graft to keep our franchise. A Time Machine is damn finicky business. Not knowing it, we might kill an important animal, a small bird, a roach, a flower even, thus destroying an important link in a growing species."

"That's not clear," said Eckels.

"All right," Travis continued, "say we accidently kill one mouse here. That means all the future families of this one particular mouse are destroyed, right?"

"Right."

"And all the families of the families of the families of that one mouse! With a stamp of your foot, you annihilate first one, then a dozen, then a thousand, a million, a *billion* possible mice!"

"So they're dead," said Eckels. "So what?"

"So what?" Travis snorted quietly. "Well, what about the foxes that'll need those mice to survive? For want of ten mice, a fox dies. For want of ten foxes, a lion starves. For want of a lion, all manner of insects, vultures, infinite billions of life forms are thrown into chaos and destruction. Eventually it all boils down to this: fifty-nine million years later, a cave man, one of a dozen on the *entire world,* goes hunting wild boar or saber-tooth tiger for food. But you, friend, have *stepped* on all the tigers in that region. By stepping on *one* single mouse. So the cave man starves. And the cave man, please note, is not just *any* expendable man, no! He is an *entire future nation.* From his loins would have sprung ten sons. From *their* loins one hundred sons, and thus onward to a civilization. Destroy this one man, and you destroy a race, a people, an entire history of life. It is comparable to slaying some of Adam's grandchildren. The stomp of your foot, on one mouse, could start an earthquake, the effects of which could shake our earth and destinies down through Time, to their very foundations. With the death of that one cave man, a billion others yet unborn are throttled in the womb. Perhaps Rome never rises on its seven hills. Perhaps Europe is forever a dark forest, and only Asia waxes healthy and teeming. Step on a mouse and you crush the Pyramids. Step on a mouse and you leave your print, like a Grand Canyon, across Eternity. Queen Elizabeth might never be born, Washington might not cross the Delaware, there might never be a United States at all. So be careful. Stay on the Path. *Never* step off!"

"I see," said Eckels. "Then it wouldn't pay for us even to touch the *grass?*"

"Correct. Crushing certain plants could add up infinitesimally. A little error here would multiply in sixty million years, all out of proportion. Of course maybe our theory is wrong. Maybe Time *can't* be changed by us. Or maybe it can be changed only in little subtle ways. A dead mouse here makes an insect imbalance there, a population disproportion later, a bad harvest further on, a depression, mass starvation, and, finally, a change in *social* temperament in far-flung countries. Something much more subtle, like that. Perhaps only a soft breath, a whisper, a hair, pollen on the air, such a slight, slight change that unless you looked close you wouldn't see it. Who knows? Who really can say he knows? We don't know. We're guessing. But until we do know for certain whether our messing around in Time *can* make a big roar or a little rustle in history, we're being damned careful. This Machine, this Path, your clothing and bodies, were sterilized, as you know, before the journey. We wear these oxygen helmets so we can't introduce our bacteria into an ancient atmosphere."

"How do we know which animals to shoot?"

"They're marked with red paint," said Travis. "Today, before our journey, we sent Lesperance here back with the Machine. He came to this particular era and followed certain animals."

"Studying them?"

"Right," said Lesperance. "I track them through their entire existence, noting which of them lives longest. Very few. How many times they mate. Not often. Life's short. When I find one that's going to die when a tree falls on him, or that drowns in a tar pit, I note the exact hour, minute, and second. I shoot a paint bomb. It leaves a red patch on his hide. We can't miss it. Then I correlate our arrival in the Past so that we meet the Monster not more than two minutes before he would have died anyway. This way, we kill only animals with no future, that are never going to mate again. You see how *careful* we are?"

"But if you came back this morning in Time," said Eckels eagerly, "you must've bumped into *us,* our Safari! How did it turn out? Was it successful? Did all of us get through—alive?"

Travis and Lesperance gave each other a look.

"That'd be a paradox," said the latter. "Time doesn't permit that sort of mess—a man meeting himself. When such occasions threaten, Time steps aside. Like an airplane hitting an air pocket. You felt the Machine jump just before we stopped? That was us passing ourselves on the way back to the Future. We saw nothing. There's no way of telling *if* this expedition was a success, *if* we got our monster, or whether all of us—meaning *you,* Mr. Eckels— got out alive."

Eckels smiled palely.

"Cut that," said Travis sharply. "Everyone on his feet!"

They were ready to leave the Machine.

The jungle was high and the jungle was broad and the jungle was the entire world forever and forever. Sounds like music and sounds like flying tents filled the sky, and those were pterodactyls soaring with cavernous gray wings, gigantic bats out of a delirium and a night fever. Eckels, balanced on the narrow Path, aimed his rifle playfully.

"Stop that!" said Travis. "Don't even aim for fun, damn it! If your gun should go off—"

Eckels flushed. "Where's our *Tyrannosaurus*?"

Lesperance checked his wrist watch. "Up ahead. We'll bisect his trail in sixty seconds. Look for the red paint, for Christ's sake. Don't shoot till we give the word. Stay on the Path. *Stay on the Path!*"

They moved forward in the wind of morning.

"Strange," murmured Eckels. "Up ahead, sixty million years, Election Day over. Keith made President. Everyone celebrating. And here we are, a million years lost, and they don't exist. The things we worried about for months, a lifetime, not even born or thought about yet."

"Safety catches off, everyone!" ordered Travis. "You, first shot, Eckels. Second, Billings. Third, Kramer."

"I've hunted tiger, wild boar, buffalo, elephant, but Jesus, this is *it*," said Eckels. "I'm shaking like a kid."

"Ah," said Travis.

Everyone stopped.

Travis raised his hand. "Ahead," he whispered. "In the mist. There he is. There's His Royal Majesty now."

The jungle was wide and full of twitterings, rustlings, murmurs, and sighs.

Suddenly, it all ceased, as if someone had shut a door.

Silence.

A sound of thunder.

Out of the mist, one hundred yards away, came *Tyrannosaurus rex*.

"Jesus God," whispered Eckels.

"Sh!"

It came on great oiled, resilient, striding legs. It towered thirty feet above half of the trees, a great evil god, folding its delicate watchmaker's claws close to its oily reptilian chest. Each lower leg was a piston, a thousand pounds of white bone, sunk in thick ropes of muscle, sheathed over in a gleam of pebbled skin like the mail of a terrible warrior. Each thigh was a ton of meat, ivory, and steel mesh. And from the great breathing cage of the upper body those two delicate arms dangled out front, arms with hands which might pick up and examine men like toys, while the snake neck coiled. And the head itself, a ton of sculptured stone, lifted easily upon the sky. Its mouth gaped, exposing a fence of teeth like daggers. Its eyes rolled, ostrich eggs, empty of all expression save hunger. It closed its mouth in a death grin. It ran, its pelvic bones crushing aside trees and bushes, its taloned feet clawing damp earth, leaving prints six inches deep wherever it settled its weight. It ran with a gliding ballet step, far too poised and balanced for its ten tons. It moved into a sunlit arena warily, its beautifully reptile hands feeling the air.

"My God!" Eckels twitched his mouth. "It could reach up and grab the moon."

"Sh!" Travis jerked angrily. "He hasn't seen us yet."

"It can't be killed." Eckels pronounced this verdict quietly, as if there could be no argument. He had weighed the evidence and this was his considered opinion. The rifle in his hands seemed a cap gun. "We were fools to come. This is impossible."

"Shut up!" hissed Travis.

"Nightmare."

"Turn around," commanded Travis. "Walk quietly to the Machine. We'll remit one half your fee."

"I didn't realize it would be this *big*," said Eckels. "I miscalculated, that's all. And now I want out."

"It *sees* us!"

"There's the red paint on its chest!"

The Thunder Lizard raised itself. Its armored flesh glittered like a thousand green coins. The coins, crusted with slime, steamed. In the slime, tiny insects wriggled, so that the entire body seemed to twitch and undulate, even while the monster itself did not move. It exhaled. The stink of raw flesh blew down the wilderness.

"Get me out of here," said Eckels. "It was never like this before. I was always sure I'd come through alive. I had good guides, good safaris, and safety. This time, I figured wrong. I've met my match and admit it. This is too much for me to get hold of."

"Don't run," said Lesperance. "Turn around. Hide in the Machine."

"Yes." Eckels seemed to be numb. He looked at his feet as if trying to make them move. He gave a grunt of helplessness.

"Eckels!"

He took a few steps, blinking, shuffling.

"Not *that* way!"

The Monster, at the first motion, lunged forward with a terrible scream. It covered one hundred yards in four seconds. The rifles jerked up and blazed fire. A windstorm from the beast's mouth engulfed them in the stench of slime and old blood. The Monster roared, teeth glittering with sun.

Eckels, not looking back, walked blindly to the edge of the Path, his gun limp in his arms, stepped off the Path, and walked, not knowing it, in the jungle. His feet sank into green moss. His legs moved him, and he felt alone and remote from the events behind.

The rifles cracked again. Their sound was lost in shriek and lizard thunder. The great lever of the reptile's tail swung up, lashed sideways. Trees exploded in clouds of leaf and branch. The Monster twitched its jeweler's hands down to fondle at the men, to twist them in half, to crush them like berries, to cram them into its teeth and its screaming throat. Its boulder-stone eyes leveled with the men. They saw themselves mirrored. They fired at the metallic eyelids and the blazing black iris.

Like a stone idol, like a mountain avalanche, *Tyrannosaurus* fell. Thundering, it clutched trees, pulled them with it. It wrenched and tore the metal Path. The men flung themselves back and away. The body hit, ten tons of cold flesh and stone. The guns fired. The Monster lashed its armored tail, twitched its snake jaws, and lay still. A fount of blood spurted from its throat. Somewhere inside, a sac of fluids burst. Sickening gushes drenched the hunters. They stood, red and glistening.

The thunder faded.

The jungle was silent. After the avalanche, a green peace. After the nightmare, morning.

Billings and Kramer sat on the pathway and threw up. Travis and Lesperance stood with smoking rifles, cursing steadily.

In the Time Machine, on his face, Eckels lay shivering.

He had found his way back to the Path, climbed into the Machine.

Travis came walking, glanced at Eckels, took cotton gauze from a metal box, and returned to the others, who were sitting on the Path.

"Clean up."

They wiped the blood from their helmets. They began to curse too. The Monster lay, a hill of solid flesh. Within, you could hear the sighs and murmurs as the furthest chambers of it died, the organs malfunctioning, liquids running a final instant from pocket to sac to spleen, everything shutting off, closing up forever. It was like standing by a wrecked locomotive or a steam shovel at quitting time, all valves being released or levered tight. Bones cracked; the tonnage of its own flesh, off balance, dead weight, snapped the delicate forearms, caught underneath. The meat settled, quivering.

Another cracking sound. Overhead, a gigantic tree branch broke from its heavy mooring, fell. It crashed upon the dead beast with finality.

"There," Lesperance checked his watch. "Right on time. That's the giant tree that was scheduled to fall and kill this animal originally." He glanced at the two hunters. "You want the trophy picture?"

"What?"

"We can't take a trophy back to the Future. The body has to stay right here where it would have died originally, so the insects, birds, and bacteria can get at it, as they were intended to. Everything in balance. The body stays. But we *can* take a picture of you standing near it."

The two men tried to think, but gave up, shaking their heads.

They let themselves be led along the metal Path. They sank wearily into the Machine cushions. They gazed back at the ruined Monster, the stagnating mound, where already strange reptilian birds and golden insects were busy at the steaming armor.

A sound on the floor of the Time Machine stiffened them. Eckels sat there, shivering.

"I'm sorry," he said at last.

"Get up!" cried Travis.

Eckels got up.

"Go out on that Path alone," said Travis. He had his rifle pointed. "You're not coming back in the Machine. We're leaving you here!"

Lesperance seized Travis' arm. "Wait—"

"Stay out of this!" Travis shook his hand away. "This son of a bitch nearly killed us. But it isn't *that* so much. Hell, no. It's his *shoes*! Look at them! He ran off the Path. My God, that *ruins* us! Christ knows how much we'll forfeit! Tens of thousands of dollars of insurance! We guarantee no one leaves the Path. He left it. Oh, the damn fool! I'll have to report to the government. They might revoke our license to travel. God knows *what* he's done to Time, to History!"

"Take it easy, all he did was kick up some dirt."

"How do we *know*?" cried Travis. "We don't know anything! It's all a damn mystery! Get out there, Eckels!"

Eckels fumbled his shirt. "I'll pay anything. A hundred thousand dollars!"

Travis glared at Eckels' checkbook and spat. "Go out there. The Monster's next to the Path. Stick your arms up to your elbows in his mouth. Then you can come back with us."

"That's unreasonable!"

"The Monster's dead, you yellow bastard. The bullets! The bullets can't be left behind. They don't belong in the Past; they might change something. Here's my knife. Dig them out!"

The jungle was alive again, full of the old tremorings and bird cries. Eckels turned slowly to regard that primeval garbage dump, that hill of nightmares and terror. After a long time, like a sleepwalker, he shuffled out along the Path.

He returned, shuddering, five minutes later, his arms soaked and red to the elbows. He held out his hands. Each held a number of steel bullets. Then he fell. He lay where he fell, not moving.

"You didn't have to make him do that," said Lesperance.

"Didn't I? It's too early to tell." Travis nudged the still body. "He'll live. Next time he won't go hunting game like this. Okay." He jerked his thumb wearily at Lesperance.

"Switch on. Let's go home."

1492. 1776. 1812.

They cleaned their hands and faces. They changed their caking shirts and pants. Eckels was up and around again, not speaking. Travis glared at him for a full ten minutes.

"Don't look at me," cried Eckels. "I haven't done anything."

"Who can tell?"

"Just ran off the Path, that's all, a little mud on my shoes—what do you want me to do—get down and pray?"

"We might need it. I'm warning you, Eckels, I might kill you yet. I've got my gun ready."

"I'm innocent. I've done nothing!"

1999. 2000. 2055.

The Machine stopped.

"Get out," said Travis.

The room was there as they had left it. But not the same as they had left it. The same man sat behind the same desk. But the same man did not quite sit behind the same desk.

Travis looked around swiftly. "Everything okay here?" he snapped.

"Fine. Welcome home!"

Travis did not relax. He seemed to be looking at the very atoms of the air itself, at the way the sun poured through the one high window.

"Okay, Eckels, get out. Don't ever come back."

Eckels could not move.

"You heard me," said Travis. "What're you *staring* at?"

Eckels stood smelling of the air, and there was a thing to the air, a chemical taint so subtle, so slight, that only a faint cry of his subliminal senses warned him it was there. The colors, white, gray, blue, orange, in the wall, in the furniture, in the sky beyond the window, were . . . were . . . And there was a *feel*. His flesh twitched. His hands twitched. He stood drinking the oddness with the pores of his body. Somewhere, someone must have been screaming one of those whistles that only a dog can hear. His body screamed silence in return. Beyond this room, beyond this wall, beyond this man who was not quite the same man seated at this desk that was not quite the same desk . . . lay an entire world of streets and people. What sort of world it was now, there was no telling. He could feel them moving there, beyond the walls, almost, like so many chess pieces blown in a dry wind. . . .

But the immediate thing was the sign painted on the office wall, the same sign he had read earlier today on first entering.

Somehow, the sign had changed:

TYME SEFARI INC.
SEFARIS TU ANY YEER EN THE PAST.
YU NAIM THE ANIMALL.
WEE TAEK YU THAIR.
YU SHOOT ITT.

Eckels felt himself fall into a chair. He fumbled crazily at the thick slime on his boots. He held up a clod of dirt, trembling. "No, it *can't* be. Not a *little* thing like that. No!"

Embedded in the mud, glistening green and gold and black, was a butterfly, very beautiful and very dead.

"Not a little thing like *that*! Not a butterfly!" cried Eckels.

It fell to the floor, an exquisite thing, a small thing that could upset balances and knock down a line of small dominoes and then big dominoes and then gigantic dominoes, all down the years across Time. Eckels' mind whirled. It *couldn't* change things. Killing one butterfly couldn't be *that* important! Could it?

His face was cold. His mouth trembled, asking: "Who—who won the presidential election yesterday?"

The man behind the desk laughed. "You joking? You know damn well. Deutscher, of course! Who else? Not that damned weakling Keith. We got an iron man now, a man with guts, by God!" The official stopped. "What's wrong?"

Eckels moaned. He dropped to his knees. He scrabbled at the golden butterfly with shaking fingers. "Can't we," he pleaded to the world, to himself, to the officials, to the Machine, "can't we take it *back,* can't we *make* it alive again? Can't we start over? Can't we—"

He did not move. Eyes shut, he waited, shivering. He heard Travis breathe loud in the room; he heard Travis shift his rifle, click the safety catch, and raise the weapon.

There was a sound of thunder.

Science Fiction

To most people, science is a mystery and scientists are the chief detectives. They peer through microscopes into a universe invisible to most of us. Scientists gaze through telescopes across distances that are calculated in light years. They wrestle with invisible foes and propose theories that we often cannot understand. Science and technology change our lives and the way we live.

Writers of science fiction often take the latest scientific theories of technological advances and imagine how they will affect our world and our behavior. Isaac Asimov, one of the foremost writers of science fiction, defined science fiction as "that branch of literature which is concerned with the impact of scientific advance upon human beings." In other words, science fiction is concerned with how science affects us.

For example, scientists predict that people will one day live in outer space. Science-fiction writers, in turn, wonder what kind of a society we will establish. Scientists invent androids, and science-fiction writers imagine a society run by androids. Scientists may one day create life, and science-fiction writers ask what kind of life it will be.

Science fiction is more than just galactic adventures and spectacular special effects. It is a way of looking into the future and examining choices. Of course, it is also entertainment. People enjoy science fiction not because it is science, but because it is good reading.

In this lesson we will look at four ways in which author Ray Bradbury develops "A Sound of Thunder" to make it seem believable to us.

1 ◆ It presents things that are strange and unusual. Outer space, alien creatures, and future worlds are standard fare in science fiction.

2 ◆ It has an element of science. A sound scientific principle or a believable scientific theory forms the basis of a story.

3 ◆ It deals with human nature or society. Even alien creatures from an unknown planet will display humanlike qualities.

4 ◆ It tells a good story. The science-fiction writer must hold your interest just as any other good storyteller must.

1 ◆ Science Fiction and the Unusual

Science fiction can always be counted on to contain the unusual—new life-forms, other planets, future eras. Science-fiction fans always enjoy reading and thinking about these strange, scary, and incredible things.

Science-fiction stories are not usually set in the "familiar" world of today. By setting a story in another place or time, or merely altering our own world, an author can create a society that is different from what we know. This society might be totally different, or different in only one small way. The author steps back from the world we live in and looks at it as an outsider might. And that, of course, is what the author hopes you will do as well. This technique is called *distancing*. Through distancing you are able to escape your own narrow world and look at things from a new viewpoint.

Readers are encouraged to compare the world of the story with the world we actually live in and see the similarities as well as the differences. Is the author's imaginary world better than our own? If so, how might we make our own world better? Is the author's imaginary world a wasteland? If it is, what can we do to make sure our own world doesn't end up the same way?

Take a look at the world of the future that Ray Bradbury has created in "A Sound of Thunder." What is unusual about it? What comparisons with our own world might this story lead you to make?

> Eckels glanced across the vast office at a mass and tangle . . . of wires and steel boxes, at an aurora that flickered now orange, now silver, now blue. . . .
>
> "A real Time Machine." He shook his head. "Makes you think. If the election had gone badly yesterday, I might be here now running away from the results. Thank God Keith won. He'll make a fine President of the United States."

The most unusual element of the world that Bradbury has created is the Time Machine. There is no such thing, of course, as a machine that takes people back in time. Yet it is fascinating to think about time travel. What might one find? What might happen if a time traveler stepped into the past?

A familiar element of this imaginary world is the presidential election. We can assume that in the year 2055 the President of the

United States is still elected by the people. But this election contained a danger yet unknown to us. One of the candidates was a tyrant, a possible dictator.

Right at the outset, then, the author has distanced us from the world of the story. It is not the world we know—it is an imaginary world of the future. Bradbury also leads us to compare the world of today with the world of the story. This comparison forces us to think about the importance of leadership in our lives. We are able to imagine the disastrous and frightening results of being governed by a tyrant.

1♦Exercise A

Read the following passage and answer the questions about it using what you have learned in this part of the lesson. Use your writing notebook or a separate piece of paper for your answers.

> The Machine slowed; its scream fell to a murmur. The Machine stopped.
>
> The sun stopped in the sky.
>
> The fog that had enveloped the Machine blew away and they were in an old time, a very old time indeed, three hunters and two Safari Heads with their blue metal guns across their knees.
>
> "Christ isn't born yet," said Travis. "Moses has not gone to the mountain to talk with God. The Pyramids are still in the earth, waiting to be cut out and put up. *Remember* that. Alexander, Caesar, Napoleon, Hitler—none of them exists."
>
> The men nodded.
>
> "That"—Mr. Travis pointed—"is the jungle of sixty\ million two thousand and fifty-five years before President Keith."

1. How does the author "distance" the reader from the world of the story? Explain your answer.

2. The author refers to Christ, Moses, Alexander, Caesar, Napoleon, and Hitler. Why does he refer to these men? What do they have in common?

Now check your answers using the suggestions in the Answer Key starting on page 457. Review this part of the lesson if you don't understand why an answer was wrong.

1♦Writing on Your Own

Look at the list you wrote for Create Your Own Science-Fiction Story on page 359 that tells about your own story idea. Now do the following:

1. Create a setting for your story. How is the setting unusual or different from the world as we know it? Consider the following elements:

   ☐ When is your story set? Is it set in the present day, or perhaps 200 years in the future?

   ☐ Where is your story set? Is it set on Earth, on another planet, or in outer space?

   ☐ What is the environment like? Is it dark or light, hot or cold, real or imagined?

2. Write a short paragraph describing the setting. Consider the above elements or any others you think are important. For example, if you are entering the world of virtual reality, what type of adventure have you chosen? Are you visiting another planet, experiencing the wonder of flight, or simply exploring unchartered territory? Remember to distance yourself and your reader from this world. You need to escape from your understanding of the world and see things from a new perspective.

3. You may want to change and rewrite your paragraph several times until you get it just the way you like it.

2 ◆ Science Fiction and Science

Every good science-fiction story contains a kernel of science. The story itself may be wildly improbable, but it must be backed up by a believable scientific theory.

There are two reasons for this "rule." The most obvious one, of course, is that without an element of science it can't be science fiction. But there's a more important reason: If the author includes something that you know to be true, then you are more inclined to go along with the rest of the story.

For example, the average reader would be insulted by a story in which a giant monster rises out of the sea and devours a city. But suppose the reader is first reminded that radiation can cause animal cells to mutate, or change—even grow. Then suppose the story involves a nuclear explosion under water, something we know has actually occurred. With these two facts in mind, you might be willing to concede that it could be possible that a giant monster was created as a result of atomic radiation. Then you could possibly imagine the giant creature rising out of the sea and swallowing up San Francisco. So you put aside the belief that the occurrence is next to impossible, and you are able to enjoy the story.

Science-fiction writers must be careful about the accuracy of the scientific facts included in their stories. If there is a glaring error in the scientific information, then it is impossible to believe the rest of the story. For instance, take the idea of time travel that is presented in "A Sound of Thunder." If the characters in the story had traveled back in time sixty million years and met John F. Kennedy, you probably would have stopped reading. You may be willing to accept the possibility of time travel, but there is a definite limit. On the other hand, to go back sixty million years and meet a dinosaur, you might say to yourself, "Sure, why not?" and continue reading.

Another element of science can be found in the following passage from the story. What theory do you find here that is generally believed to be true? What effect does this theory have on the rest of the story?

> "A Time Machine is damn finicky business. Not knowing it, we might kill an important animal, a small bird, a roach, a flower even, thus destroying an important link in a growing species."

Most people accept or are aware of the scientific theory of evolution. This theory says that life on earth developed slowly over millions of years, with each small change leading to other changes. That is what Travis is talking about in that passage. But if you interrupt this chain of life, then the link you have removed could cause an entirely different series of events. And that, of course, is exactly what happens when Eckels steps off the path and crushes a butterfly. The butterfly was a link in the evolutionary chain. If you accept the idea of evolution, you will not find it hard to believe that this one minor mishap could have devastating consequences.

2 ◆ Exercise B

Read the following passages and answer the questions about them using what you have learned in this part of the lesson. Use your writing notebook or a separate piece of paper for your answers.

Passage A
[Travis instructs the hunters before they leave the time machine.]
"This Machine, this Path, your clothing and bodies, were sterilized, as you know, before the journey. We wear these oxygen helmets so we can't introduce our bacteria into an ancient atmosphere."

Passage B
"Can these guns get a dinosaur cold?" Eckels felt his mouth saying.

"If you hit them right," said Travis on the helmet radio. "Some dinosaurs have two brains, one in the head, another far down the spinal column. We stay away from those. That's stretching luck. Put your first shots into the eyes, if you can, blind them, and go back into the brain."

1. A scientific fact or procedure is present in each of the two passages. What are they?

2. Do these passages make the story more believable? Why or why not? Support your answer.

Now check your answers using the suggestions in the Answer Key starting on page 457. Review this part of the lesson if you don't understand why an answer was wrong.

2♦Writing on Your Own

Look at the list you have written for Create Your Own Science-Fiction Story on page 359 that tells about your own story idea. Now do the following:

1. Science fiction is not just a combination of far-fetched ideas. For a science-fiction story to be believable, it must contain scientific facts we know to be true. Make up a list of possible scientific facts that would work with your story idea.

2. Choose one of the ideas you have listed above. In a short paragraph include your scientific fact. For example, if you chose virtual reality, you may want to include facts about it. How is virtual reality used now? How do scientists think it will be used in the future? Whatever subject you choose, you may want to find out more about it to make your story more believable.

3. You may want to change and rewrite your paragraph several times until you get it just the way you like it.

Most science fiction contains a lesson or an opinion about modern society. This sort of "statement" is usually implied, not stated outright. It is *suggested* in the message of the story. That is why science-fiction writers always use ideas that are familiar when inventing new creatures or planets. When you think about their creations, chances are they will remind you of someone or some place you already know. At this point, you are able to understand the author's implied message because you can relate to it.

In "A Sound of Thunder" Ray Bradbury comments on the kind of leaders a society chooses. You can best understand his message if you know something about history. The story was written in 1952, not long after World War II. The brutal reign of Adolf Hitler in Germany was still fresh in people's minds.

In the following passage, a minor character in the story describes two candidates for President of the United States in the year 2055. What kind of leader would each make? Which of these candidates do you think the author would have voted for?

> "Thank God Keith won," [said Eckels.] "He'll make a fine President of the United States."
>
> "Yes," said the man behind the desk. "We're lucky. If Deutscher had gotten in, we'd have the worst kind of dictatorship. There's an anti-everything man for you, a militarist, anti-Christ, anti-human, anti-intellectual. People called us up, you know, joking but not joking. Said if Deutscher became President they wanted to go live in 1492."

The candidate named Keith sounds honest and trustworthy. He's undoubtedly the one the author would have voted for. But the other, Deutscher, is described as "anti-everything," a tyrant interested only in his own wants and ready to wage war against those who challenge him. It's no coincidence, considering when the story was written, that this candidate has a German-sounding name— Deutscher. The author wanted readers to connect Deutscher with Hitler.

The author's attitude is clear. Leaders like Deutscher and Hitler are a threat to peace and progress. The author suggests that even minor changes in society could result in completely different kinds of leaders—

leaders associated with social unrest. This is the implied message about society that Bradbury makes in "A Sound of Thunder."

Science fiction may convey other kinds of messages also. An author may comment on a new scientific discovery by predicting how that discovery could be misused in the future. In Exercise C, Bradbury issues a sober warning. See if you can figure out what kind of statement he is making in this passage.

3 ♦ Exercise C

Read the following passage and answer the questions about it using what you have learned in this part of the lesson. Use your writing notebook or a separate piece of paper for your answers.

> [Travis says,] "Maybe Time *can't* be changed by us. Or maybe it can be changed only in little subtle ways. . . . Who knows? Who really can say he knows? We don't know. We're guessing. But until we do know for certain whether our messing around in Time *can* make a big roar or a little rustle in history, we're being damned careful."

1. What is Travis' main concern in this passage? Do you agree or disagree with his concerns? Why?

2. What is the author's implied message concerning scientific progress?

Now check your answers using the suggestions in the Answer Key starting on page 457. Review this part of the lesson if you don't understand why an answer was wrong.

3 ♦ Writing on Your Own

Look at the list you have written for Create Your Own Science-Fiction Story on page 359 that tells you about your own story idea. Now do the following:

1. Select an item from your list and think of what message you would want to tell your readers. For example, if you chose virtual reality,

you may want to examine what would happen if that discovery fell into the wrong hands. How could something created to benefit people end up changing or destroying their lives?

2. Write a short paragraph explaining how your scientific idea has changed society. Is it for the better? Will it destroy society? Why? Your paragraph should include your lesson or implied statement.

3. You may want to change and rewrite your paragraph several times until you get it just the way you like it.

4 ♦ Science Fiction and Storytelling

The incredible creatures and places presented in science-fiction stories are entertaining. The scientific facts used as a basis for the stories are informative. And the statements about people and society cause us to think about our world. But when you come right down to it, the real reason people read science fiction is to enjoy a good story. Above all, then, a science-fiction writer must be a good storyteller.

Like any other teller of tales, authors of science fiction must be able to create characters a reader can believe in. Plots must be exciting and suspenseful. Language should be vivid and precise.

Without a doubt, Ray Bradbury is a master storyteller. He is able to create vivid images in the minds of his readers. That is why his science fiction is so popular. As an example, read this description of Tyrannosaurus rex. How does this passage add suspense, excitement, and interest to the story?

> Out of the mist, one hundred yards away, came *Tyrannosaurus rex*. . . .
>
> It came on great oiled, resilient, striding legs. It towered thirty feet above half of the trees, a great evil god, folding its delicate watchmaker's claws close to its oily reptilian chest. Each lower leg was a piston, a thousand pounds of white bone, sunk in thick ropes of muscle, sheathed over in a gleam of pebbled skin like the mail of a terrible warrior. Each thigh was a ton of meat, ivory, and steel mesh. And from the great breathing cage of the upper body those two delicate arms dangled out front, arms with hands which might pick up and examine men like toys, while the snake neck coiled. And the head itself, a ton of sculptured stone, lifted easily upon the sky. Its mouth gaped, exposing a fence of teeth like daggers. Its eyes rolled, ostrich eggs, empty of all expression save hunger. It closed its mouth in a death grin.

Notice how menacing and dangerous the creature seems. It is huge, towering above the treetops. It is strong, with "thick ropes of muscle." It is evil, with hands "which might pick up and examine men like toys." Above all, it is hungry, with "a fence of teeth like daggers."

Can such a creature be stopped by mere bullets? you wonder. Or will the hunters end up destroyed? The author has created dramatic suspense in this scene. What will happen next? Who will win? This kind of suspense, which keeps readers turning pages, is the mark of a good storyteller.

Another equally important skill for a writer is the ability to write a vivid description. Read the passage in Exercise D. How does the author make you "see" this dying prehistoric creature and think about dinosaurs in a way you have never thought about them before?

4 ◆ Exercise D

Read the following passage and answer the questions about it using what you have learned in this part of the lesson. Use your writing notebook or a separate piece of paper for your answers.

> The Monster lay, a hill of solid flesh. Within, you could hear the sighs and murmurs as the furthest chambers of it died, the organs malfunctioning, liquids running a final instant from pocket to sac to spleen, everything shutting off, closing up forever. It was like standing by a wrecked locomotive or a steam shovel at quitting time, all valves being released or levered tight. Bones cracked; the tonnage of its own flesh, off balance, dead weight, snapped the delicate forearms, caught underneath. The meat settled, quivering.

1. Authors use comparisons to help readers clearly visualize events in a story. In the passage, Ray Bradbury compares the dinosaur to something in the twentieth century. What does Bradbury compare the dinosaur to? Why do you think he makes this comparison?

2. Think about the terms the author uses to describe this creature: a hill of flesh, chambers, malfunctioning organs, liquids, tonnage, meat. Does his description help you clearly see the creature? Write a few sentences describing this creature in your own words.

Now check your answers using the suggestions in the Answer Key starting on page 457. Review this part of the lesson if you don't understand why an answer was wrong.

4♦Writing on Your Own

Look at the list you have written for Create Your Own Science-Fiction Story on page 359 that tells you about your own story idea. Now do the following:

1. A good author includes an element of suspense or conflict in a story. Without conflict, you would merely be reporting a series of events. Create a list of possible conflicts that could arise in your story. Perhaps your idea poses an environmental threat, pits man against machine, or questions our entire social structure.

2. Choose one of the conflicts you have created to add suspense to your story. What has gone wrong? Will the results be disastrous? Or will the social structure of that world be changed as a result? Write a paragraph that adds suspense to your story while examining issues important to your story idea. For example, what if some individuals never return from the world of virtual reality? Where have their minds really gone? Will an unknown, dangerous force be created by these "lost" minds?

3. You may want to change and rewrite your paragraph several times until you get it just the way you like it.

Now go on to Reviewing and Interpreting the Story.

Answer these questions without looking back at the story. Choose the best answer to each question and put an *x* in the box beside it, or write your answer on a separate piece of paper.

Remembering .Facts

1. Some dinosaurs are more difficult to kill than others because they

   ☐ a. run very fast.

   ☐ b. are able to outwit their attacker.

   ☐ c. can blend in with the jungle and hide from hunters.

   ☐ d. have two brains.

2. How do the hunters know which dinosaurs they can shoot?

   ☐ a. They are all dinosaur experts.

   ☐ b. The correct dinosaur has been marked with red paint.

   ☐ c. They have all seen pictures of which dinosaurs they may kill.

   ☐ d. The tour guides are there to point out the correct dinosaurs.

Following the Order of Events

3. What is the first thing Eckels notices when he returns from the time safari?

   ☐ a. a strange smell in the air

   ☐ b. the mud on his boots

   ☐ c. a dead butterfly

   ☐ d. the sign on the office door

4. Just before returning to the present, Travis orders Eckels to

  ☐ a. take a photo of the dead dinosaur.

  ☐ b. bury the dinosaur.

  ☐ c. pay ten thousand dollars.

  ☐ d. retrieve the bullets.

Understanding Word Choices 5. "The cave man . . . is not just any <u>expendable</u> man, no! He is an entire future nation." Which of the following words is closest in meaning to *expendable*?

  ☐ a. dependable

  ☐ b. agreeable

  ☐ c. disposable

  ☐ d. defendable

6. "With the death of that one cave man, a billion others yet unborn are <u>throttled</u> in the womb." Another word for *throttled* is

  ☐ a. created.

  ☐ b. nourished.

  ☐ c. enslaved.

  ☐ d. strangled.

7. Why is it so important that the hunters remain on the Path?

   ☐ a. There is a heavy fine for leaving the Path.

   ☐ b. By disturbing *anything* in the past, they could change the future.

   ☐ c. The hunters are protected from harm only if they remain on the Path.

   ☐ d. The guides are afraid someone will get lost in the dense jungle.

8. What had Eckels done to change the course of time?

   ☐ a. He left the Path.

   ☐ b. He removed the bullets from the dead dinosaur.

   ☐ c. He did not follow the rules given to him by Travis.

   ☐ d. He killed a butterfly.

9. "If Deutscher had gotten in, we'd have the worst kind of dictatorship. There's an <u>anti-everything</u> man for you. . . ." What is meant by *anti-everything*?

   ☐ a. He firmly supports the causes he believes in.

   ☐ b. His main concern is for the people he represents.

   ☐ c. He does not support and is against the needs of the people.

   ☐ d. He is against taking any aggressive action.

10. "The same man sat behind the same desk. But the same man did not quite sit behind the same desk." What is the author telling you?

   ☐ a. Although it is the same man, there is something slightly different about him.

☐ b. It is not the same man, only someone who looks similar.

☐ c. It is the same man, but a different desk.

☐ d. Everything has changed, nothing is the same.

Understanding Character 11. When facing the mighty dinosaur, Eckels is

☐ a. determined to shoot it on his own.

☐ b. terrified and wants out of the safari.

☐ c. disappointed because it is an easy kill.

☐ d. sorry he wasted his money.

12. Which group of adjectives best describes Travis?

☐ a. kind and sympathetic

☐ b. cold and calculating

☐ c. brave and intolerant

☐ d. fearful and weak

Understanding Setting 13. Why is it necessary that the story begin and end in the same place?

☐ a. The author does not want to confuse the reader.

☐ b. The subtle differences in the same setting will be recognized by the travelers.

☐ c. If the travelers were to remain in the past, the future would be at risk.

☐ d. The travelers must report back to Safari headquarters following their adventure.

14. "The jungle was high and the jungle was broad and the jungle was the entire world forever and forever." What feelings does the author want to create?

☐ a. sorrow and despair

☐ b. anger and fear

☐ c. awe and amazement

☐ d. joy and happiness

Understanding Feelings 15. How does Eckels seem to feel about Deutscher's election as president at the end of the story?

☐ a. He is happy at this turn of events.

☐ b. He feels terrified by this change.

☐ c. He thinks Deutscher will be good for the country.

☐ d. He doesn't care who is president.

16. Travis blames Eckels for the change in the world. How does Travis respond?

☐ a. He decides to quit time travel.

☐ b. He wants the world to know about Eckels' mistake.

☐ c. He decides to give his support to President Deutscher.

☐ d. He kills Eckels.

Now check your answers using the Answer Key starting on page 457. Make no mark for right answers. <u>Correct</u> any wrong answers you may have by putting a check mark (✓) in the box next to the right answer. Count the number of questions you answered correctly and plot the total on the Comprehension Scores graph on page 468.

Next, look at the questions you answered incorrectly. What types of questions were they? Count the number you got wrong of each type and enter the numbers in the spaces below.

Remembering Facts   _____

Following the Order of Events   _____

Understanding Word Choices   _____

Understanding Important Ideas   _____

Understanding Levels of Meaning   _____

Understanding Character   _____

Understanding Setting   _____

Understanding Feelings   _____

Now use these numbers to fill in the Comprehension Skills Profile on page 469.

Discussion Guides

The questions below will help you think about the story and the lesson you have just read. If you don't discuss these questions in class, try to think about them or discuss them with your classmates. Perhaps you will want to write a few paragraphs in answer to the questions.

Discussing Science Fiction

1. In what ways are the people and the society of the year 2055 a lot like people and society today?

2. What are some of the incredible elements of the future presented in "A Sound of Thunder"? How do the familiar elements of the story help make the incredible elements more believable?

3. What scientific facts or theories are included in this story?

Discussing the Story

4. Eckels, the big game hunter, learns something about himself in the course of the story. What does he learn?

5. At the end of the story, the man behind the desk is a little bit different from how he was at the beginning. In what way has he changed?

6. Author Ray Bradbury suggests that killing a butterfly could change the world millions of years later. How, then, might the world of 2055 be different if the Nazis hadn't been in power during World War II?

Discussing the Author's Work

7. Ray Bradbury was careful to do *none* of the following:

   ☐ make the dinosaur cute and lovable

   ☐ make the world of the future a place of total peace and happiness

   ☐ place the dinosaur in a desert or arctic setting

   Why would it have been *bad* science fiction if the author had done any of these things?

8. Reread the paragraph about time travel that begins, "A touch of the hand . . ." on page 362. In what way is the language of this paragraph poetic? What feelings does it express about time travel—fear? disinterest? fascination? awe? Point out some figures of speech and discuss what they add to the passage.

9. Bradbury hints that scientists don't know for sure where their work may lead them. Name some fields of modern science that could possibly have harmful effects on the world? Does this possibility mean that we should not investigate these areas further? Explain your opinion.

Writing Exercise

Read all the instructions before you begin writing. If you have any questions about how to begin the writing assignment, review Using the Writing Process beginning on page 445, or confer with your writing coach.

1. Review the passages you wrote in the four exercises Writing On Your Own. If you haven't done those exercises yet, build your story idea now by following the instructions for each exercise.

2. At this point, you already have many of the elements needed to compose your science-fiction story. You have a setting that contains both the familiar and the unfamiliar. You also have a proven scientific fact to give your story credibility. There is a certain distance between the world as we know it and the world you have created. You know how your idea affects society. Finally, you have chosen a conflict to give your story some suspense.

   Now it is time to bring everything together for your story. There are a few things you need to consider. Who or what is going to be your main character? You will need to give a description of this character. Your character must fit the setting, your story must adhere to the known scientific fact, and your plot must create suspense and conflict. Most important, use your imagination but don't go overboard. Remember, anything goes as long as your readers can relate to it.

3. Write, revise, correct, and rewrite your story until you are sure you have got it just the way you want it.

Unit 10   Judgments and Conclusions:
         Discussing Stories

A Cap for Steve
BY MORLEY CALLAGHAN

About the Illustration

What do you think is happening in this scene? Point out
some details in the drawing to support your response.

Here are some questions to help you think about the
story:

◆ Where is this scene taking place?

◆ How do you think the boy feels about the ball player?

◆ What do you think the man with the boy is talking
about?

Unit 10

Introduction

About the Story

Baseball is often called the great American pastime, but you can find baseball-crazy kids just about anywhere. Canadian author Morley Callaghan introduces us to Steve Diamond, a shy twelve year old who loves baseball more than anything in the world. He eats, sleeps, and dreams the game. And as far as his father is concerned, that's just the beginning of the problem.

Like many parents, Steve's father, Dave, worries a lot about making ends meet. He gets impatient about money, and his son's love for baseball doesn't help matters much. Even though a few extra dollars would make a big difference to the family budget, Steve spends his time playing ball instead of holding down a part-time job. Dave gets more and more annoyed, but neither he nor his son really confronts the developing conflict.

Despite Dave's scorn for the game, Steve finally convinces his dad to take him to watch the Phillies play. But to everyone's amazement, the awestruck boy comes home with a souvenir cap. Before long, that cap teaches both Steve and Dave a few lessons about growing up, and helps them—and us—think about some important life values.

This story is a simple one. It isn't filled with action or danger, and the characters are regular everyday people. But they deal with problems that are familiar to everyone. Like many teenagers, Steve learns that his father isn't perfect. That discovery is painful for father and son, yet it helps the two of them begin to build a stronger relationship. Dave learns that money shouldn't always come first, and Steve learns the importance of being quick to forgive. As you read the story, you may come to other conclusions about their relationship.

Toronto is the setting for almost all of Morley Callaghan's writing, and his vivid descriptions of the city have inspired many other Canadian writers. Born there in 1903, Callaghan grew up in the city, where he spent some time working for the *Toronto Star*. There he met the famous writer Ernest Hemingway, who encouraged him to concentrate on writing. Throughout his long career, Callaghan wrote many novels and short stories, some of which became best-sellers and won awards. If you are interested in reading more of his stories, you might look for the collections *Now that April's Here* and *Morley Callaghan's Stories*. Patricia Morley has written a biography of him called *Morley Callaghan*.

About the Lesson

The lesson that follows the story is about making judgments and drawing conclusions. The ideas in this lesson won't be entirely new because you've been making judgments and drawing conclusions about every story in this book—and probably every story you've ever read. But the lesson will help you assemble your thoughts and form a clear opinion about your reading.

Before you discuss a story, you make some judgments about what you have read and come to some conclusions about the story as a whole. For example, you decide whether or not you like the story and come up with reasons that support your opinion. You think about the characters and the settings and decide how they affect you. You consider the conflicts and the action, and you decide what they mean. Then you assemble in your mind the facts and details that the author has presented. From these facts and details you form ideas about the meaning of the story and its importance or value. These ideas are inferences that you make from the story, and from the inferences you form opinions about the story as a whole—including plot, characters, and theme.

The following questions will prepare you for a discussion of "A Cap for Steve."

◆ What details do you learn about Dave at the beginning of the story? How do his attitudes and personality influence the events in the story?

◆ Do you always approve of Steve's behavior? Or do you think he has some growing up to do?

◆ What makes Dave take money from Mr. Hudson?

◆ At the end of the story, Dave feels that he has failed his son. But he also feels "strangely exalted" by his role as a father. How is it possible for one person to have such different feelings about the same event?

Analyzing Your Own Story

Throughout this book you have worked on exercises that have helped you understand how a story is built. Now here is your chance to think about your own work. Use your writing notebook or a separate piece of paper and try the following suggestions:

1. Reread the stories you have written in previous chapters, and choose one that you like. It should have at least two characters.

2. Think about the relationship between two major characters. Do they seem to share some important emotion—for example, love, hate, or jealousy—or does each person seem isolated and alone? What details of plot or character description help to create that relationship? How is the setting involved? Make a list of the details that work to support the relationship between the characters.

3. Now think about how you could intensify that relationship. For example, if two characters have a history of jealousy and competition, how can you improve the story to emphasize that history? What details of plot or character description can you add? How can the setting contribute? Make a list of your ideas.

A Cap for Steve

by Morley Callaghan

Dave Diamond, a poor man, a carpenter's assistant, was a small, wiry, quick-tempered individual who had learned how to make every dollar count in his home. His wife, Anna, had been sick a lot, and his twelve-year-old son, Steve, had to be kept in school. Steve, a big-eyed, shy kid, ought to have known the value of money as well as Dave did. It had been ground into him.

But the boy was crazy about baseball, and after school, when he could have been working as a delivery boy or selling papers, he played ball with the kids. His failure to appreciate that the family needed a few extra dollars disgusted Dave. Around the house he wouldn't let Steve talk about baseball, and he scowled when he saw him hurrying off with his glove after dinner.

When the Phillies came to town to play an exhibition game with the home team and Steve pleaded to be taken to the ball park, Dave, of course, was outraged. Steve knew they couldn't afford it. But he had got his mother on his side. Finally Dave made a bargain with them. He said that if Steve came home after school and worked hard helping to make some kitchen shelves he would take him that night to the ball park.

Steve worked hard, but Dave was still resentful. They had to coax him to put on his good suit. When they started out Steve held aloof, feeling guilty, and they walked down the street like strangers; then Dave glanced at Steve's face and, half-ashamed, took his arm more cheerfully.

As the game went on, Dave had to listen to Steve's recitation of the batting average of every Philly that stepped up to the plate; the time the boy must have wasted learning these averages began to *appall* him. He showed it so plainly that Steve felt guilty again and was silent.

After the game Dave let Steve drag him onto the field to keep him company while he tried to get some autographs from the Philly players, who were being hemmed in by gangs of kids blocking the way to the club-house. But Steve, who was shy, let the other kids block him off from the players. Steve would push his way in, get blocked out, and come back to stand mournfully beside Dave. And Dave grew impatient. He was wasting valuable time. He wanted to get home; Steve knew it and was worried.

Then the big, blond Philly outfielder, Eddie Condon, who had been held up by a gang of kids tugging at his arm and thrusting their score cards at him broke loose and made a run for the club-house. He was jostled, and his blue cap with the red peak, tilted far back on his head, fell off. It fell at Steve's feet, and Steve stooped quickly and grabbed it. "Okay, son," the outfielder called, turning back. But Steve, holding the hat in both hands, only stared at him.

"Give him his cap, Steve," Dave said, smiling apologetically at the big outfielder who towered over them. But Steve drew the hat closer to his chest. In an awed trance he looked up at big Eddie Condon. It was an embarrassing moment. All the other kids were watching. Some shouted. "Give him his cap."

"My cap, son," Eddie Condon said, his hand out.

"Hey, Steve," Dave said, and he gave him a shake. But he had to jerk the cap out of Steve's hands.

"Here you are," he said.

The outfielder, noticing Steve's white, worshipping face and pleading eyes, grinned and then shrugged. "Aw, let him keep it," he said.

"No, Mister Condon, you don't need to do that," Steve protested.

"It's happened before. Forget it," Eddie Condon said, and he trotted away to the club-house.

Dave handed the cap to Steve; envious kids circled around them and Steve said, "He said I could keep it, Dad. You heard him, didn't you?"

"Yeah, I heard him," Dave admitted. The wonder in Steve's face made him smile. He took the boy by the arm and they hurried off the field.

On the way home Dave couldn't get him to talk about the game; he couldn't get him to take his eyes off the cap. Steve could hardly believe in his own happiness. "See," he said suddenly, and he showed Dave that Eddie Condon's name was printed on the sweat-band. Then he went on dreaming. Finally he put the cap on his head and turned to Dave with a slow, proud smile. The cap was away too big for him; it fell down over his ears. "Never mind," Dave said. "You can get your mother to take a tuck in the back."

When they got home Dave was tired and his wife didn't understand the cap's importance, and they couldn't get Steve to go to bed. He swaggered around wearing the cap and looking in the mirror every ten minutes. He took the cap to bed with him.

Dave and his wife had a cup of coffee in the kitchen, and Dave told her again how they had got the cap. They agreed that their boy must have an attractive quality that showed in his face, and that Eddie Condon must have been drawn to him—why else would he have singled Steve out from all the kids?

But Dave got tired of the fuss Steve made over that cap and of the way he wore it from the time he got up in the morning until the time he went to bed. Some kid was always coming in, wanting to try on the cap. It was childish, Dave said, for Steve to go around assuming that the cap made him important in the neighborhood, and to keep telling them how he had become a leader in the park a few blocks away where he played ball in the evenings. And Dave wouldn't stand for Steve's keeping the cap on while he was eating. He was always scolding his wife for accepting Steve's explanation that he'd forgotten he had it on. Just the same, it was remarkable what a little thing like a ball cap could do for a kid, Dave admitted to his wife as he smiled to himself.

One night Steve was late coming home from the park. Dave didn't realize how late it was until he put down his newspaper and watched his wife at the window. Her restlessness got on his nerves. "See what comes from encouraging the boy to hang around with those park loafers," he said. "I don't encourage him," she protested. "You do," he insisted irritably, for he was really worried now. A gang hung around the park until midnight. It was a bad park. It was true that on one side there was a good district with fine, expensive apartment houses, but the kids from that neighborhood left the park to the kids from the poorer homes. When his wife went out and walked down to the corner it was his turn to wait and worry and watch at the open window. Each waiting moment tortured him. At last he heard his wife's voice and Steve's voice and he relaxed and sighed; then he remembered his duty and rushed angrily to meet them.

"I'll fix you, Steve, once and for all," he said. "I'll show you you can't start coming into the house at midnight."

"Hold your horses, Dave," his wife said. "Can't you see the state he's in?" Steve looked utterly exhausted and beaten.

"What's the matter?" Dave asked quickly.

"I lost my cap," Steve whispered; he walked past his father and threw himself on the couch in the living room and lay with his face hidden.

"Now, don't scold him, Dave," his wife said.

"Scold him. Who's scolding him?" Dave asked, indignantly. "It's his cap, not mine. If it's not worth his while to hang on to it, why should I scold him?" But he was implying resentfully that he alone recognized the cap's value.

"So you are scolding him," his wife said. "It's his cap. Not yours. What happened, Steve?"

Steve told them he had been playing ball and he found that when he ran the bases the cap fell off; it was still too big despite the tuck his mother had taken in the band. So the next time he came to bat he tucked the cap in his hip pocket. Someone had lifted it, he was sure.

"And he didn't even know whether it was still in his pocket," Dave said sarcastically.

"I wasn't careless, Dad," Steve said. For the last three hours he had been wandering around the homes of the kids who had been in the park at the time; he wanted to go on, but he was too tired. Dave knew the boy was apologizing to him, but he didn't know why it made him angry.

"If he didn't hang on to it, it's not worth worrying about now," he said, and he sounded offended.

After that night they knew that Steve didn't go to the park to play ball; he went to look for the cap. It irritated Dave to see him sit around listlessly, or walk in circles, trying to force his memory to find a particular incident which would suddenly recall to him the moment when the cap had been taken. It was no attitude for a growing, healthy boy to take, Dave complained. He told Steve firmly once and for all that he didn't want to hear any more about the cap.

One night, two weeks later, Dave was walking home with Steve from the shoemaker's. It was a hot night. When they passed an ice-cream parlor Steve slowed down. "I guess I couldn't have a soda, could I?" Steve said. "Nothing doing," Dave said firmly. "Come on now," he added as Steve hung back, looking in the window.

"Dad, look!" Steve cried suddenly, pointing at the window. "My cap! There's my cap! He's coming out!"

A well-dressed boy was leaving the ice-cream parlor; he had on a blue ball cap with a red peak, just like Steve's cap. "Hey, you!" Steve cried, and he rushed at the boy, his small face fierce and his eyes wild. Before the boy could back away Steve had snatched the cap from his head. "That's my cap!" he shouted.

"What's this?" the bigger boy said. "Hey, give me my

cap or I'll give you a poke on the nose."

Dave was surprised that his own shy boy did not back away. He watched him clutch the cap in his left hand, half crying with excitement as he put his head down and drew back his right fist: he was willing to fight. And Dave was proud of him.

"Wait, now," Dave said. "Take it easy, son," he said to the other boy, who refused to back away.

"My boy says it's his cap," Dave said.

"Well, he's crazy. It's my cap."

"I was with him when he got this cap. When the Phillies played here. It's a Philly cap."

"Eddie Condon gave it to me," Steve said. "And you stole it from me, you jerk."

"Don't call me a jerk, you little squirt. I never saw you before in my life."

"Look," Steve said, pointing to the printing on the cap's sweatband. "It's Eddie Condon's cap. See? See, Dad?"

"Yeah. You're right, Son. Ever see this boy before, Steve?"

"No," Steve said reluctantly.

The other boy realized he might lose the cap. "I bought it from a guy," he said. "I paid him. My father knows I paid him." He said he got the cap at a ball park. He groped for some magically impressive words and suddenly found them. "You'll have to speak to my father," he said.

"Sure, I'll speak to your father," Dave said. "What's your name? Where do you live?"

"My name's Hudson. I live about ten minutes away on the other side of the park." The boy appraised Dave, who wasn't any bigger than he was and who wore a faded blue windbreaker and no tie. "My father is a lawyer," he said boldly. "He wouldn't let me keep the cap if he didn't think I should."

"Is that a fact?" Dave asked belligerently. "Well, we'll see. Come on. Let's go." And he got between the two boys and they walked along the street. They didn't talk to each other. Dave knew the Hudson boy was waiting to get to the protection of his home, and Steve knew it, too, and he looked up apprehensively at Dave. And Dave, reaching for his hand, squeezed it encouragingly and strode along, cocky and belligerent, knowing that Steve relied on him.

The Hudson boy lived in that row of fine apartment houses on the other side of the park. At the entrance to one of these houses Dave tried not to hang back and show he was impressed, because he could feel Steve hanging back. When they got into the small elevator Dave didn't know why he took off his hat. In the carpeted hall on the fourth floor the Hudson boy said, "Just a minute," and entered his own apartment. Dave and Steve were left alone in the corridor, knowing that the other boy was preparing his father for the encounter. Steve looked anxiously at his father, and Dave said, "Don't worry, Son," and he added resolutely, "No one's putting anything over on us."

A tall balding man in a brown velvet smoking-jacket suddenly opened the door. Dave had never seen a man wearing one of those jackets, although he had seen them in department-store windows. "Good evening," he said, making a deprecatory gesture at the cap Steve still clutched tightly in his left hand. "My boy didn't get your name. My name is Hudson."

"Mine's Diamond."

"Come on in," Mr. Hudson said, putting out his hand and laughing good-naturedly. He led Dave and Steve into his living room. "What's this about that cap?" he asked. "The way kids can get excited about a cap. Well, it's understandable, isn't it?"

"So it is," Dave said, moving closer to Steve, who was awed by the broadloom rug and the fine furniture. He wanted to show Steve he was at ease himself, and he wished Mr. Hudson wouldn't be so polite. That meant Dave had to be polite and affable, too, and it was hard to manage when he was standing in the middle of the floor in his old windbreaker.

"Sit down, Mr. Diamond," Mr. Hudson said. Dave took Steve's arm and sat him down beside him on the chesterfield. The Hudson boy watched his father. And Dave looked at Steve and saw that he wouldn't face Mr. Hudson or the other boy; he kept looking up at Dave, putting all his faith in him.

"Well, Mr. Diamond, from what I gathered from my boy, you're able to prove this cap belonged to your boy."

"That's a fact," Dave said.

"Mr. Diamond, you'll have to believe my boy bought that cap from some kid in good faith."

"I don't doubt it," Dave said. "But no kid can sell something that doesn't belong to him. You know that's a fact, Mr. Hudson."

"Yes, that's a fact," Mr. Hudson agreed. "But that cap means a lot to my boy, Mr. Diamond."

"It means a lot to my boy, too, Mr. Hudson."

"Sure it does. But supposing we called in a policeman. You know what he'd say? He'd ask you if you were willing to pay my boy what he paid for the cap. That's usually the way it works out," Mr. Hudson said, friendly and smiling, as he eyed Dave shrewdly.

"But that's not right. It's not justice," Dave protested. "Not when it's my boy's cap."

"I know it isn't right. But that's what they do."

"All right. What did you say your boy paid for the cap?" Dave said reluctantly.

"Two dollars."

"Two dollars!" Dave repeated. Mr. Hudson's smile was still kindly, but his eyes were shrewd, and Dave knew the lawyer was counting on his not having the two dollars; Mr. Hudson thought he had Dave sized up, he had looked at him and decided he was broke. Dave's pride was hurt, and he turned to Steve. What he saw in Steve's face was more powerful than the hurt to his pride: it was the memory of how difficult it had been to get an extra nickel, the talk he heard about the cost of food, the worry in his mother's face as she tried to make ends meet, and the bewildered embarrassment that he was here in a rich man's home, forcing his father to confess that he couldn't afford to spend two dollars. Then Dave grew angry and reckless. "I'll give you the two dollars," he said.

Steve looked at the Hudson boy and grinned brightly. The Hudson boy watched his father.

"I suppose that's fair enough," Mr. Hudson said. "A cap like this can be worth a lot to a kid. You know how it is. Your boy might want to sell—I mean be satisfied. Would he take five dollars for it?"

"Five dollars?" Dave repeated. "Is it worth five dollars, Steve?" he asked uncertainly.

Steve shook his head and looked frightened.

"No, thanks, Mr. Hudson," Dave said firmly.

"I'll tell you what I'll do," Mr. Hudson said. "I'll give you ten dollars. The cap has a sentimental value for my boy, a Philly cap, a big-leaguer's cap. It's only worth about a buck and a half really," he added. But Dave shook his head again. Mr. Hudson frowned. He looked at his own boy with indulgent concern, but now he was embarrassed. "I'll tell you what I'll do," he said. "This cap—well, it's worth as much as a day at the circus to my boy. Your boy should be recompensed. I want to be fair. Here's twenty dollars," and he held out two ten-dollar bills to Dave.

That much money for a cap, Dave thought, and his eyes brightened. But he knew what the cap had meant to Steve; to deprive him of it now that it was within his reach would be unbearable. All the things he needed in his life gathered around him; his wife was there, saying he couldn't afford to reject the offer, he had no right to do it; and he turned to Steve to see if Steve thought it wonderful that the cap could bring them twenty dollars.

"What do you say, Steve?" he asked uneasily.

"I don't know," Steve said. He was in a trance. When Dave smiled, Steve smiled too, and Dave believed that Steve was as impressed as he was, only more bewildered, and maybe even more aware that they could not possibly turn away that much money for a ball cap.

"Well, here you are," Mr. Hudson said, and he put the two bills in Steve's hand. "It's a lot of money. But I guess you had a right to expect as much."

With a dazed, fixed smile Steve handed the money slowly to his father, and his face was white.

Laughing jovially, Mr. Hudson led them to the door. His own boy followed a few paces behind.

In the elevator Dave took the bills out of his pocket. "See, Stevie," he whispered eagerly. "That windbreaker you wanted! And ten dollars for your bank! Won't Mother be surprised?"

"Yeah," Steve whispered, the little smile still on his face. But Dave had to turn away quickly so their eyes wouldn't meet, for he saw that it was a scared smile.

Outside, Dave said, "Here, you carry the money home, Steve. You show it to your mother."

"No, you keep it," Steve said, and then there was nothing to say. They walked in silence.

"It's a lot of money," Dave said finally. When Steve didn't answer him, he added angrily, "I turned to you, Steve. I asked you, didn't I?"

"That man knew how much his boy wanted that cap," Steve said.

"Sure. But he recognized how much it was worth to us."

"No, you let him take it away from us," Steve blurted.

"That's unfair," Dave said. "Don't dare say that to me."

"I don't want to be like you," Steve muttered, and he darted across the road and walked along on the other side of the street.

"It's unfair," Dave said angrily, only now he didn't mean that Steve was unfair, he meant that what had happened in the prosperous Hudson home was unfair, and he didn't know quite why. He had been trapped, not just by Mr. Hudson, but by his own life. Across the road Steve was hurrying along with his head down, wanting to be alone. They walked most of the way home on opposite sides of the street, until Dave could stand it no longer. "Steve," he called, crossing the street. "It was very unfair. I mean, for you to say . . ." but Steve started to run. Dave walked as fast as he could and Steve was getting beyond him, and he felt enraged and suddenly he yelled, "Steve!" and he started to chase his son. He wanted to get hold of Steve and pound him, and he didn't know why. He gained on him, he gasped for breath and he almost got him by the shoulder. Turning, Steve saw his father's face in the street light and was terrified; he circled away, got to the house, and rushed in, yelling, "Mother!"

"Son, Son!" she cried, rushing from the kitchen. As soon as she threw her arms around Steve, shielding him, Dave's anger left him and he felt stupid. He walked past them into the kitchen.

"What happened?" she asked anxiously. "Have you both gone crazy? What did you do, Steve?"

"Nothing," he said sullenly.

"What did your father do?"

"We found the boy with my ball cap, and he let the boy's father take it from us."

"No, no," Dave protested. "Nobody pushed us around. The man didn't put anything over us." He felt tired and his face was burning. He told what had happened; then he slowly took the two ten-dollar bills out of his wallet and tossed them on the table and looked up guiltily at his wife.

It hurt him that she didn't pick up the money, and that she didn't rebuke him. "It is a lot of money, Son," she said slowly. "Your father was only trying to do what he knew was right, and it'll work out, and you'll understand." She was soothing Steve, but Dave knew she felt that she needed to be gentle with him, too, and he was ashamed.

When she went with Steve to his bedroom, Dave sat by himself. His son had contempt for him, he thought. His son, for the first time, had seen how easy it was for another man to handle him, and he had judged him and had wanted to walk alone on the other side of the street. He looked at the money and he hated the sight of it.

His wife returned to the kitchen, made a cup of tea, talked soothingly, and said it was incredible that he had forced the Hudson man to pay him twenty dollars for the cap, but all Dave could think of was Steve was scared of me.

Finally, he got up and went into Steve's room. The room was in darkness, but he could see the outline of Steve's body on the bed, and he sat down beside him and whispered, "Look, Son, it was a mistake. I know why. People like us—in circumstances where money can scare us. No, no," he said, feeling ashamed and shaking his head apologetically; he was taking the wrong way of showing the boy they were together; he was covering up his own failure. For the failure had been his, and it had come out of being so separated from his son that he had been blind to what was beyond the price in a boy's life. He longed now to show Steve he could be with him from day to day. His hand went out hesitantly to Steve's shoulder. "Steve, look," he said eagerly. "The trouble was I didn't realize how much I enjoyed it that night at the ball park. If I had watched you playing for your own team—the kids around here say you could be a great pitcher. We could take that money and buy a new pitcher's glove for you, and a catcher's mitt. Steve, Steve, are you listening? I could catch you, work with you in the lane. Maybe I could be your coach . . . watch you become a great pitcher." In the half-darkness he could see the boy's pale face turn to him.

Steve, who had never heard his father talk like this, was shy and wondering. All he knew was that his father, for the first time, wanted to be with him in his hopes and adventures. He said, "I guess you do know how important that cap was." His hand went out to this father's arm. "With that man the cap was—well it was just something he could buy, eh Dad?" Dave gripped his son's hand hard. The wonderful generosity of childhood—the price a boy was willing to pay to be able to count on his father's admiration and approval—made him feel humble, then strangely exalted.

Judgments and Conclusions: Discussing Stories

You and your class have been involved in many discussions about the stories in this book. We hope you have enjoyed those discussions and have learned something about yourself as well as the stories. This lesson encourages you to continue discussing literature. It helps you think about some reasons for talking about stories and about some ways to discuss what you read. The lesson also concentrates on judgments and conclusions. When you make a judgment or draw a conclusion, you include yourself in the story experience. You put yourself into the story.

People discuss all kinds of things—stories, novels, plays, movies, TV programs, computer games, music, art—and they discuss them in a variety of ways. A teacher may discuss a story with a student, but they probably don't talk about it in the same way that two friends do. And the two friends probably don't talk about the story in the same way a newspaper columnist does in a book review. Discussing stories is not just a school exercise. It's something you will do, something you will learn from, for the rest of your life.

A discussion is often a search for answers to certain questions. Did I enjoy the story? Why did I like it? Is the author a skillful writer? Are the ideas behind the story interesting to think about? Are they important? Do I agree with them? Why do the characters behave this way? These are just a few of the many questions people ask about stories, and every person has different answers.

Discussion makes stories more than entertainment. It makes them part of learning. It's like thinking out loud, sharing your thoughts with others. You compare the story with experiences in your own life. You make judgments and come to conclusions. And in this way you learn something new from each story you read.

People who read a great deal are usually good at solving problems and thinking creatively. But they don't limit themselves just to reading. They think about what they read and try to learn from it. They decide how the ideas they find in their reading fit into the general scheme of life.

In this lesson we will look at one of the many ways to think about a story and discuss it. This approach has four steps:

1 ♦ You put yourself into the story situation.

2 ♦ You make inferences, or draw connections, between facts and details.

3 ♦ You ask questions about the story.

4 ♦ You make judgments and draw conclusions about what you have read and discussed.

1 ♦ Putting Yourself into the Story

A story is an experience, something that happens in your mind as you read. Just as you can think about experiences in real life, you can think about the experience in a story. But to make a story an experience, you must put yourself into the story situation. You must share in the story, and you do that with the help of the author's skill and your own imagination. Let's review some of the techniques an author uses to help you become part of the story:

Setting. You see in your mind's eye where the story takes place. You understand what it feels like to be in the situation that the author describes.

Characters. You picture the characters. You understand how they feel. You predict how they will act in certain situations. You care about what happens to them.

Plot. You become involved in the events, the conflicts, and the action. You feel excitement, sorrow, tension, or relief.

Once you have become involved in the story, you can think about it and talk about it. And one of the first things you are likely to talk about is how the story made you *feel.* How does the setting make you feel? How do you feel about the characters? How do you feel about the outcome of the plot? Try discussing your feelings about this passage from "A Cap for Steve."

> Dave Diamond, a poor man, a carpenter's assistant, was a small, wiry, quick-tempered individual who had learned how to make every dollar count in his home. His wife, Anna, had been sick a lot, and his twelve-year-old son, Steve, had to be kept in school. Steve, a big-eyed, shy kid, ought to have known the value of money as well as Dave did. It had been ground into him.
>
> But the boy was crazy about baseball, and after school, when he could have been working as a delivery boy or selling papers, he played ball with the kids. His failure to appreciate that the family needed a few extra dollars disgusted Dave. Around the house he wouldn't let Steve talk about baseball, and he scowled when he saw him hurrying off with his glove after dinner.

That passage begins the story. In it, you immediately learn about three very different characters and their living situation, and you get a taste of the conflict that is to come. Already you can ask yourself some questions:

Setting. What do you learn about the family's living situation? What do you learn about the place in which they live?

Characters. What do you learn about Dave, Anna, and Steve?

Plot. What will be the major conflict of the story? How do you feel about that conflict after reading this passage?

Not every reader will have the same answers to those questions. Everyone will feel a bit different about the story, depending on age, family background, and interests. Those differences of opinion are what makes a discussion interesting.

Think about your answers and then compare them to the answers that follow. You'll probably notice some differences.

Setting. The family is poor, so the house or apartment is probably small and plain without many luxuries. They seem to live in the neighborhood of a town or city because there are enough local kids to make up a baseball team. There are also jobs for delivery boys and paper sellers.

Characters. Dave works as a carpenter's assistant and doesn't make much money. He is small and thin, and he gets angry easily. He worries about taking care of his family. He thinks Steve should help out more and gets annoyed when he doesn't.

Anna is often sick, which worries her husband.

Steve is twelve years old. He is shy and has big eyes; and he seems quiet and maybe a bit innocent. He loves baseball and doesn't seem to realize that his father wants him to get a job.

Plot. Obviously the conflict will involve baseball and money. It's difficult at this point to know whether to sympathize with Dave or with Steve. Dave works hard and cares about his family, but he doesn't share in his son's interests. Steve seems like a good kid who loves baseball, but maybe he's old enough to start thinking about his family as well as himself.

There are usually no pat answers to questions raised by a story. Neither are there pat answers to many questions raised in real life. We have options and choices. But by thinking carefully about a situation, you can see those choices and come up with a thoughtful, reasonable conclusion.

1 ◆ Exercise A

Read the following passage and answer the questions about it using what you have learned in this part of the lesson. Use your writing notebook or a separate piece of paper for your answers.

> One night Steve was late coming home from the park. Dave didn't realize how late it was until he put down his newspaper and watched his wife at the window. Her restlessness got on his nerves. "See what comes from encouraging the boy to hang around with those park loafers," he said. "I don't encourage him," she protested. "You do," he insisted irritably, for he was really worried now. . . . When his wife went out and walked down to the corner it was his turn to wait and worry and watch at the open window. Each waiting moment tortured him. At last he heard his wife's voice and Steve's voice, and he relaxed and sighed; then he remembered his duty and rushed angrily to meet them.

1. What do you learn about Dave's relationship with his wife? How does he really feel about her concern? How does he pretend to feel?

2. Are you annoyed with Dave or do you sympathize with him? Is it possible to feel both? Why?

Now check your answers using the suggestions in the Answer Key starting on page 457. Review this part of the lesson if you don't understand why an answer was wrong.

1 ◆ Writing on Your Own

Look at the lists you developed for Analyzing Your Own Story on page 403. Now do the following:

1. Reread the details on both lists, thinking once again about character

relationships. Now choose a scene from your story (one or two paragraphs) to work on.

2. Rewrite the scene, emphasizing an emotion (or lack of emotion) shared by the characters. You may keep most of your original material or you may completely rework it. In any case, use your list of ideas to help you improve the scene.

3. You may want to rewrite the scene several times until you get it just the way you like it.

2 ◆ Making Inferences

When you are experiencing something new, the first thing you do is size up the situation. What am I dealing with? Am I safe? Can I trust the people? Will I be happy here? Will I be bored? Will there be trouble? How should I act? You pick up the information you need to answer those questions from the details around you.

For example, imagine arriving at a party where you don't know anyone very well. The person throwing the party greets you at the door, takes you inside, and offers you something to eat. She introduces you to a group of friendly people who include you in their conversation. There's good music playing, and people are dancing and laughing. You relax and come to a conclusion: "I'm going to have a good time."

Your reasoning told you what the details meant. Based on your knowledge and experience, you *inferred* certain meanings from what you saw. Your inferences were affected by the facts and details around you. Like a detective, you gathered together clues, made judgments, and came to a conclusion.

You do the same thing when you read. It doesn't matter if you're reading a story, a newspaper, or a passage in a history textbook. Making inferences works the same way. In "A Cap for Steve" you make inferences about Dave, Steve, and Anna—even Mr. Hudson and Eddie Condon—from the facts and details in the story. The author has carefully chosen those facts and details to lead you to certain inferences, to help you think about the characters in a certain way, and to share important ideas.

What inferences can you make about Eddie Condon in the following passage?

> Then the big, blond Philly outfielder, Eddie Condon, who had been held up by a gang of kids tugging at his arm and thrusting their score cards at him, broke loose and made a run for the club-house. He was jostled, and his blue cap with the red peak, tilted far back on his head, fell off. It fell at Steve's feet, and Steve quickly stooped and grabbed it. "Okay, son," the outfielder called, turning back. But Steve, holding the hat in both hands, only stared at him. . . .
>
> "My cap, son," Eddie Condon said, his hand out.
>
> "Hey, Steve," Dave said, and he gave him a shake. But he had to jerk the cap out of Steve's hands.

"Here you are," he said.

The outfielder, noticing Steve's white, worshipping face and pleading eyes, grinned and then shrugged. "Aw, let him keep it," he said.

"No, Mister Condon, you don't need to do that," Steve protested.

"It's happened before. Forget it," Eddie Condon said, and he trotted away to the club-house.

You can make several inferences about Eddie Condon from this brief passage. For one thing, you can infer that he is popular with kids and that he is not always patient about it. "Broke loose and made a run for the club-house" hints that he's trying to escape from the crowd. So why does he give Steve the cap? Why does Steve, out of all the kids on the field, attract his attention? Think about this sentence: "The outfielder, noticing Steve's white, worshipping face and pleading eyes, grinned and then shrugged." The sentence lets you know that Eddie Condon is softhearted beneath his impatience. He gives in to those "pleading eyes." The sentence also reminds you that famous people can be vain. You can infer that Steve's "worshipping face" has a part in softening Eddie, and he decides to let Steve keep the cap.

But making inferences isn't limited to helping you learn more about characters. It can also help you explore deeper issues in a story, as in the following passage:

The other boy realized he might lose the cap. "I bought it from a guy," he said. "I paid him. My father knows I paid him." He said he got the cap at the ball park. He groped for some magically impressive words and suddenly found them. "You'll have to speak to my father," he said.

"Sure, I'll speak to your father," Dave said. "What's your name? Where do you live?"

"My name's Hudson. I live about ten minutes away on the other side of the park." The boy appraised Dave, who wasn't any bigger than he was and who wore a faded blue windbreaker and no tie. "My father is a lawyer," he said boldly. "He wouldn't let me keep the cap if he didn't think I should."

You can infer a lot about the Hudson boy's values in this passage. He believes that paying for the cap gives him a right to keep it, and he feels superior to Dave who is small and poorly dressed. The boy gropes "for some magically impressive words." He mentions his father is a lawyer, a man of power and importance. The author includes these facts and details about the Hudson boy because he wants Dave—and you—to think carefully about money and power.

2 ◆ Exercise B

Read the following passage and answer the questions about it using what you have learned in this part of the lesson. Use your writing notebook or a separate piece of paper for your answers.

> The Hudson boy lived in that row of fine apartment houses on the other side of the park. At the entrance to one of these houses Dave tried not to hang back and show he was impressed, because he could feel Steve hanging back. When they got into the small elevator Dave didn't know why he took off his hat. . . .
>
> "Come on in," Mr. Hudson said, putting out his hand and laughing good-naturedly. He led Dave and Steve into his living room. "What's this about that cap?" he asked. "The way kids can get excited about a cap. Well, it's understandable, isn't it?"
>
> "So it is," Dave said, moving closer to Steve, who was awed by the broadloom rug and the fine furniture. He wanted to show Steve he was at ease himself, and he wished Mr. Hudson wouldn't be so polite. That meant Dave had to be polite and affable, too, and it was hard to manage when he was standing in the middle of the floor in his old windbreaker.

1. What can you infer about Dave's feelings in this passage? What is he trying to show Steve? What is he trying to show Mr. Hudson?

2. From what you know about Dave's personality, what can you infer about the statement "he wished Mr. Hudson wouldn't be so polite"? What would Dave like to do?

Now check you answers using the suggestions in the Answer Key starting on page 457. Review this part of the lesson if you don't understand why an answer was wrong.

2◆Writing on Your Own

Look at the lists you developed for Analyzing Your Own Story on page 403. Then reread the scene you wrote in 1◆ Writing on Your Own. Now do the following:

1. Ask a classmate to read the scene and make inferences about the relationship between the characters. Think about those inferences. Do you agree with them or do you think your classmate misunderstood your meaning? Is there any way you can make your ideas clearer?

2. Rewrite the scene, thinking carefully about the inferences you want a reader to draw about the characters. If you need to, make notes about your ideas before you write and use them to help you rework the passage.

3. You may want to change and rewrite the scene several times until you get it just the way you like it.

3 ◆ Asking Questions about the Story

You've probably been through this before. A teacher says, "Let's discuss the story you just read," and suddenly the room becomes silent. No one can think of a thing to say, even the people who are usually talkative.

Many people have a hard time thinking about ways to discuss a story. But if you try to think of the story as an experience in your life, then you can talk about it just like any other experience. But you have to prepare yourself by reading the story carefully and knowing the facts and details.

The easiest way to start a discussion is to answer the question, Did you like the story? Then you can go ahead and use other questions to help you discuss the specifics. The list that follows the passage shows some of the many questions you can ask about a story. Let's use some of those questions to discuss this passage from "A Cap for Steve."

> [Mr. Hudson has just paid twenty dollars for the cap.]
> In the elevator Dave took the bills out of his pocket. "See, Stevie," he whispered eagerly. "That windbreaker you wanted! And ten dollars for your bank! Won't Mother be surprised?"
> "Yeah," Steve whispered, the little smile still on his face. But Dave had to turn away quickly so their eyes wouldn't meet, for he saw that it was a scared smile.
> Outside, Dave said, "Here, you carry the money home, Steve. You show it to your mother."
> "No, you keep it," Steve said, and then there was nothing to say. They walked in silence.
> "It's a lot of money," Dave said finally. When Steve didn't answer him, he added angrily, "I turned to you, Steve. I asked you, didn't I?"
> "That man knew how much his boy wanted that cap," Steve said.
> "Sure. But he recognized how much it was worth to us."
> "No, you let him take it away from us," Steve blurted.

Did you like the story? Start with your overall impression of the story. What did you like about it? What didn't you like? Were you able to get involved in the story? You don't need to go along with the teacher's opinion or anyone else's. In fact, a discussion is always more interesting when people disagree. But you need to have reasons for your opinion. You need to show that you have thought carefully about characters, settings, plot, and the author's style.

What were the important conflicts and actions? What happened in the passage? How did the characters respond to the conflict? What problems did they have to face? Did the author do a good job of showing you those problems?

Dave and Steve have just made twenty dollars by selling the cap to Mr. Hudson and his son. They are walking home with the money. But are they happy? Dave is pretending to be happy. He reminds Steve about the windbreaker he wanted. And Steve can put ten dollars in the bank. Dave wants Steve to take charge of the money. But underneath it all, you begin to feel that Dave is uncomfortable. Steve hardly even pretends to be happy. He is scared by what has happened, and he is also angry.

What conflicts are developing in this passage? There is the conflict between Dave and Steve, who disagree about the money. Each person also struggles with internal conflicts. Dave wants to be happy, but he feels guilty. And Steve wants to trust his father but is angry and disappointed with his father's actions.

What characters did you like? Or what characters did you hate? Trying to understand the people in a story can be as much fun as trying to understand people in real life.

In this passage you may sympathize with Steve, who has lost both his cap and his trust in his father. You may sympathize with Dave, who loves his son and feels guilty about his own behavior. Or you may sympathize with both characters. In their own way Dave and Steve are trying to do the right thing, but neither one is perfect. Like most of us, they have a lot to learn.

What important ideas did the author present? When you begin to talk seriously about characters, conflicts, and plot, you naturally find yourself talking about the ideas behind them.

The passage from "A Cap for Steve" asks you to think about several important ideas. One, of course, is the value of money. Does a boy's dream equal two ten-dollar bills, or is a dream something that money can't buy? Money is an important theme throughout the story, but the author also wants you to consider some other ideas. Are parents always right, or do they sometimes make mistakes? Do children ever need to put their families ahead of themselves? Should we disguise our feelings, or is it better to tell others exactly how we feel? Everyone who reads "A Cap for Steve" will have different answers to those questions.

How does the story relate to your own life? This can be one of the most interesting questions to discuss. How are the characters similar to people you know? How do the serious ideas in the story affect your life? Have you even been in Dave's or Steve's position? Have you ever felt like the Hudson boy? Have you ever disagreed with your parents? By thinking carefully about these issues in the story, you can learn more about yourself.

3 ◆ Exercise C

Read the following passage and answer the questions about it using what you have learned in this part of the lesson. Use your writing notebook or a separate piece of paper for your answers.

> "What happened?" she [Anna] asked anxiously. "Have you both gone crazy? What did you do, Steve?"
>
> "Nothing," he said sullenly.
>
> "What did your father do?"
>
> "We found the boy with my ball cap, and he let the boy's father take it from us."
>
> "No, no," Dave protested. "Nobody pushed us around. The man didn't put anything over us." He felt tired and his face was burning. He told what had happened; then slowly he took the two ten-dollar bills out of his wallet and tossed them on the table and looked up guiltily at his wife.
>
> It hurt him that she didn't pick up the money, and that she didn't rebuke him. "It is a lot of money, Son," she said slowly. "Your father was only trying to do what he knew was right, and it'll work out, and you'll understand." She was soothing Steve, but Dave knew she felt that she needed to be gentle with him, too, and he was ashamed.

1. Just one character in this passage is able to see the big picture. The other characters only see things from their own points of view. Name the character who understands the whole problem, and write a sentence that supports your choice.

2. Despite the conflict in this passage, it's easy to see that all of the characters care about each other. How can you tell?

Now check your answers using the suggestions in the Answer Key starting on page 457. Review this part of the lesson if you don't understand why an answer was wrong.

3♦Writing on Your Own

Look at the lists you developed for Analyzing Your Own Story on page 403. Then reread the passage you wrote for 2♦Writing on Your Own. Now do the following:

1. Ask yourself the following questions: What important conflict does this scene show? What's going on between the characters and why? How can I make that conflict even clearer? Make a list of your thoughts.

2. Now rewrite the scene, making the conflict between the characters as clear as you can.

3. You may want to change and rewrite your paragraph several times until you get it just the way you like it.

4 ♦ Making Judgments and Drawing Conclusions

Judgments and *conclusions* are words that make reading sound very technical. But don't let the words give you that impression. As we have said throughout this unit, you make judgments and draw conclusions all the time. They are part of the mental process that goes on every minute of your life. They are as automatic as breathing. When you see a tree in your path, you conclude that you must walk around it. When you look at your watch, you judge how much time you have to get to school. When you try a new food, you make a judgment about whether or not you like it. When you try on clothes in a store, you draw some conclusions about what looks good on you.

The more experience you have in life, the better your judgments and conclusions become. Experiences give you more facts on which to base your judgments. Reading is a good way to gain more experience. It provides you with information and introduces you to events that you couldn't—or wouldn't want to—get any other way. And these experiences help you make decisions in your life.

Making judgments and drawing conclusions are not really steps you take when you read. You do those things naturally while you read and after you finish. Every time you answer a question in this book or in a class discussion, you make a judgment and come to a conclusion. You can't talk about the setting of a story without making judgments about place and time. You can't talk about characters until you have drawn some conclusions about them. After you finish a story, you look back at all the facts and details and make some judgments about the story as a whole. You conclude that you like or dislike the story based on those judgments.

The conflicts in "A Cap for Steve" are familiar to everyone. We all disagree with our parents at some point in our lives, and we all must admit that we've made some mistakes. Sometimes those disagreements and mistakes ruin lives, but sometimes they help us grow. What judgments and conclusions can we make about the future of the Diamond family? Think about the following passage:

> Finally, he [Dave] got up and went into Steve's room. The room was in darkness, but he could see the outline of Steve's body on the bed, and he sat down beside him and whispered, "Look, Son, it was a mistake. I know why. People like us—in circumstances where money can scare

us. No, no," he said, feeling ashamed and shaking his head apologetically; he was taking the wrong way of showing the boy they were together; he was covering up his own failure. For the failure had been his, and it had come out of being so separated from his son that he had been blind to what was beyond the price in a boy's life. He longed now to show Steve he could be with him from day to day. His hand went out hesitantly to Steve's shoulder.

Here, for the first time, you see Dave being honest with himself. Yes, he is awkward and uncomfortable, but he knows that he needs to admit his own mistakes in order to save his relationship with Steve. After reading that passage, what judgments can you make about him? You judge that he loves his son very much and that he finally realizes the importance of Steve's dream. You judge that he truly wants to become part of Steve's life. So what conclusions can you draw about the Diamond family? You conclude that Steve and Dave will probably become closer as a result of their conflict.

4 ◆ Exercise D

Read the following passage and answer the questions about it using what you have learned in this part of the lesson. Use your writing notebook or a separate piece of paper for your answers.

"Steve, look," he [Dave] said eagerly. "The trouble was I didn't realize how much I enjoyed it that night at the ball park. If I had watched you playing for your own team— the kids around here say you could be a great pitcher. We could take that money and buy a new pitcher's glove for you, and a catcher's mitt. Steve, Steve, are you listening? I could catch you, work with you in the lane. Maybe I could be your coach . . . watch you become a great pitcher." In the half-darkness he could see the boy's pale face turn to him.

Steve, who had never heard his father talk like this, was shy and wondering. All he knew was that his father, for the first time, wanted to be with him in his hopes and adventures. He said, "I guess you do know how important that cap was." His hand went out to his father's arm.

432   A Cap for Steve

"With that man the cap was—well it was just something he could buy, eh Dad?" Dave gripped his son's hand hard. The wonderful generosity of childhood—the price a boy was willing to pay to be able to count on his father's admiration and approval—made him feel humble, then strangely exalted.

1. What judgment can you make about Steve's talent for playing baseball? Why?

2. This passage tells you a lot about the lessons that Dave has learned. But can you draw any conclusions about Steve? What lessons has he learned? How does he show his father what he has learned?

Now check your answers using the suggestions in the Answer Key starting on page 457. Review this part of the lesson if you don't understand why an answer was wrong.

4 ◆ Writing on Your Own

Look at the lists you wrote for Analyzing Your Own Story on page 403. Then reread the scenes you wrote in the three Writing on Your Own exercises. Now do the following:

1. You can make judgments and draw conclusions about other people's stories, but it's also important to think honestly about your own writing. After reading the passage you wrote in 3◆Writing on Your Own, ask yourself the following questions: Do I like this passage? Why or why not? What works in it? What doesn't?

2. Write a paragraph or two about your own writing, telling why you like or dislike what you have done. Be honest! If you love it, say so. If you don't, explain what would make it better.

3. You may want to change and rewrite your paragraph several times until you get it just the way you like it.

Now go on to Reviewing and Interpreting the Story.

Reviewing and Interpreting the Story

Answer these questions without looking back at the story. Choose the best answer to each question and put an *x* in the box beside it, or write your answer on a separate piece of paper.

Remembering Facts

1. What does Steve have to do before Dave agrees to take him to the ball game?

   ☐ a. sell newspapers after school

   ☐ b. help build some kitchen shelves

   ☐ c. practice his pitching

   ☐ d. make some deliveries for Mr. Hudson

2. How does Steve lose his cap?

   ☐ a. Someone takes it out of his pocket.

   ☐ b. He loses it on the way to the shoemaker's.

   ☐ c. Dave takes it away from him.

   ☐ d. It tears when he slides to home plate.

Following the Order of Events

3. How much money does Mr. Hudson first offer Dave for the cap?

   ☐ a. ten dollars

   ☐ b. five dollars

   ☐ c. six dollars

   ☐ d. twenty dollars

4. How much does Dave end up taking for the cap?

   □ a. ten dollars

   □ b. five dollars

   □ c. two dollars

   □ d. twenty dollars

Understanding
Word Choices

5. In Mr. Hudson's house, Dave and Steve sit down together on the <u>chesterfield</u>. What is a *chesterfield*?

   □ a. a rug

   □ b. a boat

   □ c. a sofa

   □ d. a table

6. Dave "wished Mr. Hudson wouldn't be so polite. That meant Dave had to polite and <u>affable</u>, too." What does *affable* mean?

   □ a. pleasant and friendly

   □ b. proud and silent

   □ c. noisy and rude

   □ d. sad and depressed

Understanding
Important Ideas

7. In Mr. Hudson's house, Steve's face shows that he is embarrassed about being poor. How does Steve's embarrassment affect Dave's behavior about the cap?

   □ a. He starts to understand Steve's love for baseball.

   □ b. Money suddenly seems very important to him.

   □ c. He begins to feel jealous of his son.

   □ d. It convinces him to buy the cap back.

8. Why doesn't Anna get angry with Dave after he sells Steve's cap?

☐ a. She believes that money is more important than baseball.

☐ b. She loves Dave more than she loves her son.

☐ c. She understands that he was trying to do the right thing.

☐ d. She is afraid to start an argument.

Understanding Levels of Meaning

9. At the beginning of the story the author says that Dave "had learned how to make every dollar count in his home." How does that small piece of information prepare you for the rest of the story?

☐ a. It lets you know that Dave is a generous man.

☐ b. It tells you that money is very important to him.

☐ c. You learn that Dave lets other people push him around.

☐ d. It tells you that money is very important to Steve.

10. "Just the same, it was remarkable what a little thing like a ball cap could do for a kid, Dave admitted to his wife as he smiled to himself." Why does the author include that sentence in the story? What does he want you to know?

☐ a. Even though Dave is annoyed by the cap, he realizes that it's good for Steve.

☐ b. Dave wants Anna to stop getting upset about the baseball cap.

☐ c. Dave will never admit that a baseball cap might be more important than money.

☐ d. Anna and Dave have decided to take the cap away from Steve.

11. Which adjective best describes Anna?

☐ a. happy-go-lucky

☐ b. understanding

☐ c. overworked

☐ d. bad-tempered

12. "Mr. Hudson thought he had Dave sized up; he had looked at him and decided he was broke." How does Mr. Hudson judge other people?

☐ a. by actions

☐ b. by personality

☐ c. by age

☐ d. by looks

13. The author doesn't include many details about the Diamond home, but he shows us just what the Hudson home looks like. Why?

☐ a. The Diamonds are probably about to move.

☐ b. He wants us to see how wealthy the Hudsons are.

☐ c. Anna and Dave never think about furniture.

☐ d. The author thinks the Hudsons are better than the Diamonds.

14. As Steve and Dave walk home with the money, they begin to quarrel. Then Steve crosses to the opposite side of the street. How does the setting— Dave and Steve with a street between them— support the conflict?

   ☐ a. You worry that Steve will get hit by a car.

   ☐ b. You understand why Dave took the money from Mr. Hudson.

   ☐ c. The street reminds you of a baseball diamond.

   ☐ d. The street divides them just as their quarrel does.

Understanding Feelings

15. Which description best shows Dave's feelings when he visits the Hudson's apartment?

   ☐ a. proud and uncomfortable

   ☐ b. tired and bored

   ☐ c. cheerful and friendly

   ☐ d. mean and spiteful

16. How does Steve feel about his father at the end of the story?

   ☐ a. He can't forgive him.

   ☐ b. He doesn't believe him.

   ☐ c. He is surprised and hopeful.

   ☐ d. He thinks his father is perfect.

Now check your answers using the Answer Key starting on page 457. Make no mark for right answers. <u>Correct</u> any wrong answers you may have by putting a check mark (✓) in the box next to the right answer. Count the number of questions you answered correctly and plot the total on the Comprehension Scores graph on page 468.

Next, look at the questions you answered incorrectly. What types of questions were they? Count the number you got wrong of each type and enter the numbers in the spaces below.

Remembering Facts   _____

Following the Order of Events   _____

Understanding Word Choices   _____

Understanding Important Ideas   _____

Understanding Levels of Meaning   _____

Understanding Character   _____

Understanding Setting   _____

Understanding Feelings   _____

Now use these numbers to fill in the Comprehension Skills Profile on page 469.

Discussion Guides

The questions below will help you think about the story and the lesson you have just read. If you don't discuss these questions in class, try to think about them or discuss them with your classmates. Perhaps you will want to write a few paragraphs in answer to the questions.

Making Judgments and Conclusions

1. Dave is difficult to get along with, and he makes a lot of mistakes. But he also has many good qualities. Why did the author create such a complicated character? What conclusions can you draw about the author's purpose?

2. You have already made some judgments about the future of the Diamond family. What judgments can you make about the future of the Hudson family?

3. Is Anna important to the story, or could the author have left her out? Explain your conclusion.

Discussing the Story

4. Even though baseball is important to this story, we never see Steve play. We don't even learn much about the Phillies game. Why didn't the author include more baseball action?

5. At the time this story was written, twenty dollars was a lot of money, even for a rich man like Mr. Hudson. Why does he want to spend so much money on a baseball cap for his son?

6. At the end of the story, Dave tries to get Steve to believe that he has changed his ways. He says he wants to be a better father and spend more time with his son. Do you think he's telling the truth, or is he fooling himself and Steve? Has he really changed?

Discussing the Author's Work

7. Many of Morley Callaghan's stories and novels are noted for their "hard-boiled realism." The phrase refers to writing that is very realistic and sometimes includes ugly or unpleasant details. It also means writing that avoids getting too emotional or sentimental. Do

you think "A Cap for Steve" is an example of hard-boiled realism? Why or why not?

8. Before becoming a full-time writer, Callaghan spent some time working as a journalist for the *Toronto Star*. Think about his very realistic writing style. Do you think his background as a newspaper writer might have influenced his stories? How?

9. Morley Callaghan often used his stories and novels to talk about serious issues such as honesty, responsibility, and power. Do you think he had any of those issues in mind when he wrote "A Cap for Steve"? Find some examples from the story that support your answer.

Writing Exercise

Read all the instructions before you begin writing. If you have any questions about how to begin the writing assignment, review Using the Writing Process beginning on page 445, or confer with your writing coach.

1. Review the passages you wrote in the four Writing on Your Own exercises.

2. You've gotten to know your two characters pretty well by now. You've thought a lot about how you want them to relate to each other and what you want your readers to think about them. They're probably almost like old friends—sometimes you like them, and sometimes they drive you crazy.

   Many authors use their favorite characters in several different stories or novels. Try reusing your two characters by writing about them in a different situation. For example, if you originally wrote about them lost in a cave together, you could now start an argument between them in a grocery store aisle. Or if they were originally playing a game of pool, they could now be rescuing their grandmother from a grizzly bear.

   Keeping in mind everything you have learned about short stories in this book, write a new story about your two characters. Remember to think about the following things:

   ◆ Developing plot and conflict

   ◆ Creating a setting for the action

◆ Using your imagination to develop lively and interesting characters

◆ Developing an underlying message or meaning in the story

3. Write, revise, correct, and rewrite your story until you are sure you have got it just the way you want it.

Using the
Writing Process

Using the Writing Process

The following reference section will help you with the writing exercises in this book. It explains the major steps in the writing process. Read this section carefully so that you understand the process thoroughly. At the end of this section is a checklist. Whenever you are asked to complete a writing assignment, you can refer to the checklist as a reminder of the things you should think about when you are working on an assignment. This reference is an information source. Use it whenever you feel it would be helpful to review part or all of the process.

Whatever kind of job you do, from carpentry to sewing to cutting the grass, it will be easier if you have a good method for doing the job. People who write—students, authors, reporters, business executives, to list a few—also have to have a method that enables them to write easily and well. Even writing simple notes or memos requires a method.

How to Use a Writing Process

Different writers use different methods, but there are certain techniques that all writers use to make their work easier and their finished product better. These techniques have been put together in a list that is called "the writing process." A "process," of course, is just another name for a method.

Keep in mind that writing is not simply the act of filling a piece of paper with words. It is a form of communication. The purpose of writing is to put *ideas* across to other people. Since ideas come from your mind, not your pen, the writing process begins with the work that takes place in your mind: the creation and organization of ideas. Next, you're ready to actually set the words down on paper. The final stage is polishing your ideas and the words you use to express them.

In this section you will read about the stages and steps that make up a "writing process." These are techniques that writers use to make their job easier and the results better. But this doesn't mean that all writers follow this list exactly as it is written here.

Remember that every writer is different and every writing project is different. You can't always follow the list in one particular way.

Finish step 1 and go on to step 2. Do step 2 and then step 3. Writing doesn't work that way. Some authors write an opening paragraph before they do anything else. Then they make a plan and go after their facts and ideas. Some writers don't find a focus for their writing until they have assembled all of their ideas. Others find their focus first.

To help you understand the process that writers use, we will group the process into three main stages: prewriting, writing, and revising. Remember that the steps in each stage blend into the next, and sometimes a writer moves back and forth through the process. When you write, your goal should be to produce a clear and lively work that expresses interesting ideas. The writing process can help you every time you write and with everything you write.

Stage 1: Prewriting

What will I write about? You will need to think of a subject or an idea. Suppose your teacher says, "Write a story for me. It's due next week." What do you do? Panic, of course.

What is there to write about? How much should I write? Where do I start? With all the things you've done in your life, in spite of all the books you've read and all the movies you've seen, your mind goes blank. Or so many things go through your mind that you become thoroughly confused.

Welcome to the writing club. This is how *all* writing begins.

What should you do? The best thing you can do at this point is to sit back in your chair and think. Let your mind wander. Scribble down ideas as they come to you—even if the ideas seem dumb or farfetched. Good ideas often develop from a crazy thought. You may want to sit around with a few friends and throw ideas at one another as you think of them. This technique is called *brainstorming*. It might go like this:

> "She said we could write about anything we want."
> "How about writing about my vacation at the lake?" (Write down *vacation*.)
> "Nah! Everybody writes about a vacation. We need something different." (Write down *different*.)
> "Different? How about *weird*? How about a weird vacation?" (Write down *weird*.)
> "Yeah! I did see a cave this summer. Maybe I walked into a cave and couldn't find my way out."

"And you walked for miles in the dark."

"And suddenly there was a bright light. And I saw that there was a big underground city!"

By brainstorming you have turned your modest idea about your vacation into a great idea for a science-fiction story.

Once you start brainstorming, the ideas can come quickly. So now it's time to get things under control by finding a *focus* for your story.

What will I focus on? Pick your best ideas. Sometimes good writing is ruined because the writer tries to do too much. You might decide that aliens live in the underground city. You want to tell how they captured you. You want to describe how they got there, what they look like, what they did to you, what you did, how you became their ruler, how you escaped and brought an alien friend back with you, and how you took him to school to meet your friends . . . and on and on. Stop! It's too much.

There are many good ideas here. What you want to do is pick out what you think is your best idea and zero in on that. Focus on that one idea just as you focus a camera on a subject. If you concentrate on describing the beauty of the underground city, you will probably have more than enough for your story. If you skip the city and just tell how you brought this wonderful cave person to school, you have a great story by itself.

The point is not to overload your story with too many ideas. Writing is always easier and better if you concentrate on telling about a few things thoroughly and well. When you wander back and forth through too many ideas, you soon become lost and confused. Your reader will also be confused and will soon lose interest in your story.

How will I organize my ideas? Plan your writing. There is very little you can do in life without first making a plan. Even a simple bike ride needs a plan. Where will you go? When? What route? How far? What will you wear? Will it be a leisurely ride, or are you out to set a speed record?

Writing, like any other activity, calls for careful planning. You begin to plan as soon as you decide what to write about and find your facts. Then you do more planning as you decide what facts and ideas you will include in your story? And there are other steps to consider.

Who is my audience? You may write one way for your friends and another way for your teacher. Who will be reading your work? Will the story be serious or funny? What ideas or feelings do you want to emphasize?

As you write, you continue to plan. You may change your mind about your plan just as a coach changes a game plan as the game progresses. Which words will you choose? An idea that seemed good at first may need to be dropped later.

Prewriting is not as hard or as complicated as it may sound. It helps to write down a few notes about your *plan* when you begin: the subject, a few important ideas, where to look for information you need, and who you might interview.

The important part of this stage is to have a plan. Think ahead about what you want your writing to be about, how you want it to sound, who will read it, and how to get it down on paper.

How do I gather facts and ideas? You have already read about brainstorming for ideas when you are searching for a subject to write about. You can also brainstorm to think of facts and ideas you want to include in your writing. Write these ideas down as you think of them. You can pick and choose from your list later.

Freewriting is another way that writers generate ideas. To freewrite, quickly jot down anything that pops into your head. Here is the way Jack London may have done freewriting in preparing his story "To Build a Fire":

> "Cold. Very cold. Way below zero. A man and dog are out in the cold. Is a man made for such weather? Is a dog? The man gets in trouble. How? Wet. He gets wet."

As you freewrite, you are often able to see the basic ideas of a story or article emerge.

Then there is research. You may think that you can make up everything in a story out of your head. Most times you can't. If you are writing about an adventure in a cave, you will want to describe a cave accurately so that it is believable to your readers. Do some research at the library. Interview people who have seen caves to add realistic touches to your story.

Facts and ideas are gathered in four ways: thinking, reading, listening, and observing.

◆ Thinking means brainstorming and freewriting.

- Reading means research in books, magazines, newspapers, encyclopedias, and other sources of information.

- Listening means interviewing, listening to tapes and to people with special knowledge.

- Observing means carefully looking at a scene, carefully looking at an event, or carefully watching a movie or television show to gather ideas. While you are observing, imagine describing those scenes. What details do you see? What observations can you make?

How do I organize my facts and ideas? There are several ways to organize your information. Some writers make *lists* (informal outlines) of the facts and ideas they have gathered and rearrange the list until they have the information in the correct order that will work well in their writing.

Other writers make formal *outlines,* designating the most important ideas I, II, III, IV, etc., and related details as A, B, C, 1, 2, 3, and so on. An outline is a more formal version of a list, and like a list, the items in an outline can be rearranged until you get the correct order. Outlines help you organize and group your ideas.

Mapping or *clustering* is another helpful technique used by many writers. With this method you write down your main idea in a circle or a rectangle and then show how other facts and ideas are connected to that main idea. Here is an example of how a cluster may evolve from a major idea:

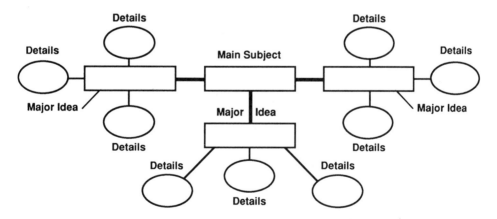

Do you see how a cluster map relates ideas? The farther you branch out, the more detailed you get. When you get to the point where you

are ready to write your story or article, you can use the cluster map as a guide to grouping your ideas.

Stage 2: Writing

How do I get my thoughts on paper? What do you do when you step onto the basketball court? You might stretch a bit and then you take the ball and start dribbling, passing, and shooting. You don't stand there and agonize over how you are going to play, or worry that you might lose. You start playing.

Once you have your subject, your plan, and your facts and ideas, the worst thing you can do is worry about the writing—how to start, where to start, how good or bad it might be, what the teacher *really* wants, writer's block, or a hundred other things that only make you panic.

Now is the time to get your thoughts on paper. Like freewriting, quickly writing down your story will make you feel more at ease with writing itself. Once your story is written down, then you can rewrite, revise, and polish.

How will I get started? Start with an opening sentence or paragraph. It can become a guide for the rest of your story or essay.

Here is an opening sentence that was used in a story about a midair collision: "A Boeing 747 collided with a smaller plane over San Diego today and crashed in flames to the ground, killing at least 144 people . . ." With this sentence, you know you will have to tell the details of the crash, why it happened, and how it happened.

You expect something different with this opening sentence: "I ran out in the driveway the other night waving a bag of cold spareribs and shouting to one of my grown kids." Obviously, this story is going to be funny. Humorist Erma Bombeck, who wrote that sentence, knew her story would have to carry on the humorous tone and probably include a few wisecracks about why a mother would want to chase her grown kid with a bag of spareribs.

Now let's look at the opening sentence from Frank O'Connor's "First Confession": "All the trouble began when my grandfather died and my grandmother—my father's mother—came to live with us." The writer has set the tone of the story. He will have to describe what the trouble is and why it began when his grandmother moved in with his family.

What is a rough draft? You are finally ready to turn all of your prewriting work into a story or essay. This will be your *rough draft*— your sloppy copy. Working from your outline or cluster map, your goal is to turn your loose facts and ideas into sentences and paragraphs that will work together. Write quickly. Refer to your outline and writing plan frequently so that you stay on track and avoid the delays caused by wondering what to write next.

At this stage don't worry too much about choosing exactly the right word or about crafting a sentence perfectly. Cross out, draw arrows showing how you are changing the order of ideas, and make notes to yourself in the margin. In the middle of what might look like a mess, you'll be surprised to find that a story is taking shape.

You're like an artist who is sculpturing your likeness in clay. After the artist's first effort, there is what looks like a muddy pile in the middle of the table. But the general shape is right. It certainly looks like a head. The ears are where the ears should be, and the nose is familiar. With polishing, the rough shape will eventually look like you.

There is nothing that slows a writer down more than thinking that the first draft will be the only draft—that it has to be the neatest and best effort—the one others will read. Your first attempt should be rough and unfinished: a *rough* draft. Plan to revise your draft two or three times. It sounds like a lot of work, but it would be disappointing to come this far and not finish the job of editing, revising, and polishing you story.

Stage 3: Revising

How should I begin my revision? Now you're ready to revise your work. You want to look for ways to polish your writing. Don't be fooled into thinking that revision is a waste of time. Professional writers revise their writing over and over again. They know that careful revision makes a big difference in the final product.

When you are revising, answer these questions:

Is my writing clear and logical? Reread your entire first draft. Make sure the sentences and paragraphs follow one another in logical order. Run-on sentences get confusing: "I entered the cave and it was so dark I couldn't see and all of a sudden a bat flew past me and I was sure it was a vampire because I could see its big teeth and I remembered this movie where a vampire captured this girl and my cousin who was with me said something that made me spill my popcorn." Wait a minute! What's going on in that sentence? You will need to decide what is important and then throw out the rest.

You may need to rewrite sentences or paragraphs, or even add new information. Check your prewriting plan to make sure you have included everything important.

Is my language interesting? Have you chosen strong verbs, nouns, and adjectives? For example, avoid using the verb *to be (is, are, being, become)* more than you have to. Choose precise actions, such as *jumped, ran, grinned, sobbed.* Instead of saying *thing,* choose the exact noun: *bucket, bathrobe, liberty, violence.* The adjectives *beautiful* and *nice* are boring. Replace them with *elegant, tidy, prim, joyous.*

Take out words that repeat the same ideas. For example, don't say "bright and intelligent." The words are synonyms. Choose one word or the other.

What errors do I look for? Check for correct spelling, grammar, and punctuation. If you mention a date or a place, check an encyclopedia to make sure it is correct. Your handwriting must be clear. If your reader can't read your handwriting, he or she is going to lose interest in your ideas.

Be sure to have your editor or writing coach read your work. An editor looks for errors in grammar and spelling. Poor spelling and errors in grammar are confusing to your readers. Your editor or coach can often find problems that you have missed.

Editors should be kind, helpful, and encouraging—not cross, mean, or critical. If you are asked to edit someone else's writing, always start with a compliment or a positive comment. Remember that other writers have the same personal feelings about their work that you have about yours.

A Writing Checklist

☐ What is my topic? Is it focused enough? Should it be broader or narrower?

☐ What is my purpose for writing? What do I want to say about the subject? What are my feelings and ideas about it?

☐ Do I have a prewriting plan? Who is my audience? How do I want my writing to sound?

☐ What do I have to do to gather my facts and ideas? Think? Read? Interview? Research?

☐ How will I organize my ideas? a list? an outline? a cluster map?

☐ How will I develop my ideas? Do I have an opening sentence or paragraph?

☐ Do I need to add more information? Switch the order of paragraphs? Take out unnecessary information?

☐ Do all the sentences in one paragraph relate to one idea? Do I have to rearrange the order of ideas? Eliminate or add information?

☐ Have I used active, precise words? Is my language interesting? Do the words explain what I mean to say?

☐ Is the grammar correct? Have I used correct spelling and punctuation? Have I checked my facts?

☐ Is my final draft clear and legible?

Answer Key

Unit 1: **First Confession**

———————————— **The Short Story** ————————————

1 ♦ Exercise A

1. Jackie blames his grandmother "And all because of that old woman!"

2. Answers will vary.

2 ♦ Exercise B

1. Answers will vary. "She became the raging malicious devil she really was."

2. Answers will vary.

3 ♦ Exercise C

1. Answers will vary. Jackie is facing the moment he has been dreading.

2. Answers will vary.

4 ♦ Exercise D

1. Answers will vary. Some readers may feel that Nora deserved to be disappointed because she was so mean to Jackie.

2. Answers will vary. Because the priest didn't condemn him, Jackie learned more about life and religion.

——————— **Reviewing and Interpreting the Story** ———————

1. d	5. c	9. d	13. c
2. c	6. a	10. b	14. a
3. a	7. c	11. b	15. c
4. a	8. c	12. d	16. a

Unit 2: **Raymond's Run**

―――――――――――――――― **Character** ――――――――――――

1 ✦ Exercise A

1. It is a negative description: "big mouth," "fat," and "stupid."

2. Squeaky resents Mary Louise because she is now friendly with Squeaky's rival.

2 ✦ Exercise B

1. Answers will vary. Squeaky is not afraid of a fight. She is willing to stand up for herself and Raymond.

2. Answers will vary. The girls act as a group; they don't make independent decisions. Squeaky is different because she is independent.

3 ✦ Exercise C

1. Mr. Pearson is awkward and unorganized. Answers will vary.

2. Answers will vary. Squeaky is angry that Mr. Pearson would suggest such a thing.

4 ✦ Exercise D

1. Squeaky has changed because she learns to care about other people.

2. Answers will vary. Squeaky realizes that the feelings of other people and their respect are important to her.

―――――――― **Reviewing and Interpreting the Story** ――――――

1. b	5. a	9. d	13. d
2. d	6. c	10. a	14. b
3. a	7. d	11. b	15. d
4. c	8. b	12. b	16. a

Unit 3: **To Build a Fire**

————————————— **Plot** —————————————

1 ♦ Exercise A

1. The man does not stop to consider that as a human he can live only within certain limits of heat and cold.

2. The cold and the strangeness should have alerted the man to the dangers surrounding him. However, they did not make any impression on the man at all.

2 ♦ Exercise B

1. He should have built a fire to thaw himself out.

2. The man once again underestimates the danger of the cold. He is surprised by how quickly his fingers and toes are freezing.

3 ♦ Exercise C

1. He realizes and accepts the fact that he is going to die. Once he has accepted death, he realizes he can die in panic or die with calmness and dignity.

2. He decides not to panic and to accept the fact that he will die.

4 ♦ Exercise D

1. Answers will vary.

2. The dog knows the man cannot provide for him, and he leaves to return to the camp.

————————— **Reviewing and Interpreting the Story** —————————

1. a	5. c	9. d	13. c
2. c	6. a	10. b	14. a
3. a	7. d	11. c	15. c
4. d	8. a	12. a	16. d

Unit 4: **Marigolds**

―――――――――――――― **Setting** ――――――――――――――

1♦ Exercise A

1. Answers will vary.

2. Answers will vary. The house scares the children.

2♦ Exercise B

1. The setting begins with a picture of the house and moves to a picture of the marigolds. "crumbling decay," "dusty brown yard," "sorry gray house"; "dazzling," "bright blossoms," "warm and passionate and sun-golden"

2. Answers will vary. The first part of the setting is depressing, but the second part makes the reader feel warm and alive. Two very different images are created in your mind.

3♦ Exercise C

1. Smell: "fresh smell of early morning and of dew-soaked marigolds"
Hearing: "tearing," "sobbing," "crying"

2. Answers will vary. Lizabeth "leaped furiously" into the flowers—"trampling and pulling and destroying." Then she was "sitting in the ruined little garden . . . crying and crying."

4♦ Exercise D

1. Reality: listening to her father; covering her ears
Memory: description of the father with his children

2. Answers will vary. She is learning that parents aren't always as strong as we imagine they are.

―――――――― **Reviewing and Interpreting the Story** ――――――――

1. a	5. d	9. c	13. c
2. c	6. b	10. b	14. b
3. b	7. c	11. d	15. c
4. a	8. a	12. a	16. d

Unit 5: **The Treasure of Lemon Brown**

———————————————— **Use of Language** ————————————————

1 ♦ Exercise A

1. Answers will vary. Students should list ungrammatical word use and unusual words, phrases, and spellings.
2. Answers will vary. He explains who Jesse is, and he asks a question at the end.

2 ♦ Exercise B

1. Answers will vary. Almost every word in the passage contributes to the suspense.
2. Answers will vary. You can feel Greg's tension.

3 ♦ Exercise C

1. The first sentence contains a metaphor: "tires hissing." The metaphor compares *tires* to a snake or some other hissing animal. The second sentence contains a simile: "words, like the distant thunder." The simile compares the sound of the words to the sound of thunder.
2. Answers will vary.

4 ♦ Exercise D

1. "They used to say I sung the blues so sweet that if I sang at a funeral, the dead would commence to rocking with the beat." The exaggeration emphasizes Lemon's sweet singing.
2. Hard times taps Lemon on the shoulder. The personification creates a vivid picture. It also tells us a little bit about the way Lemon handles his problems.

———————————— **Reviewing and Interpreting the Story** ————————————

1. b	5. c	9. d	13. c
2. b	6. b	10. c	14. a
3. a	7. d	11. b	15. a
4. d	8. a	12. c	16. b

Unit 6: The Moustache

──────────────── Theme ────────────────

1 ◆ Exercise A

1. a wax museum

2. Cormier describes the patients standing and sitting as "frozen forever in these postures." Answers will vary.

2 ◆ Exercise B

1. pride

2. Mike realizes for the first time that older people have real lives and feelings of guilt, just as he does. Answers will vary.

3 ◆ Exercise C

1. her appearance; her false cheerfulness; her wink; she spoke to Mike as if his grandmother wasn't there

2. Neither Mike nor the attendant thought of the grandmother as a real person with real feelings.

4 ◆ Exercise D

1. Mike wants to ask if his parents really love each other and if there is anything to forgive between them.

2. Answers will vary. Shaving his moustache shows that Mike realizes there is much more to growing up than his outward appearance.

──────── Reviewing and Interpreting the Story ────────

1. d	5. a	9. b	13. c
2. d	6. c	10. c	14. a
3. a	7. b	11. b	15. c
4. c	8. c	12. d	16. b

Unit 7: **Sucker**

————————————— **Tone and Mood** —————————————

1 ✦ Exercise A

1. good feeling; get on my nerves; excited; waiting expression; seriously; roughly

2. One is warm and close; the other is cool and distant.

2 ✦ Exercise B

1. he closed his mouth; his eyes got narrow; his fists shut; never such a look; getting older; hard look; his face was hard

2. Sucker's feeling changed from admiration to hatred. If you were Peter you might feel ashamed, guilty, or regretful.

3 ✦ Exercise C

1. The house and the night are quiet, dark, and cold.

2. Answers will vary. Perhaps you are relieved that you are not out in the storm.

4 ✦ Exercise D

1. Answers will vary. Pete felt humiliated by Maybelle, and he took that anger out on Sucker.

2. Answers will vary. The calm tone made the insults sound more intense and convincing.

————————— **Reviewing and Interpreting the Story** —————————

1. b	5. c	9. d	13. b
2. a	6. a	10. a	14. c
3. d	7. c	11. b	15. b
4. d	8. b	12. d	16. c

Unit 8: **Naftali the Storyteller and His Horse, Sus**

———————————— **The Folk Story** ————————————

1 ♦ Exercise A

1. Answers will vary. "If stories weren't told or books weren't written, man would live like the beasts, only for the day."

2. He studied, learned, and listened. Answers will vary.

2 ♦ Exercise B

1. Answers will vary.

2. The death of one thing provides life for another. In that sense, life is eternal.

3 ♦ Exercise C

1. The skills are reading and studying. Answers will vary.

2. His parents told him stories when he was little. Books were expensive and in short supply, so they were considered treasures.

4 ♦ Exercise D

1. Answers will vary. He feels that stories are our history, and knowing ourselves is more important than money.

2. He sought to spread knowledge everywhere through stories.

———————————— **Reviewing and Interpreting the Story** ————————————

1. d	5. c	9. b	13. b
2. b	6. a	10. a	14. a
3. c	7. a	11. c	15. d
4. d	8. d	12. d	16. c

Unit 9: **A Sound of Thunder**

——————————— **Science Fiction** ———————————

1 ❖ Exercise A

1. The author "distances" the reader by placing the story in another time. This world is not the world of the present: "Christ isn't born yet," "Moses has not gone to the mountain to talk with God," "The Pyramids are still in the earth," "Alexander, Caesar, Napoleon, Hitler—none of them exists."

2. Answers will vary. They all helped shape the world.

2 ❖ Exercise B

1. Passage A: clothing and bodies sterilized; Passage B: "Some dinosaurs have two brains, one in the head, another far down the spinal column."

2. Answers will vary.

3 ❖ Exercise C

1. Travis does not want to alter the past. Answers will vary.

2. Scientists can't always predict how their discoveries will effect humanity.

4 ❖ Exercise D

1. He compares it to a locomotive. Answers will vary.

2. Answers will vary.

——————————— **Reviewing and Interpreting the Story** ———————————

1. d	5. c	9. c	13. b
2. b	6. d	10. a	14. c
3. a	7. b	11. b	15. b
4. d	8. d	12. c	16. d

Unit 10: **A Cap for Steve**

———— Judgments and Conclusions: Discussing Stories ————

1 ◆ Exercise A

1. Answers will vary. Dave understands her worry because he is also worried. He pretends to be annoyed.

2. Answers will vary.

2 ◆ Exercise B

1. Answers will vary. He is trying to show both Steve and Mr. Hudson that he is comfortable in the fancy apartment and able to take care of himself.

2. Answers will vary. We know Dave is hot-tempered, so we can infer that he might like to start an argument.

3 ◆ Exercise C

1. Anna: "Your father was only trying to do what he knew was right, and it'll work out, and you'll understand." Other sentence choices may also support your answer.

2. Answers will vary. Anna wants to soothe both Steve and Dave. Steve tries to tell Anna how he feels. Dave is concerned about the way Anna and Steve see his actions.

4 ◆ Exercise D

1. Answers will vary. ". . . the kids around here say you could be a great pitcher."

2. Answers will vary. Steve shows his father he has learned to forgive other people for their mistakes.

———————— Reviewing and Interpreting the Story ————————

1. b	5. c	9. b	13. b
2. a	6. a	10. a	14. d
3. b	7. d	11. b	15. a
4. d	8. c	12. d	16. c

Comprehension
Scores Graph
&
Comprehension
Skills Profile

Comprehension Scores

Use this graph to plot your comprehension scores. At the top of the graph are the names of the stories in the book. To mark your score for a unit, find the name of the story you just read and follow the line beneath it down until it crosses the line for the number of questions you got right. Put an *x* where the lines meet. As you mark your score for each unit, graph your progress by drawing a line to connect the *x*'s. The numbers on the right show your comprehension percentage score.

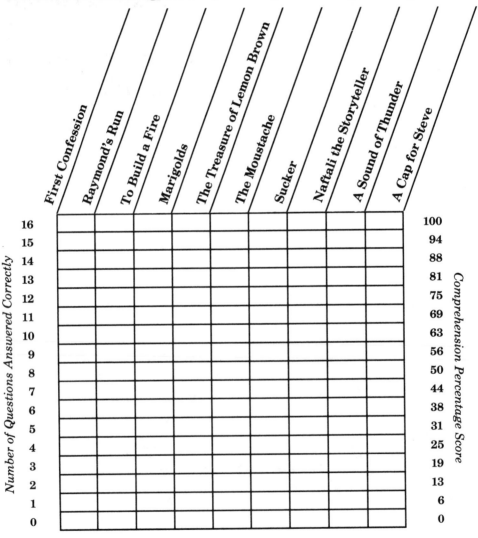

Comprehension Skills Profile

Use this profile to see which comprehension skills you need to work on. Fill in the number of incorrect answers for each skill every time you complete a unit. For example, if you have two incorrect answers for Remembering Facts, you will blacken two spaces above that skill label. The numbers on the left side show your total number of wrong answers for each comprehension skill. The profile will show you which kinds of questions you consistently get wrong. Your instructor may want to give you extra help with these skills.

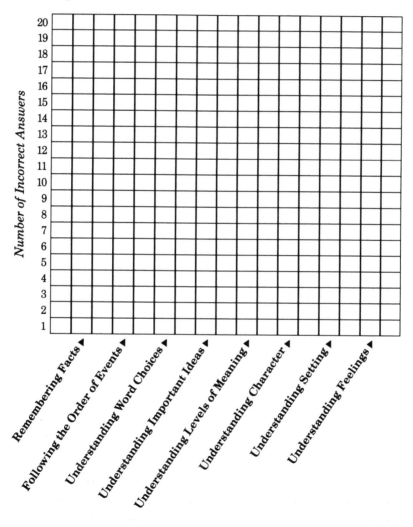